A BRIEF HISTORY OF THE NEW YORK YANKEES

RONALD A. MAYER

Mechanicsburg, PA USA

Published by Sunbury Press, Inc.
Mechanicsburg, Pennsylvania

www.sunburypress.com

Copyright © 2025 by Ronald A. Mayer.
Cover Copyright © 2025 by Sunbury Press, Inc.

Sunbury Press supports copyright. Copyright fuels creativity, encourages diverse voices, promotes free speech, and creates a vibrant culture. Thank you for buying an authorized edition of this book and for complying with copyright laws by not reproducing, scanning, or distributing any part of it in any form without permission. You are supporting writers and allowing Sunbury Press to continue to publish books for every reader. For information contact Sunbury Press, Inc., Subsidiary Rights Dept., PO Box 548, Boiling Springs, PA 17007 USA or legal@sunburypress.com.

For information about special discounts for bulk purchases, please contact Sunbury Press Orders Dept. at (855) 338-8359 or orders@sunburypress.com.

To request one of our authors for speaking engagements or book signings, please contact Sunbury Press Publicity Dept. at publicity@sunburypress.com.

FIRST SUNBURY PRESS EDITION: March 2025

Set in Adobe Garamond | Interior design by Crystal Devine | Cover by Lawrence Knorr | Edited by Anaya Montgomery.

Publisher's Cataloging-in-Publication Data
Names: Mayer, Ronald A., author.
Title: A brief history of the New York Yankees / Ronald A. Miller.
Description: First trade paperback edition. | Mechanicsburg, PA : Sunbury Press, 2025.
Summary: This brief history of the New York Yankees is a fast and enjoyable read. No longer do you have to struggle through a 400 plus page history to learn about the greatest dynasty in sports history. It is all here from their beginning as the Highlanders through 2023. Every American League Pennant (40) and World Series (27) is covered. From the historic purchase of Babe Ruth to Aaron Judge and his record breaking 62 home run season including Gehrig, DiMaggio, Mantle and other Hall of Fame stars. A must read for New York Yankee fans.
Identifiers: ISBN 979-8-88819-291-7 (softcover).
Subjects: SPORTS & RECREATION / Baseball / History | POETRY / Subjects & Themes / General.

Designed in the USA
0 1 1 2 3 5 8 13 21 34 55

For the Love of Books!

Dedicated to my wife Arlene,
you are a beautiful person both inside and out,
I love you

Also by
Ronald A. Mayer

The 1937 Newark Bears: A Baseball Legend

Perfect! 14 Pitchers of "Perfect" Games

The New Jersey Book of Lists (With Gerald Tomlinson)

*Christy Mathewson:
A Game-by-Game Profile of a Legendary Pitcher*

*The 1923 New York Yankees:
A History of Their First World Championship Season*

*The 1932 New York Yankees:
The Story of a Legendary Team a Remarkable Season
And a Wild World Series*

*Baseball Memories:
A Collection of 101 Poems Celebrating Immortal Players, Classic
Games and Wacky Events of the National Pastime*

*Carl Hubbell:
Five Fabulous Seasons that Paved the Way to Cooperstown*

Contents

A Very, Very Humble Beginning. 1

The Highlanders, New Owners Ruppert and Huston, New
Manager Huggins (1903–1919). 4

Babe Ruth Arrives, First World Championship, New Stadium
(1920–1923). 12

Three Years before Fame and The Greatest Team Ever!
(1924–1927). 21

Another Championship, Huggins Dies, a Transition Season
(1928–1930). 28

Joe McCarthy Arrives, another Championship (1931–1932). 33

Three Second Place Finishes, Ruth Departs (1933–1935). 38

Joe D Arrives, Four More Championships, Ruppert and
Gehrig Die (1936–1939). 44

A Narrow Miss, another Winning Streak (1940–1943) 57

War Ends, New Ownership, another World Championship
(1944–1948). 65

Stengel, Mantle Arrive, Joe D Retires, Five Championships
(1949–1953). 73

A Pause, Four Pennants and Two Championships (1954–1958). . . 85

Five Pennants, Two Championships, Casey Fired,
CBS New Owners (1959–1964) 97

Yankees Dynasty Crumbles, Steinbrenner New Owner
(1965–1975). 113

Four Pennants, Two Championships, Managerial Madness
(1976–1981). 121

Fourteen-year Dry Spell, Managerial Madness Continues (1982–1995) 136

Torre, Jeter Arrive, Six Pennants, Four Championships (1996–2003) 154

A-Rod Arrives, Boston Comeback, Three More East Titles (2004–2007) 186

A New Joe and Stadium, A Pennant and Championship (2008–2017) 195

Girardi Gone, Boone New Manager, Championship Drought (2018–2023) 221

Soto Arrives, Another Pennant (41), Championship Drought Continues (2024). 249

Appendix A: New York Yankees Pennants/World Series/ Managers 275

Bibliography. 277

About the Author. 282

A Very, Very Humble Beginning

This is a story about an unsung baseball team
Humbled at the start now held in high esteem
Therefore, let's start way back from day one
So as to enlighten . . . and have some fun

On February 2, 1876, the National League began
Formed by William Hulbert, a wealthy businessman
The NL replaced the mismanaged National Association
With eight large city teams . . . not to be outdone

Boston, Chicago, and Philadelphia to name three
Along with Hartford, Louisville, and Cincinnati
Plus, Brooklyn and St. Louis to round out the eight
The NL was now defined and ready to celebrate

Regrettably, owners ruled the clubs with an iron fist
Making it difficult for players to coexist
Thrown games were known as early as 1877
These crooked players were not destined for heaven

Schedules were never completed by weak teams
Those out of the race, left with crushed dreams
Rival teams popped up as a genuine threat
Most were fought off with a determined mindset

Two upstart leagues survived for only one year
No support, Union Association (1884) did disappear
The Player's League of 1890 followed suit
As their plans for a labor union left it destitute

The American Association did have success
For a period (1882–1891) until a rival did oppress
The Player's League raided their talented athletes
This affected their attendance and their gate receipts

Years later, the NL increased to 12 teams
Hoping expansion would fill their financial dreams
But the 12-club league wasn't quite working
Forcing the owners to operate on a shoestring

So back to eight teams they did uncork
One was the Giants of old New York
And Boston, Philadelphia, Pittsburgh, plus
Brooklyn, Cincinnati, Chicago, and St. Louis

A flourishing minor circuit was the Western League
This in time would create a lasting intrigue
Byron Bancroft Johnson was their president
Who in 1900 did create an unusual event

This was the year Johnson renamed the loop
Calling it the American League, now to regroup
Eight teams would make up the new AL
In large cities it would do monetarily well

The AL clubs were Detroit, Baltimore, and Washington
Philadelphia, Boston, Milwaukee, almost done
In Cleveland and Chicago, Johnson added a franchise,
A year later came the very ultimate prize

The AL was granted major league status in 1901
And now began the vicious competitive fun
The AL raided NL rosters unmercifully
Boosting attendance much to AL glee

Immortals like McGraw, McGinnity, and Young
Jumped to the AL as the balance of power swung
One of the teams in the AL was Baltimore
Managed by the umpire baiting "Mugsy" McGraw

McGraw, to say the least, was not a big Johnson fan
Leading Mugsy to implement his secret plan
Having John T. Brush of the NL Executive Committee
Buy the Baltimore club, which Brush did readily agree

Brush then released a number of key players to the NL
This was a highhanded and sneaky bombshell
Surprise! McGraw was one of the players released
Now his fortunes very quickly increased

He became the manager of the New York Giants in '02
To the AL and Ban Johnson, McGraw said adieu
Guess who bought the Giants the following year?
It was Brush, riding into New York like Paul Revere

Baltimore finished their tumultuous season
Finally dropping out of the AL for good reason
Johnson saw an opportunity in the unfilled franchise
Move it to New York? What a marvelous prize!

The Highlanders, New Owners Ruppert and Huston, New Manager Huggins (1903–1919)

It's now time to point out a little-known fact
In case you missed reading it and overreact
The New York Yankees franchise that most adore
Had its start in the city of Baltimore

In 1903, Johnson soon found local buyers
Sadly, not the most upstanding of hires
Bill Devery, former Chief of Police, reportedly corrupt
Frank Farrell, notorious gambler, generally messed up

The two unsavory owners paid $18,000 for the franchise
The team was called the Highlanders, not a huge surprise
Solely because of its unique Manhattan location
At Washington Heights, the highest gradation

At Hilltop Park the games were all played
Fans sat on wooden benches . . . no shade
15,000, was the capacity of the park
Over 100 years later it appears to be a lark

Clark Griffith managed the club from the beginning
Season after season, his teams mostly winning
Twice his team finished second, 1904 and 1906
Both times coming up empty in his bag of tricks

The Highlanders, New Owners Ruppert and Huston, New Manager Huggins (1903–1919)

First place in 1904 was painful, lost on the last day
To the manager, players and loyal fans' shocking dismay
Playing a twin-bill with Boston, one game behind
First game, top of the ninth, score 2-2, what a bind

A Boston runner on third, two out, Jack Chesbro the ace
Uncorked a wild pitch . . . to end the close race!
Chesbro's record (41-12) during the season was awesome
Completed 48 of 51 games as his performance did blossom

Wee Willie Keeler was another Highlander star
With opposing pitchers, he would successfully spar
Willie led the Highlanders with a .343 average in '04
Commenting on his success, his peers could not ignore

Sam Crawford, said, "He only used half his bat"
Choking up, slapping the ball, like a pesky gnat
Wee Willie said it best . . . succinctly and quaint
And famously . . . "Hit 'em where they ain't"

In 1905, a 22-year-old named Hal Chase
Joined the Highlanders to play first base
He would become one of the team's great players
He also became one of the most nefarious betrayers

At first base he was claimed a defensive magician
Had few equals, if any, at that position
He was gracious, charming, and urbane
Also, described as having a "corkscrew brain"

Hal Chase was basically a dishonest person
His gambler friends made his actions worsen
His teammates believed he was throwing games
Manager Frank Chance also made such brash claims

Chance had his fill of the crooked Hal Chase
So, in June 1913, he told him to pack his suitcase
Off he went to the mighty Chicago White Sox
Jumped to the Federal League to open Pandora's Box

Chase was alleged to be the evil impresario
Behind the gamblers and the players of Chicago
It was during the 1919 World Series fix
As one of his many dirty and illegal tricks

Back to the mediocre Highlanders of 1908
Where the club finished last, owners irate
Clark Griffith was out, Kid Elberfeld was now in
Followed by George Stallings and Hal Chase, a sin

Bringing us to 1912 and manager Harry Wolverton
Who finished last (50-102), still not done
Leading this managerial merry-go-round to Frank Chance
And a fresh look and an entirely different circumstance

In 1913, two exciting events quickly took place
The Highlanders to the Polo Grounds, more space
As new tenants the club would, of course, pay rent
For use of the improved structure, money well spent

The renting of the Polo Grounds was not a lark
It was payback from the Giants' use of Hilltop Park
Sadly, in 1911 the Polo Grounds went up in flames
So, the Highlanders offered Hilltop for their games

The other change involved the Highlanders name
The now famous New York Yankees it became
How the iconic name came to be is unclear
What is . . . millions of fans the name now revere

The Highlanders, New Owners Ruppert and Huston, New Manager Huggins (1903–1919)

The name change and new location
Brought both frustration and elation
For the Yankees were still playing ugly ball
Time for a major ownership overhaul

Owners Devery and Farrell were losing dough
Also quarrelling, trying to make the franchise grow
It became time to seek a new buyer or two
Which they did in 1915 as they said, "adieu"

New owners, Ruppert and Huston, were successful men
As witnessed in their business dealings time and time again
Both were wealthy, as expected, and strong willed
With dreams of a successful team to build

Jacob Ruppert worked at his father's brewery, age 19
By age 31, he was deep into the political scene
Elected to the U.S. Congress from New York, district 15
He served four terms, accomplishments at best routine

He rose to colonel in the 7th Regiment, National Guard
At whatever endeavor, the colonel worked hard
The brewery was where he made his most success
Beginning as a "barrel washer" he did confess

As a young man he worked 12-hour days
Earning $10 a week, always looking up, never sideways
To vice president and general manager, he progressed
And then to president, a man self-possessed

Tillinghast L'Hommedieu Huston was his majestic name
An engineering captain in the U.S. Army brought fame
In Cuba, Huston made his substantial monetary score
Rebuilding harbors after the Spanish-American war

Huston was untidy, personable, and chatty
"Cap" was a big man and somewhat fatty
He loved to chat with players and writers of the game
While his partner was often aloof, some do claim

For $460,000 Ruppert and Huston bought a weak team
Looking back to 1915, the price doesn't seem extreme
Ruppert was installed as the Yankees president
The stronger personality of the two, it meant

Huston, of course, was then named vice-president
And at the time, Cap seemed to be content
To select a new manager was their first mission
Choosing Wild Bill Donovan for the position

As a pitcher, Donovan compiled a record of 185-139
An impressive mark and that's the bottom line
In 1914, as player-manager, he led the Providence Grays
To the International League pennant and well-earned praise

But after three unsuccessful seasons with the Yanks,
Ruppert and Huston quite emphatically said no thanks
Now came the novice owner's first major dispute
The colonel was either clever or unfairly cute

Ruppert wanted Miller Huggins to lead
Huston wanted a crony, so he disagreed
Cap wanted Brooklyn manager Wilbert Robinson
That's when Ruppert did a sneaky end run

President Wilson declared war on Germany April 16, 1917
And unwittingly affected the Yankees managerial scene
The next day Huston reenlisted and was shipped to France
Creating an opportunity for Ruppert, his agenda to advance

The Highlanders, New Owners Ruppert and Huston, New Manager Huggins (1903–1919)

Ruppert hired Miller Huggins while Huston was far away
When he heard the news, he was furious over the power play
In telegrams accusing Ruppert of everything under the sun
But once Huggins was signed, Cap in France was outdone

The diminutive Miller Huggins stood 5'6" tall
At second base for the Reds and Cards, a fireball
He weighed 120 pounds on his best day
For 13 years in the NL, however, he did play

Not a power hitter was little "Hug"
For the fences he did not slug
But in 1912, he batted .304 with glee
Also led the NL in walks four times, did he

From 1913-17 he was the player-manager of St. Louis
His managerial record of 346-415 was tortuous
Apparently, Ruppert saw something in the little guy
Other than Ban Johnson's advice, no reason why

Despite his size, Hug could hold his own
And when needed, could provide real backbone
From the University of Cincinnati with a law degree
This served him well when discussions were weighty

He was a loner, and never one of the boys
No family, no hobbies, baseball offered all the joys
In 1918, Hug's first Yankees' season at the helm
He finished fourth, 60-63, that did not overwhelm

Six home runs qualified as the Yankees power maker!
It was he of the nickname, "Home Run Baker"
He also hit .306 along with Wally Pipp at .304
Other than these two, the Yankees were quite a bore

In 1919, an improved Yankees team finished third
Leading the AL with 45 homers, now seems absurd
20-game winner Bob Shawkey deserved much praise
Plus, the 1.65 ERA of controversial pitcher Carl Mays

In 1919, over 619,000 watched the Yanks set a new mark
And in time, forced New York to build their own ballpark
But that was four years away and given little thought
At the time, with a new club, winning was eagerly sought

Just for a moment, let's turn the calendar back to 1914
And imagine we are in a brand-new time machine
There is a young Red Sox pitcher noted to be uncouth
His name, soon to be a household word, is "Babe" Ruth

Ruth played for Boston from 1914 to 1919
Pitching with skill and hitting in between
During that six-year span, his record was 89-46
Along with a .308 batting average he would intermix

Ruth also hit 49 home runs in those six years
29 in 1919 to lead the league, dazzling his peers
In fact, the 29 dingers set a new major league mark
As the "Sultan of Swat" Ruth would soon embark

In 1919, Ruth also led the league with 113 RBIs
Plus 103 runs scored and all that implies
The Babe would soon enjoy sudden fame
That could be argued made him bigger than the game

Actually, 1919 was a turning point in Ruth's career
Ed Barrow, Boston manager, would be the seer
Turned Ruth into a full-time outfielder in 1919
A move that created a home run hitting machine

The Highlanders, New Owners Ruppert and Huston, New Manager Huggins (1903-1919)

Enter Boston Red Sox owner Harry Frazee
A man who loved to produce Broadway shows, did he
Sadly, for Red Sox fans, the shows were mostly turkeys
Leaving Frazee and Boston financially on their knees

Babe Ruth Arrives, First World Championship, New Stadium (1920–1923)

Due to Frazee's Broadway flops he needed cash
This was serious and not mere balderdash
So, for $125,000 the Yankees bought Ruth
The day after Christmas, **1919**, that's the truth

Huggins and Ruth were at odds from the get-go
It made for an interesting and entertaining combo
Ruth's behavior was often erratic and headstrong
Ignoring Huggins' authority and thus to get along

The Yankees quickly signed Ruth to a two-year contract
At $20,000 per year, fans by the thousands he did attract
His **1920** season can only be described as awesome
But surprisingly didn't help the Yankees pennant outcome

Let's leave Ruth for a moment to note two profound events
Two highly capable persons to tackle baseball's discontents
Landis, appointed baseball commissioner in 1920
Barrow named Yankees president, a baseball cognoscente

Paul Krichell came with former Boston manager Barrow
A coach, and later super scout, quite a dynamo
Later he discovered a Columbia first baseman named Lou
Signed Gehrig to a Yankees contract . . . and it's all so true

In '20 Ruth hit a whopping .376 with 54 out of the park
Setting for many years a new home run benchmark
He also drove in 135 runs and scored an incredible 158
Despite his unreal stats, third place was the Yankee's fate

Babe Ruth Arrives, First World Championship, New Stadium (1920–1923)

Even with 20-game winners Carl Mays and Bob Shawkey
The rest of the staff did not measure up, a sad reality
But **1921** would be a different and exciting story
As the Yankees won their **first AL pennant** and glory

Ruth topped his performance of the previous year
With a .378 batting average, 168 RBIs, now in high gear
He also hit at the time, an unheard of 59 four baggers
Discouraging other power hitters once proud swaggers

Aiding Ruth was left-fielder Bob Meusel in his breakout year
Whacking 24 homers and driving in 138, he did persevere
Carl Mays (27-9), most American League wins, so gutsy
Bob Shawkey (18-12), Waite Hoyt (19-13), gifts from Frazee

On to the World Series to face their unhappy landlord
Yes, the Giants versus the Yankees, a Series unexplored
It was the best-of-nine, the last time this format was allowed
In 1922, the best-of-seven was employed and forever endowed

The Yankees began the Series with skill and desire
Winning the first two games with much to admire
From the pitching of Carl Mays and Waite Hoyt
Both throwing 3-0 shutouts, exceptionally adroit

Game three, the Giants' bats finally came alive
Led by Ross Youngs' four ribbies they won 13-5
There was one other loss to affect the game
Ruth not himself during the Series, what a shame

Game two, the Babe scraped his elbow stealing a base
It became infected, had to be lanced, hard to replace
In game four, the Giants narrowly won, 4-2
The Series now tied as the excitement grew

Game five, Ruth was back batting third
In inning four he accomplished the absurd
He bunted and was safe at first
A surprise move and totally unrehearsed

Ruth eventually scored putting the Yankees in front
The final score was 3-1 and started with Ruth's bunt
Hoyt went all the way, giving up 10 hits for the win
As the Giants comeback would now begin

McGraw's club took the Series, winning the next three!
By scores of 8-5, 2-1, and 1-0 . . . what a pity
For Yankee fans to be so close and their first
It would take two seasons to quench the winning thirst

Ruth and Meusel planned on a barnstorming tour
The reason was the inviting financial allure
Landis, clearly and emphatically said absolutely not
Both ignored the commissioner and off they did trot

Landis fined both players their World Series money
And suspended them for six weeks, not very funny
As one author claimed and others would agree
It established Landis as having "unforgiving authority"

Despite Ruth and Meusel missing about 30 games
The **1922** season did not go up in flames
The Yankees obtained several Boston players of note
Thanks to Frazee for keeping the Yankees afloat

The Yankees obtained pitchers Joe Bush and Sam Jones
Along with shortstop Everett Scott with little undertones
In a separate acquisition with the Philadelphia A's
The Yankees purchased Whitey Witt, in center to graze

Babe Ruth Arrives, First World Championship, New Stadium (1920–1923)

It turned out to be a very, very tight pennant race
But the Yanks topped St. Louis by a game and first place
It was their **second straight AL pennant**, more to come
As of 2024, 41 would be the remarkable sum

In 110 games, 35 homers Ruth did blast
From the previous year of 59, quite a contrast
"Bullet" Joe Bush, the recent acquisition from the Sox
Turned in an excellent 26-7 as hitters he did outfox

McGraw and his Giants won their eighth NL pennant
Would face the Yankees in the World Series, their tenant
Huggins and his Yankees were looking for sweet revenge
Sadly, they played like the prehistoric men of Stonehenge

The Giants swept the Yankees four straight!
Excelling both on the mound and at the plate
Game two (tied at three) called because of darkness
Closest the Yankees came . . . fans to impress

As a team the Yankees batted a weak .203
Ruth, no homers, hit .118, what a pity
As the Giants pitching did dominate
In short order sealed the Yankees' fate

McGraw was still annoyed over the Yankees celebrity
Outdrawing his team by wide margins, no hyperbole
Ergo, McGraw gave the Yankees the proverbial boot
Ruppert, not a happy tenant, would build a substitute

In **1923**, the Yankees completed their new ballpark
Eventually it became a widely celebrated landmark
Built with concrete and 2,300 tons of structural steel
The first three-tier ballpark, at the time, simply surreal

A record crowd of 62,000 attended that April day
And it was reported 25,000 more were turned away
The cost at around $2.5 million was spent to the hilt
For a palace called, "The House That Ruth Built"

In today's dollars it appears a small amount of dough
Not true, compared to the items of '23 listed below
Bread 9¢, milk 14¢, eggs 24¢, that's right
Including a New York City hotel for $3.00 a night

Ticket scalpers were prevalent even back then
They were caught by alert cops time and time again
They were called speculators then, but did connive
One tried to sell a $1.10 grandstand ticket for $1.25

Opening day 1923, the stadium packed as mentioned before
Including Ruppert, Huston, Landis, and celebrities galore
The Yankees versus the Red Sox, a mean, nasty rivalry
Years later would develop into ugly games requiring a referee

But on this exciting, historic April spring day
The Yankees whipped Boston with sound play
They were leading 1-0 in the third frame
The Yankees looking for more, their aim

On base were Joe Dugan and Whitey Witt
While thousands screamed for Ruth to hit
Howard Ehmke on the mound for the Sox
Ruth with a 2-2 count waiting in the box

On the next pitch Ruth homered to right
Yankee fans lit up the Stadium, what a sight
Hats were tossed in the air with unabashed joy
While Ruth circled the bases waving like a little boy

Babe Ruth Arrives, First World Championship, New Stadium (1920–1923)

The final score was New York 4, Boston 1
As ace Shawkey gave up three hits and a run
The veteran right-hander would win 16 in 1923
But this victory, setting the pace, was a key

The Yankees romped through the AL, winning by 16
By seasons' end, it was a proud and glorious scene
It was Miller Huggins' **third straight AL flag**
With the World Series yet played, no time to brag

New York won with a deadly combination
Long ball and timely hitting, plus a deep rotation
Ruth hit .393 with 41 homers and 130 RBIs
It was obvious to all, the Babe was the franchise

Despite Ruth's greatness, his teammates let's not ignore
Wally Pipp drove in 109 while hitting a respectable .304
Meusel chipped in with 91, an off year for Bob
Newcomer, Witt, hit .314, scored 113, a commendable job

But it wasn't all hitting that won for the Yanks
The pitching staff must be given some thanks
Sad Sam Jones would lead the pitching with 21-8
Followed by Herb Pennock (19-6), a HOF great

A record of 19-15 was recorded by Bullet Joe
His outpitch, a blazing fastball, he could throw
17-9 with a team leading 3.02 ERA, the mark of Hoyt
Who would identify a batter's weakness, then exploit

Beside Hug winning the AL flag for the third time
Ruppert made a significant financial move, so sublime
For years he and Huston have had a clash or two
Mostly Huston not forgiving Ruppert of the Huggins' coup

Early in the season Ruppert finalized the deal
He bought out Huston, the press did reveal
The price for Huston's half was about $1¼ million
Making Cap Huston a rich, free, and easy civilian

The buyout was finalized on May 24, 1923
At last, Cap Huston from baseball was free
His mood was relaxed, light, and breezy
In part, he said, "I am just going to take it easy"

After eight years of the partnership, it was now over
Ruppert, sole owner of a winning team now in clover
Plus, Ed Barrow running the team, a Sox escapee
Ruppert was about to create baseball's greatest dynasty

And now off to the World Series we go
Again, to face the Giants wouldn't you know
Despite Ruth, the Giants had the edge at the plate
Frankie Frisch (.348) and Youngs (.336) did a wait

Also, George Kelly (.307) and Dave Bancroft at .304
Not finished, these were McGraw's hitting core
Let's not forget Casey Stengel (.339) as a substitute
Who would turn out to be quite a World Series hoot

Rosy Ryan (16-5) and Jack Scott (16-7) were the best
The rest of the Giant pitchers were not as blessed
McGraw badly wanted his third straight Series victory
Since it would be the first time in baseball history

And this tale will tell how badly he wanted to win
Under no terms, on or off the field, would he give in
Lou Gehrig rejoined the Yankees after September 1
Thus, was officially ineligible to play, he was done

Babe Ruth Arrives, First World Championship, New Stadium (1920-1923)

First baseman Pipp was nursing an injured ankle
Hug wanted Lou to take his place despite any rankle
Luckily a precedent was established in 1920 for all to see
But the opposing manager would have to agree

McGraw knew Gehrig finished hitting a mighty .423
His well-known hatred for the Yankees, all could see
McGraw's answer to Huggins rendered him awestruck
"If the Yankees have had an injury, it's their hard luck"

The Stadium was the venue for the World Series, game one
Over 55,000 packed the park determined to have fun
As the game entered the ninth, tied at four
With two out, Stengel to hit the Giant fans did implore

Casey answered the call, lining a pitch to left center
And heading for second was the tormentor
He didn't stop even at third, he headed for the plate
The relay was close, but Casey slid safely home, it was fate

The Giants won 5-4, frustrating the Yankees once more
Game two, at home, the Giants were looking for an encore
But Ruth took over, blasting two homers, Yanks winning 4-2
Pennock pitched a complete game, as batters he did subdue

Game three, Art Neft blanked the Yanks on six hits
It was Stengel again giving the Yankees fits
A scoreless game after six, Casey once again at bat
Swatted a homer to right, just clearing the fence at that

Circling the bases, at the Yankees, he thumbed his nose
Down through the years, so the laughable story goes
Commissioner Landis fined Casey fifty dollars for his silliness
". . . Stengel just can't help being Stengel," he did confess

After game three, the fun for the Giants terminated
During the next three games Yankee superiority dictated
Game four, a Yankee six run second inning chased Jack Scott
The final score was 8-4, as the Yankee bats were getting hot

Game five over after two innings, Yankee bats still alive
Joe Dugan's three-run homer, the Giants couldn't survive
The final score was 8-1, over before it started, a blowout
As Joe Bush's three-hit gem left the outcome never in doubt

In game six, the Yankees were trailing after seven, 4-1
Their only tally came in the first, a Ruth home run
Top of the eighth, Giants pitchers couldn't stop the Yankees
Singles, walks, an error scored five, out came the hankies

Sam Jones, in relief preserved Pennock's second win
Now the well-deserved celebration would begin
It was the **Yankees first World Championship** supreme
And the beginning of baseball's most storied team

Three Years Before Fame and the Greatest Team Ever! (1924–1927)

In **1924**, the Yankees high expectations to repeat
Were foiled by Washington and took a backseat
The Senators won their first AL pennant ever!
Beating out New York by two games, quite an endeavor

Although the Yankees lost, they did find some delight
When Washington in seven, McGraw's Giants did smite
Despite losing the pennant, Yankee fans rooted for Ruth
Who excited the enthusiastic crowds, especially the youth

And the Babe gave the fans lots to cheer about
A league-leading .378 and 46 homers he did clout
But Ruth wasn't the only Yankee whose stats did soar,
Bob Meusel hit .325 and like Ruth, drove in 124

Herb Pennock led the rotation with pitches so nasty
With 21-9 and an earned run average of 2.83
Hoyt, Bush, and Shawkey won 18, 17, and 16 respectively
Hard to lose with this hitting and pitching, many would agree

The good news was Lou Gehrig's call up late in September
With Ruth they would form a hitting combo to remember
In 1924, Gehrig batted 12 times with six hits
Driving in five runs in 10 games, already giving pitchers fits

More good news when Earle Combs was obtained
The 25-year-old speedster, center field he was ordained
A huge contributor to future great Yankee teams
At the same time, fulfilling his Hall of Fame dreams

The Yankees were hungry for another pennant in **1925**
But Ruth's off the field lifestyle they could not survive
It happened just before the season was underway
Ruth's endless eating, drinking, and womanizing did betray

He collapsed one day with excruciating stomach pain
Sadly, his and the Yankees season it would stain
Before a diagnosis of an ulcer, rumors in the press swirled
It was dubbed, "The Bellyache Heard 'Round the World"

Ruth wouldn't play his first game until June first
Mediocre play and ignoring rules, his season cursed
Huggins had seen and witnessed more than enough
Hug exploded; it was well past time to get tough

Hug suspended Ruth and slapped him with a $5,000 fine
Outraged, the Babe went to Ruppert and Barrow to whine
Both supported their manager one hundred percent
Ruth apologized to Hug, later reinstated, ending an ugly event

Hugs' happy moments were with Gehrig at first base
Who began a streak that was "impossible" to erase
So, all the experts, with certainty, did proclaim
Until Cal Ripken Jr. set his sights and took aim

Gehrig, as fans know, played in 2,130 games straight
Ripken played in 2,632 consecutive games, how great
It's doubtful Cal's record will ever be broken
Having said that, it will not be the last word spoken

The Yankees embarrassing seventh place finish
In 1925 did not change their play in '26 to diminish
Also, a trade made in August 1925 would enrich
Gaining a shortstop who had to make a position switch

Three Years Before Fame and the Greatest Team Ever! (1924–1927)

His name is Tony Lazzeri who switched to second base
With Hugs' teaching, Tony quickly did embrace
Lazzeri would team up with young Mark Koenig at short
To form a double play combo, opposing rallies to abort

The Yankees (91-63) finished **1926** in first place
Early on they were running away with the race
In August however, the team went into a spin
And their lead over Cleveland began to thin

But the Yankees prevailed, nosing out Cleveland by three
It was **pennant number four** in Hug's short history
Many contributed to this satisfying and unexpected win
Lazzeri hit only .275, however, 117 runs he drove in

Gehrig, playing a full season, batted .313 with 109 RBIs
But a healthy and somewhat contrite Ruth took the prize
The Babe drove in 153 with 47 home runs, hitting .372
A nice recovery from last seasons' embarrassing miscue

Pennock with a 23-11 record led the pitching rotation
Plus, Shocker (19-11), Hoyt (16-12), part of the foundation
The pitching staff wasn't very deep beyond the big three
Fourth in the mix was Jones (9-8), but slumping badly

In the World Series the Cardinals would be the Yankees foe
In boxing lingo, the Yankees were favored to win by a kayo
In the opening game, before over 61,000, Pennock won 2-1
Gehrig, in the bottom of the sixth, drove in the winning run

Game two, Grover Alexander stopped the Yankees cold
The score 6-2, allowing four hits did the 39-year-old
Game three shifted to a jam-packed Sportsman's Park
For St. Louis was Jesse Haines, a knuckler his trademark

Haines and the Cardinals won 4-0 to take the lead
Game four, all Babe Ruth, everyone did concede
Three home runs, four ribbies off the Babe's bat
The final score 10-5, to the Sultan of Swat tip your hat

The fifth game was a rematch, Sherdel and Pennock
After nine innings the game was in a 2-2 deadlock
In the 10th, Lazzeri drove in the winning run, a sac fly
Hug was looking for one more victory to say bye-bye

St. Louis, managed by Rogers Hornsby, would not give in
He called on Alexander once more for the critical win
"Pete" threw a complete game in HOF style, winning 10-2
Now on to game seven and a World Series brand new

Haines against Hoyt in this must win game
The outcome to determine shame or fame
Bottom of the seventh, the Cards were ahead 3-2
The Yankees had the bases full, two out, and overdo

Now Haines had developed a blister on his hand
Hornsby made a gutsy decision, certainly unplanned
"The Rajah" called on Alexander for the third time
To face Lazzeri, the hard-hitting rookie, so sublime

Remember, Pete pitched nine innings the day before
The count went to 1-2 on Tony, the crowd in an uproar
The next pitch a back-breaking curve, Lazzeri struck out
One of the memorable moments in the Series, no doubt

Pete blanked the Yanks in the eighth to keep the 3-2 lead
In the ninth, two out, Pete walked Ruth, wise indeed
Ruth, in a rare mistake, played the role of a big lout
He tried to steal second and was easily thrown out

Three Years Before Fame and the Greatest Team Ever! (1924–1927)

In St. Louis, Alexander the hero was all the rave
Accounting for two victories and a crucial save
Off the field, there is another great story to be told
Involving Johnny Sylvester, a New Jersey 11-year-old

It would take too long to tell the story properly
And a digression from this brief poetic history
There is much written about what he and Ruth did
Check out Charlie Poekel's book, *Babe & the Kid*

The **1927** New York Yankees began the season 6-0
And continued winning with skill and gusto
From opening day until the very last game
They held first place to widespread acclaim

By early July, the Yankees opened a 12-game lead
And kept on winning which was almost guaranteed
By seasons end, finishing with a record of 110-44
19 games ahead of Mack's A's, and plaudits galore

The **Yankees fifth AL pennant** and wanting more
As the decades passed, it was time to keep score
The 1927 Yankees had talent at every position
And winning was clearly their only mission

Gehrig led the club, hitting an astounding .373
With 47 home runs, another incredible reality
Plus 173 RBIs, what a year's experience will do
Along with the MVP award for Columbia Lou

Ruth hit 60 home runs, at the time, an unbelievable feat
On the day he hit #60, over 60,000 jumped out of their seat
It was a celebration that wasn't seen in New York for years
Ruth was so loved there might have even been joyful tears

The "Bambino" drove in 165 runs while batting .356
Like Gehrig, it was a devastating and deadly mix
Meusel batted .337 with 103 runs batted in
These three could drive a pitcher to the looney bin

Lazzeri hit .309, 18 homers, drove in 102, there's more
Lead-off man Combs led the league with hits galore
Exactly 231 and triples too, with a speedy 23
Koenig hit .285, Dugan .269, weak? Only comparatively

The team makeup was stable and fixed like 1926
Except for three catchers who made up the mix
Collins, Grabowski, and Bengough shared the role
Calling a good game with minimum damage control

The '27 Yankees also had great pitching arms aplenty
They led the American League with an ERA of 3.20
Hoyt (22-7), Pennock (19-8), and Shocker (18-6), all fearless
Followed by Ruether (13-6) and Pipgras (10-3) to impress

Enter Wilcy Moore (19-7), with an ERA of 2.28 and 13 saves
In the role of a starter and reliever gaining well-earned raves
No wonder the '27 Yanks were called the greatest ever
Other fans may disagree, but Yankee partisans . . . never

Before the World Series, a word about "Murder's Row"
A term applied to the heart of the Yankees lineup below
Combs, Ruth, Gehrig, Meusel, and Lazzeri
The true origin of the term still a mystery

In 1927, the Yankees ran over the American League
Leaving little excitement during the season or intrigue
No difference in the World Series; it was a bore
As the Yankees in quick order beat Pittsburgh in four

Three Years Before Fame and the Greatest Team Ever! (1924–1927)

There was a tale about the Pirate players that circulated
Watching New York in batting practice, confidence deflated
At that moment, Pittsburgh lost hope of winning at all
True or not, it might have led the Pirates to their downfall

Hoyt won game one 5-4, with help from Wilcy Moore
Pipgras won game two 6-2, Hug now looking encore
He got his wish . . . and then some in game three
With Pennock close to pitching a perfecto . . . a reality

The veteran lefty, after 7⅓, was pitching a perfect game
Until the great Pie Traynor singled in the eighth frame
The final score was 8-1, with Pennock hurling a three-hitter
Gone was the first World Series perfecto and its glitter

Huggins chose Wilcy Moore to pitch game four
The manager couldn't ask for any more
Wilcy and the Yankees won a close game, 4-3
On a wild pitch, bottom of the ninth, you see

Five pennants, two World Championships, Hug's star rose
"What have you done for me lately," as the saying goes
Huggins would win again, but for the last time
As he suddenly and tragically died, still in his prime

Another Championship, Huggins Dies, a Transition Season (1928–1930)

Ruppert made the correct choice in Hug, it appears
Six pennants and three World Championships in eight years
The "Mighty Mite," as he was sometimes called
Once again in **1928**, Yankee fans he enthralled

The Yankees had their hands full in 1928
Their competition was steep and first rate
They beat out a Philadelphia team soon to dominate
From 1929-1931 with player after player, oh so great

The Yankees beat the A's by 2½ games for the flag
About the victory there was not much to brag
The Yankees and A's were tied in early September
When the A's lost a twin bill, Mack would always remember

The twin-bill at the Stadium, the Yanks and A's tied
The Yankees won both, which began the A's slide
The '28 Yankees were good, not as good as the '27 team
Despite performing well, the club was lacking, it did seem

In '28, two young rookies joined the team
In their own style, both held in high esteem
Leo Durocher, a 21-year-old shortstop, his position
Who later would be a HOF manager, his ambition

The other rookie was Bill Dickey, a catcher
In pinstripes for many years, a man of stature
Hug said, ". . . one of the greatest catchers in the game"
He knew, Bill Dickey is also in the Hall of Fame

Another Championship, Huggins Dies, a Transition Season (1928–1930)

Ruth and Gehrig had extraordinary years once again
Treating a baseball diamond like a child's playpen
Ruth 54 homers, Gehrig 27, 20 less than the '27 season
Pitchers were handling him with more caution, the reason

But Lou drove in 147 while hitting a lofty .374
Settling for singles and doubles to add to the score
Ruth hit .323 and drove in 146, one less than Lou
No matter, they were baseball's most fearsome two

Meusel and Combs had fine seasons, each a real pro
Combs led the AL in triples, the second year in a row
Injuries to Lazzeri and Pennock resulted in lost time
Urban Shocker, who won 18 in '27, died in his prime

He pitched two innings in '28 and declared his retirement
He had a heart ailment, of which few knew the extent
That took his life, September 9 . . . at age 38
The autopsy showed an enlarged heart, his final fate

The Yankees faced the Cards in a World Series rematch
Looking for revenge, which they quickly did dispatch
Five players helped the Yankees win four straight
Despite a host of injuries, the Yankees did annihilate

Pennock (17-6) had a sore arm . . . could not throw
Lazzeri, also a lame throwing arm, competed like a pro
Ruth, playing on a bad ankle, not at one hundred percent
Combs had a broken finger . . . and so on it went

The Yankees used three pitchers, the sweep to complete
Hoyt, Pipgras, and Zachary turning Cardinal hopes into defeat
Hoyt pitched brilliantly, winning games one and four
Game one, a superb three-hitter winning 4-1, the final score

Pipgras won game two 9-3 for seven innings, a shutout
As the Cardinals' hopes of evening the Series, now in doubt
Tom Zachary (3-3, 3.94 ERA) won the crucial third game, 7-3
A starter who pitched 45-plus innings, picked by Hug was he

Zachary, acquired in August off waivers from Washington
He was their pitcher in '27 who gave up Ruth's 60th home run
After that game, a spirited Ruth said, mostly in fun
"Let's see some son of a bitch try to top that one"

Hoyt won game four 7-3, ending the Cards' despair
With help from Ruth and Gehrig, one destructive pair
Ruth hit three homers, Gehrig one, in this game alone
For the Series, the Cardinal pitchers they would own

For the Series, Lou hit .545, four homers, and nine RBIs
Babe had three homers, drove in four, hit .625 to terrorize
While the two-man show was getting their kicks
Hoyt, Pipgras, and Zachary were an unbeatable mix

As all know, popularity and success are often fleeting
In baseball and other sports, it's all about repeating
In **1929,** the best the Yankees could do was second place
The Philadelphia Athletics made a joke of the race

The Yankees had logical reasons for their lack of success
The most obvious, the A's abundance of talent did coalesce
Also, the Yankees had trouble replacing Dugan at third
Koenig at short was slipping, as was Meusel, came the word

There was a bright spot, however, behind the plate
Bill Dickey, second year catching would become first-rate
In 130 games he batted .324 with 10 home runs
And in time he would be one of the Yankees big guns

Another Championship, Huggins Dies, a Transition Season (1928–1930)

Dickey gave credit to Gehrig for helping him hit
In those days, most veterans didn't give a whit
"I was upper cutting on the ball," Dickey did spout
"And he [Lou Gehrig] straightened me out"

Hoyt went from 27-7 to 10-9, gone the following year
Pennock dropped from 17-6 to 9-11, reasons unclear
Adding to the Yankees misfortune, a devastating death
On September 25, Miller Huggins took his last breath

Hug's demise began when he treated a carbuncle on his cheek
With a heat lamp, later to be discovered the wrong technique
His condition was called erysipelas, a serious skin infection
While the heat lamp exacerbated his fatal condition

Hearing the bad news, Combs broke down and began to cry
At his funeral two days later, the team said its final goodbye
The loss of Hug was a shocking blow
Gehrig said, "He taught me everything I know"

Coach Art Fletcher took over, the season waning
The obvious choice, with 11 games remaining
Season over, the hunt for a manager deployed
One was rejected, the other two employed

Ruppert and Barrow put the Babe on the shelf
How can he manage a team? He can't even manage himself
Donie Bush and Eddie Collins were up for the position
Bush had signed with the Chicago White Sox, his mission

Collins, after a fabulous 25-year career, chose to give back
The HOF second baseman wanted to coach for Connie Mack
So, the Yankees went with candidate number four
For whatever reason rather than continue to explore

The player chosen was long-time Yankee, Bob Shawkey
Former New York pitcher, now coach and Yankee devotee
Shawkey was hired and Meusel sold to Cincinnati
In **1930**, the Yankees went on a rebuilding spree

The Yankees obtained Red Ruffing from the Red Sox
Giving up Cedric Durst, as Boston they did outfox
Later in the month, Hoyt and Koenig were sent to Detroit
Opening short for Lyn Lary, a move so adroit

Rookie Ben Chapman replaced Dugan at third base
Roster changes, the Depression, hardly a race
The Yankees finished 86-68 in lowly third place
A hefty 16 games back of the A's, far off the pace

After the season Bob Shawkey was fired, no surprise
And not happy over his sudden and unexpected demise
According to Shawkey, he was asked to return in '31
By both Ruppert and Barrow, verbally the deal was done

Later, on the way to the office of GM Ed Barrow
Shawkey spotted Joe McCarthy leaving, a crushing blow
At that moment, Shawkey knew he wasn't returning
He took one look, said nothing, and left in anger burning

Author Marty Appel knew Shawkey late in life
And discussed with him those days of bitter strife
Shawkey was still angry about his treatment, so rude
To Appel, he succinctly said, "I got screwed."

Joe McCarthy Arrives, Another Championship (1931–1932)

Firing Shawkey, justified or not, he got the boot
So how it was handled is really moot
The Yankees wanted McCarthy, manager of Chicago
With the Cubs since '26, his appeal to Wrigley lost its glow

There were reasons for Wrigley's unrest
In 1930, they all came together and coalesced
Rogers Hornsby wanted the manager's position
Believing he could do a better job, his admission

Wrigley remembered losing the World Series in 1929
To Philadelphia, and the way they lost, it did undermine
It happened in game four, the Cubs leading by eight
In the seventh, 10 A's did cross home plate!

The disaster was aided by two lost balls in the sun
The A's won the game 10-8, Chicago was now done
Hack Wilson was the outfielder who made the flubs
As McCarthy took some blame as manager of the Cubs

Whether McCarthy resigned from the Cubs or was fired
Was debatable, but by the Yankees he was quickly hired
It was rumored to be a two-year deal, $30,000 per year
Proved to be the right move for the Yankees and Joe's career

To Ruth, hiring Joe McCarthy was an affront
And in his criticism, he was very blunt
McCarthy never played in the major leagues, he said
While Ruth's dream of managing was crushed instead

In the minor leagues, McCarthy played 15 years
Learning the game, day in and day out from his peers
More important was his managerial experience
That over the years was successful and immense

Joe McCarthy managed in the minors for 10 years
Seven with the Louisville Colonels to raves and cheers
During McCarthy's tenure in the American Association
Won two pennants, a Little World Series laying a foundation

It paid off in 1926 when he signed with the Cubs
And on to the New York Yankees, the best of clubs
McCarthy was a disciplinarian, task master, all business
He cut out card playing, and demanded appropriate dress

He was a savvy baseball man with an acute memory
But in **1931,** McCarthy had a rude awakening for all to see
Mack's A's bulldozed to their third straight AL flag
As McCarthy's Yankees, 13½ games back, did lag

In '31, Lou Gehrig set an AL record with 185 RBIs
He also tied Ruth with 46 home runs, likewise
But the sensation of the season was a young rookie
A left-handed pitcher . . . and a tad kooky

Vernon "Lefty" Gomez won 21, lost nine
An engaging character, always with a witty line
When asked about his success, he revealed
"Clean living and a fast outfield"

1932 was an entirely different story
Won the pennant by 13 games and more glory
The Yankees won 107 games; the pitching was terrific
Gomez was 24-7, to be more specific

Joe McCarthy Arrives, Another Championship (1931–1932)

Ruffing 18-7 and George Pipgras 16-9, no joking
Johnny Allen, 17-4, a rookie skilled at provoking
In time, Allen's temper and erratic behavior did him in
It makes one wonder what he might have been

Rookie Frankie Crosetti was now at short
From the San Francisco Seals, he added support
And would remain with the Yankees for 37 years
17 as an active player, loved by all it appears

He also spent 20 as the Yankees third base coach
Making quick and critical decisions, a vital approach
Alongside the "Crow" was Joe Sewell at third base
One of the great contact hitters of the human race

He was the man most difficult to strike out
Making contact was what he was all about
In 503 at bats, he fanned three times in '32
His advice, "Keep your eye on the ball," few could do

Gehrig, at age 29, had a great season once more
His stats, except for Yankee fans, beginning to bore
He led the club in hitting .349 and runs batted in 151
Ruth, at age 37, led with 41 homers, a familiar rerun

In '32, Bill Dickey, as a Yankee was in his fifth year
And at the top of his game, he was near
He hit .310 with 15 homers and 84 RBIs
A solid season, many times he would reprise

The 1932 World Series vs Chicago was quite bitter
Today, the story would be all over twitter
In reality, it was more than bitter, it was hostile
The bench jockeying from both sides, ugly and vile

The mayhem and nasty remarks began in game one
Led by Ruth who could never be outdone
The reason was the Cubs voted Koenig a half share
Of the Series money and the Yankees thought unfair

Mark played for the Yankees and was a likeable guy
So, when Ruth called the Cubs "cheapskates," that's why
During all the taunting the Yankees won the first two
The scores 12-6 and 5-2, Ruffing and Gomez did subdue

Now on to controversial game three, and the "called shot"
Quoted from my book, *Baseball Memories*, a dubious plot
At Wrigley in game three, Charlie Root was on the mound
Ruth came to bat in the fifth, the crowd spellbound

As the Babe stepped to the plate, the score tied at four
With heckling and derisive catcalls never heard before
Ruth took two strikes from pitcher Root
He dug in, raised his arm and pointed, now the dispute!

Did he point to center field indicating a home run?
Or point two fingers at the Cub's dugout saying, not done
On the next pitch, Ruth hit a monster home run
That clout over the years has been spun and spun

The next morning a reporter dubbed it the "called shot"
Others followed suit, thickening the bogus plot
That's how the legend of the "called shot" was born
While observers and players refuted the myth with scorn

Years later Root and Ruth met on a movie set
The called shot discussed in the following vignette
Root said, "Hey, you never pointed to center field . . ."
Ruth started laughing . . . the truth revealed

". . . I didn't, but it made a hell of a story . . ."
The Babe was correct, for the debate is still laudatory
Regardless, the legend lives on, what's not to adore
Lest you forget the Yankees took the Series in four!

The Yankees did win the heated game three, 7-5
Pipgras the win, Pennock a save, Cubs barely alive
Not for long, as the Yankees won game four, 13-6
On a combo of hitting and pitching, a winning mix

The star of the '32 Series was Gehrig, without a doubt
Hitting .529 with three home runs, he did clout
Accounting for a team-leading eight runs batted in
As usual, Ruth got the headlines, and the spin

It was the **Yankees fourth World Championship**
On to 23 more, all other teams to outstrip
It was also the **Yankees seventh AL pennant**, 34 to go
Before they would reach another glorious plateau

Three Second Place Finishes, Ruth Departs (1933–1935)

In **1933**, the Yankees finished 91-59 in second place
Seven games back of Washington, winners of the AL race
The Senators (99-53) improved their team, did not standstill
Acquiring Lefty Stewart, Jack Russell, and Earl Whitehill

These three pitchers would win 49 games, almost half
Led by General Crowder (24-15), the ace of the staff
While the Yankees saw no reason to change or revise
With power from Dickey, Gehrig, and Lazzeri, it's hard to criticize

And of course, the one and only, the once great Ruth
The Babe now showing signs of aging, no longer a youth
In fact, some thought Ruth was becoming a liability
Although most fans came to see him, not all did agree

The Yanks drew over 728,000, the most in baseball
However, the Babe's stats were beginning to show a downfall
He batted .301 and hit only 34 homers, the lowest since 1925
The season of the "bellyache", when his performance took a dive

Despite Ruth's slowing, he still managed to grab a headline
On July 6, in the first major league All-Star Game, he did shine
He walloped the first home run in All-Star Game history
It was a two-run shot, resulting in the 4-2 AL victory

The '33 season was characterized by a lowlight and a highlight
First, the Yankees and Senators were in an embarrassing fight
It involved the Yankees' Chapman and Washington's Buddy Myer
With bad blood remaining from '32, it became a wildfire

Three Second Place Finishes, Ruth Departs (1933–1935)

It began with Chapman sliding hard into Myer at second
In turn, Myer kicked Chapman in the thigh, he did reckon
As Chapman began punching Myer with a series of blows
Both benches emptied defending their teammates, so it goes

It was hinted that Chapman made anti-Semitic remarks to Myer
Chapman had no love for Jews who knew if it did transpire
Both Myer and Chapman were ejected and had to vamoose
Through the Senators dugout, Chapman received verbal abuse

Resulting in Chapman and pitcher Whitehill in another bout
Causing angry Senator fans to grab bats from the dugout
While Yankee Dixie Walker went after taunting fans
Aided by Dickey, Lazzeri, and Gomez, three capable hands

Myer, Chapman, and Whitehill were suspended for five days
While fans were arrested for their mischievous ways
This wild and crazy story finally ended, it would seem
Not so, three years later, Chapman traded to another team

Guess what team Chapman was traded to, just for fun?
None other than the feisty Senators from Washington
Chapman and Myer were now teammates, how ironic
Whoever made the trade must have been demonic

On to a happier event, and it's about Lou Gehrig
On August 17, he played in his 1,308 consecutive gig
The milestone broke the previous record by Everett Scott
Playing for the Yankees in 1923, in case anyone forgot

In **1934,** the New York Yankees finished second once more
Behind the Tigers, led by Hank Greenberg, with stats to adore
At 23, he batted .339 with 26 homers and 139 ribbies
And led the AL with 63 doubles, a genuine Hercules

But there were hopeful signs for the Yankees ahead
They called up three future stars, none a retread
They were Red Rolfe, Johnny Murphy, and George Selkirk
From the Newark Bears, they came ready for serious work

For the next seven years Rolfe anchored third base
While Murphy soon became the Yankees relief ace
Selkirk helped fill in for Combs immediately in July
Who broke his shoulder crashing into a wall he would defy

In 1934, Gehrig won the prodigious Triple Crown
Forty-nine times the slugger went downtown
He also batted .363, an unheard-of average now
And drove in 166, as Phil Rizzuto would say, "Holy Cow"

Gehrig also had a Triple Crown winner as a teammate
Lefty Gomez was his name, who in '34 was simply great
He led the AL with 26 wins, 2.33 ERA, and 158 K's
Plus, pitching in over 281 innings, a season of praise

Sadly, Babe Ruth's last season as a Yankee was 1934
The most popular player ever, the fans did love and adore
His stats reflected an aging and upset superstar he'd been
He batted .288 with 22 homers and 84 runs batted in

Today, those stats would bring a multi-million-dollar contract
Those numbers, a joke when Ruth was in his prime, that's a fact
However, Ruth did leave behind some impressive milestones
On July 13, he hit homer number 700, higher than the Dow Jones

On August 12, his last appearance at Boston's Fenway
A record 46,766 attended, as 20,000 were turned away
And on September 29, as a Yankee he hit his last home run
At Washington, but the Sultan of Swat was not done

Three Second Place Finishes, Ruth Departs (1933-1935)

Since the hiring of McCarthy, the Babe was frustrated
He wanted to manage the Yanks but was repudiated
He wouldn't return to the Yankees in **1935**, he stated
Unless the long-awaited Yankee managers job awaited

The sudden ultimatum took Ruppert by surprise
But the owner to the occasion quickly did arise
From *Baseball Memories*, a poem tells the outcome
Entitled, *A Bittersweet Ending*, and Ruth, a Yankee alum

It was a very bold and final statement by Ruth
But Ruppert's rejection of him was the truth
The solution with the Boston Braves did wait
As owner Emil Fuchs held Ruth's baseball fate

With Ruppert's okay, Fuchs offered Ruth a contract
With ambiguous and vague clauses, it was stacked
Was he offered the coveted manager's position?
Only the "opportunity to manage" was the condition

Fuchs had an ulterior motive surely
To use Ruth as an attraction purely
Fuchs and the Braves were in financial straits
He needed more fans coming through the gates

Ruth quickly realized as the '35 season began
He was being used by Fuchs as a straw man
He wasn't going to be a manager, just a **player**
Emil Fuchs was a sneaky betrayer

But the proud Bambino had one memorable day left
With a baseball bat in hand, he was always so deft
Against Pittsburgh on May 25 at Forbes Field
At the plate, a harvest of homers he did yield

In the first inning off Red Lucas **#712**, he struck
As he circled the bases like a proud young buck
In the third inning off Guy Bush **#713**, he smashed
Once more circling the bases unabashed

Each time there was a runner on base
Now came the 7th inning Bush again to face
Bases were empty as Ruth clobbered **#714**
At the time, this career number was obscene

Ruth's final home run cleared the Forbes Field fence
A blast so powerful it was described as immense
Landing in the street and rolling to Schenley Park
Estimated 500 feet away, a Ruthian trademark

Ruth hit three home runs by day's end
Going 4 for 4 with 6 RBIs, his glory to extend
It truly was Babe Ruth's last and final hurrah
His next several games were a painful blah

On June 2, 1935, Babe Ruth finally retired
A shell of himself, but still widely admired
Larger than life in and out of the game
He saved baseball, many historians proclaim

The Yankees finished second in **1935**, three back
The Detroit Tigers winning with an up and down attack
They also won the World Series defeating Chicago
Their first Series win ever, with the city all aglow

It was the Yankees first season, sans the Sultan of Swat
And Gehrig was named captain, Lou was in Camelot
The first captain since Everett Scott, you see
Who left the Yankees in 1925 with a lame knee

It is hard to write the next line with a straight face
Gehrig had an "off" season, and to make the case
He batted .329 with 30 homers and 120 runs batted in
Compared to his other seasons is the key, but thin

The divisive Johnny Allen was finally sent packing
His personality there was always something lacking
He and McCarthy were never well-matched
So, a trade to Cleveland was finally hatched

Allen traded for pitchers Steve Sundra and Monte Pearson
Sadly for Cleveland, his on-field rage would have a rerun
From Cleveland, he moved on to three other teams
His temper and anger always spoiling his talent and dreams

Before leaving 1935 and the exciting years ahead, buckle down
Mention must be made of what happened in tiny Cooperstown
The **first election** to the **Hall of Fame** was held in December 1935
Electing five of the greatest players, except for one, all alive

Babe Ruth, Honus Wagner, Walter Johnson, and Ty Cobb
Plus, Christy Mathewson were selected, an easy job
Throughout the years they have been often admired
Resulting in, deservedly so, immortality acquired

Joe D Arrives, Four More Championships, Ruppert and Gehrig Die (1936–1939)

Second place finishes for the Yankees would end
When Joe DiMaggio, a Yankees contract he penned
Actually, the event took place in May 1934
And almost didn't happen . . . let' explore

The rumored price of $100,000 was needed to buy DiMaggio
And during the Depression, an exceptional amount of dough
DiMaggio was playing in the PCL for the San Francisco Seals
In love with his talent, scouts were head over heels

He was the perfect baseball player, some said
Many knew of his potential as word quickly spread
DiMaggio possessed quiet and steady leadership traits
And would be loved and worshipped by his teammates

Sports writers had a difficult time analyzing him
Was he quiet, distant, coy, or just plain grim?
One thing everyone agreed upon, he could hit
In 1933, a 61-game hitting streak, he did acquit

The Yankees wanted to sign Joe in '34, but for an injury
Stepping out of a taxi, he tore cartilage in his knee
After an orthopedist determined DiMaggio would heal
Yankee scout, Bill Essick, called George Weiss to make the deal

Weiss was in charge of the farm system since 1932
"Don't give up on DiMaggio," Essick said anew
Weiss' faith in Essick paid off for many years to come
Signing Joe for $25,000, five minor leaguers, a small sum

Joe D Arrives, Four More Championships, Ruppert and Gehrig Die (1936–1939)

Joe played for the Seals in 1935, batting .398
With 34 home runs, the Yankees await
It was time for Joe to make it on the big stage
Travelling east, the rookie was all the rage

"Joe D" was not the only new face with the Yankees in 1936
Jake Powell arrived from Washington, the outfield to fix
Also from Washington came pitcher Bump Hadley
In a January trade, he was finally set free

In 1936, the Yankees won pennant number eight
Topping Detroit by 19½ games, their second-place fate
Offensively, the Yankees (102-51) were close to the 1927 team
Six of the eight regulars batted over .300, a manager's dream

Dickey led the club with a batting average of .362
A record for catchers, but since broken by a few
Gehrig led the club with 49 homers, no surprise
Five Yankees chipped in with over 100 RBIs

Gehrig also batted .354, hitting all season long
With 152 RBIs, like All-American Jack Armstrong
And 130 walks, scoring 167 times, a fabulous season
Earning him his second MVP and for good reason

DiMaggio was one of the five with 125 RBIs
Plus 29 homers and a .323 average, stats to eulogize
The pitching rotation was good, not awesome
Ruffing with 20 wins, the leader he had become

Pearson won 19, more than twice the previous year
While Gomez with 13, off his game it did appear
Hadley won 14, Johnny Broaca 12, soon to leave baseball
His troubles in '37 due to jumping the team, the end all

Yankees versus Giants, the first Subway Series in 13 years
Welcome by the New York faithful with supportive cheers
The Yankees won the Series in six exciting games
After losing the opener to one of the great baseball names

Carl Hubbell finished the regular season on fire
Winning 16 in a row, a streak to admire
The left-hander's record was 26-6 with a 2.31 ERA
"Hub" won the first game 6-1, dominating all the way

In game two, the Yankees mauled Schumacher and the relievers
The score was 18-4, the Giant hurlers clearly underachievers
Lazzeri's grand slam was one of the game's features
The second in World Series history landing in the bleachers

Hadley tamed the Giants in game three, 2-1
With Crosetti in the eighth knocking in the winning run
Hubbell was looking to tie the Series in game four
But the Yankees had other plans in store

Despite Hubs best efforts he lost the game 5-2
Gehrig's two-run homer early, Hub's fatal miscue
While Pearson pitched a nifty seven hitter for the win
The Giants were now on proverbial ice so thin

On the brink of losing the Series in game five
The Giants won 5-4 in 10 innings to stay alive
The victory only delayed the obvious conclusion
Giving the Giants hope . . . or was it an illusion?

In game six the Yankees ended the Giants dream
Crushing them 13-5 and emerging the better team
The Yankees were leading, entering the ninth 6-5
When their hungry bats suddenly did arrive

Joe D Arrives, Four More Championships, Ruppert and Gehrig Die (1936-1939)

Five singles, one error, and three walks later
Seven runs were put on the board, a huge deflator
It was the **New York Yankees fifth World Championship**
Looking ahead, 22 more and a wonderful and joyous trip

In **1937**, the Yankees easily won their **ninth AL flag**
With a 102-52 record, while the Tigers by 13 did lag
Despite Selkirk and Powell missing valuable playing time
The Yankees played inspired baseball . . . ever so sublime

Two replacements picked up the Yanks outfield slack
Myril Hoag and Tommy Henrich added to the attack
Hoag batted .301 in 106 games, the most he played
Henrich in 67 games hit .320, a star for the next decade

Henrich's rise to fame is a very interesting one
Beginning with Cleveland trying a sneaky end run
Hiding Tommy in their farm system, they boldly dared
Until Landis, Tommy's a free agent, he declared

The Yankees signed Henrich for $25,000 it was reported
Although offered more money from others, he thwarted
"I'd been a Yankee fan since I was eight years old"
Now as a gifted Yankee player he was in their fold

Henrich played with the Yankees until 1950, his last year
With DiMaggio and Charlie Keller, an outfield to revere
Noted for his clutch hitting which was justifiable
He proudly was given the nickname "Old Reliable"

Gehrig, DiMaggio, and Dickey in '37, tough outs all
Leading the offense, the reason they are in the Hall
Gehrig hit .351 along with 158 runs batted in
And 37 homers, too bad Lou wasn't a twin

But 22-year-old Joe D looking like the future franchise
Driving in 167, an AL best 46 homers to tantalize
Oh yes, Joe D also led the league with 151 runs scored
While hitting a cool .346, no wonder he was so adored

Dickey in 140 games at the most demanding position
Hit .332 with 29 homers and 133 RBIs, man on a mission
Gomez and Ruffing led the Yankees pitching staff
Together they wrote many opposing team's epitaph

Gomez (21-11) with a 2.33 ERA bounced back from '36
It was in the World Series where "Goofy" got his kicks
Ruffing (20-7) with an earned run average of 2.98
Made this lefty/righty pitching combo simply first-rate

Second World Series in a row, the Yankees/Giants met
The Yankees won in five . . . no need to fret
Game one, Gomez against Hubbell, two of the best
As the score of 1-0 Giants into the sixth would attest

"Hubbell is going to walk our lead-off man," Joe did claim
He added, "Let's get ready for an inning to win this game"
Sure enough, McCarthy's trusted expectations came true
The Yankees scored seven, chasing Hub and saying adieu

The final score was 8-1, the same as in game two
Ruffing scattered seven hits, the Giants in a stew
Game three, Pearson and the Yankees led 5-1
Ninth, bases full, two out, Giants looking home run

McCarthy taking no chances, he yanked Pearson
Calling for Johnny Murphy as the tension had begun
The "Fireman" as he was called, pitched to one batter
Ending the game . . . it was a very simple matter

Joe D Arrives, Four More Championships, Ruppert and Gehrig Die (1936–1939)

In game four, Hubbell, as expected, kept the Giants alive
With a clutch six-hitter (7-3) to bring on game five
Gomez versus Melton, and after four tied at two all
But the fifth inning was sadly the Giant's downfall

Lazzeri tripled and scored on Gomez's clutch hit
As the Yankees took a 3-2 lead and didn't quit
An error by the Giants moved Gomez to second base
Then Gehrig doubled for an insurance run in case

The game finally ended 4-2, the Yankees did slay
Two more wins, Lefty now 5-0 in World Series play
Walter Johnson said, "Gomez is a great money pitcher"
The praise from Lefty's idol made his performance richer

Lazzeri led all hitters batting .400, but soon to be let go
For the Newark Bears had a young player named Joe
Gordon his surname and in '38 he played second
Until traded in 1946 for Allie Reynolds as Cleveland did beckon

It was the **Yankees sixth World Series Championship**
More on the horizon Yankee fans, relax, and get a grip
And of course, 32 more AL pennants and stars to deploy
Plus 21 more World Series titles to recall with joy

The Yankees made it **three straight pennants in 1938**
Finishing 99-53, winning on the mound and at the plate
The Red Sox finished a distant second, 9½ games back
Future years the bitter rivalry would create lots of flack

Joe D led the Yankees in average home runs and RBIs
Hitting .324/32/140, and at 23 now the franchise
Rookie Gordon added power as Gehrig declined
He hit 25 homers and drove in 97, his future defined

49

Gehrig hit .295/29/114, a telling season for the big guy
While fans were, no doubt, thinking age was the reason why
Sadly, all would soon find out it was much more dire
And the way Gehrig handled it . . . much to admire

Henrich, in his second season moved from left to right field
Smacking 22 homers and driving in 91, numbers he did wield
With a superb 21-7 record, Ruffing led the pitching rotation
His third season in a row of 20 or more, a solid foundation

Backed by Gomez (18-12) and 16 wins from Pearson
One was the **first no-hitter at Yankee Stadium** ever spun
The right-hander beat Cleveland 13-0, his former club
While Spud Chandler finished (14-5), no longer a sub

The Yankees now the toast of the town and way beyond
Nearing a million in attendance with a loyal fan-based bond
Setting a record on May 30, when over 80,000 fans attended
Stadium capacity much less, fire laws ignored or bended

In the NL, the Chicago Cubs won the flag
As Pittsburgh, by two games, did lag
Bill Lee (22-9) was their pitching ace
Offensively, versus the Yankees, no race

The Yankees faced the Cubs, the Fall Classic of 1932
Swept the Cubs like a banana republic coup
Also in this World Series, third game, if you recall
The Babe hit the controversial "called" home run ball

Joe was facing the Cubs again, looking for an encore of '32
While Cubs manager Hartnett aimed to shake the bugaboo
Experts thought the Cubs had little chance of winning
Right on, after four games only the Yankees were grinning

Joe D Arrives, Four More Championships, Ruppert and Gehrig Die (1936–1939)

In game one, the Yankees beat Bill Lee, the Cubs' ace
Ruffing winning 3-1, scattering nine hits, setting the pace
The Cubs hoping for a miracle started Dean in game two
But "Dizzy" was no longer the pitcher everyone knew

Diz had broken his toe in the 1937 All-Star Game
From that point on, his fast ball wasn't the same
To his credit Diz soft-pitched the Yankees, leading 3-2
In the eighth, a two-run homer to Crosetti he threw

In the ninth Dean gave up another two-run blast
DiMaggio the culprit, final score 6-3, Cub fans aghast
The lack of his famous fast ball made pitching tough
Joe D said, ". . . it was just a slow curve and control stuff"

Gomez the win, his sixth in a World Series, Murphy the save
Pearson against Bryant (19-11) game three, a shock wave
As the Yankees won 5-2 on Gordon and Dickey four-baggers
Now the Cubs, close to elimination, were serious laggers

To complete the sweep, McCarthy sent Ruffing to the mound
The Cubs responded with Lee, who the Yankees did pound
Giving up three in the second inning to lose the game 8-3
Crosetti drove in four of the eight ending a Series hot spree

The **Yankees seventh World Championship**, third in a row
The latter the first in the game's history, wouldn't you know
Amidst the great news there was a coming storm of despair
Gehrig's strange behavior, teammates and others were aware

Something was wrong with Lou; it showed in his Series play
He batted .286, no home runs or RBIs, to everyone's dismay
Some good-naturedly in jest, blamed it on his getting old
It was much more when, next year, the full story would unfold

The year **1939** for players and fans would be an emotional trip
The Yankees were seeking their **11th flag** and **eighth Championship**
But sadly, the death of Ruppert and then Gehrig's demise
Would fill the year with unforeseen lows and proud highs

Mixed emotions dominated the year 1939
Beginning with Ruppert's failing health, an early sign
Phlebitis began to take its toll the year before
Curtailing activities and health signs not to ignore

On January 12, 1939, Ruth paid the dying Ruppert a visit
A conversation the Colonel's condition did not permit
The mighty Babe left the dying owner in tears
Despite their disagreements over the many years

Sadly, Colonel Jacob Ruppert died the following day
With services held at St. Patrick's for friends to pray
While thousands lined the streets to honor the man
And the emerging New York Yankee dynasty he began

Yankees ownership was split into three pieces
A long-time lady friend of the Colonel and two nieces
However, it was the trustees who ran the team
And named Barrow president, who was held in high esteem

Spring training of '39, all eyes were fixed on Lou
The question everyone asked: was he all through?
Gehrig was clearly showing signs of slowing down
Gone was the powerful swing, once held in renown

Notably sluggish at his position, first base
His slowed reactions appeared out of place
Gehrig sensed something was not quite right
While McCarthy faced an uncomfortable plight

Joe D Arrives, Four More Championships, Ruppert and Gehrig Die (1936-1939)

Late April, Lou's failing skills left him feeling low
May 2, he told McCarthy, "I'm benching myself Joe"
Shortly after a week at the Mayo Clinic he did spend
Examined by specialists and what it would portend

The diagnosis was amyotrophic lateral sclerosis
A rare and fatal disease not easy to dismiss
Once the tragic news reached Lou's fans
The Yankees put into motion honorary plans

Soon after, "Lou Gehrig Appreciation Day" was proclaimed
Independence Day July 4, 1939, eagerly and proudly named
Over 61,000 fans attended the pageant, colorful and dramatic
Dignitaries extolling the dying player with praise so emphatic

The Yankees retired Lou's uniform number "4"
Never achieved in major league history before
Lou was presented with tributes and gifts galore
From groundskeepers, VIPs, and many more

Lou then delivered "Baseball's Gettysburg Address"
Leaving everyone in tears and an emotional mess
His immortal line repeated here for all it's worth
"I consider myself the luckiest man on the face of the earth"

Of course, there is much more to the famous speech
Humility, kindness, and love he did preach
Five months later, Lou was elected to the Hall of Fame
On June 2, 1941, he passed, a lasting tribute to the game

With Gehrig gone and Dahlgren at first base
The Yankees still steamrolled into first place
As the Red Sox finished 17 games behind
Frequently chasing the Yankees, their role defined

It was the **Yankees AL pennant number 11**
As Yankees fans relished being in baseball heaven
DiMaggio, Gordon, Selkirk, and Bill Dickey
Provided awesome power all would agree

Each drove in more than 100 runs, did they
Making the Yankees tough to outplay
DiMaggio led the league with an average of .381
At times flirting with .400 as the fan's favorite son

Let's not forget rookie Charlie Keller
His contribution, a season so stellar
"King Kong" batted .334 with 83 RBIs
Adding to the opposition's futile demise

The pitching was led by Red Ruffing, a right-hander
With a 21-7 mark, a superb season in all candor
It was Red's fourth straight season winning 20 or more
A rare pitching performance that's hard to ignore

No other Yankee hurlers came close to winning 20
But Steve Sundra and Atley Donald contributed plenty
Sundra posted an 11-1 (.917) mark with a 2.76 ERA
While Donald was 13-3, to the opposing team's dismay

Cincinnati won the pennant in the National League
Narrowly beating St. Louis, unlike the Yankees blitzkrieg
The Reds had key players, so give credit where credit is due
Of the starting lineup and star hurlers, here's a quick review

Frank McCormick batted .332 and drove in 128
The best on the club as havoc he could create
Ernie Lombardi with only 85 ribbies was next
Led the club with 20 homers, little power to flex

Joe D Arrives, Four More Championships, Ruppert and Gehrig Die (1936–1939)

Billy Werber and Ival Goodman offered plenty of speed
Not a good substitute for power, many agreed
The Reds' pitching staff perhaps was a little too thin
With two hurlers, maybe three, the World Series to win

Bucky Walters led the major leagues with 27 wins
Paul Derringer with 25, they were victory twins
That's almost where the Reds pitching story ends
But there was another hurler who paid rich dividends

His name is Gene Thompson, mainly a reliever
A right-hander and a very young overachiever
His record was 13-5, with a 2.54 era
Could be a surprise during Series play

When the press finished examining each team thoroughly
The World Series began and Cincinnati met reality
Game one, Ruffing in a pitcher's duel edged Derringer 2-1
Dickey's ninth inning single drove in the winning run

Game two, Monte Pearson pitched a stunning two-hitter
Beating Bucky Walters 4-0, as Yankee fans were aglitter
Gomez (12-8) was matched against Thompson in game three
Lefty allowed a run in the first, then was removed for a side injury

Bump Hadley (12-6) replaced Gomez as the Yankees exploded
With four runs as Keller (2), DiMaggio, and Dickey unloaded
While Hadley threw eight strong innings and won 7-3
Young Thompson took the loss, facing hitters so beastly

Suffice it to say, game four was more than exciting
And a poetic challenge putting it down in writing
No score until the top of the seventh frame
When Keller and Dickey homered, Derringer to blame

55

The Reds struck back in their half of the inning
With three runs off Sundra, now set on winning
The following inning, the Reds added another run
Off reliever Murphy, score now 4-2, but Yanks not done

In the ninth, the Yankees scored twice off Walters
To tie the game at 4-4, as the Red's ace falters
Then in the 10th, New York scored a big three
With DiMaggio's clutch, two ribbies the key

In the Reds 10th, Murphy got himself in a mess
Allowing the first two hitters to single, no less
But then Murphy regained his confidence
Retiring the side, and ending the suspense

It was the **Yankees eighth World Series Championship**
And this glorious victory was a record-setting pip
It was the New York Yankees fourth consecutive win
Along with their fourth consecutive pennant, baseball's twin

A Narrow Miss, another Winning Streak (1940–1943)

The **1940** AL pennant race was a nasty bummer
A battle among three competitive teams all summer
New York, Detroit, and Cleveland fought to the end
As the reluctant Detroit Tigers refused to bend

The Tigers finished ahead of Cleveland by one game
And the Yankees by two, what a shame
It spoiled McCarthy's goal of five straight
Themselves to blame, their play not first rate

Crosetti, Rolfe, Dickey, and Selkirk had off years
One of a manager's most dreaded fears
There was one exception, Joe DiMaggio
Giving Yankee fans something about which to crow

"Joltin' Joe" batted a cool .352 at the young age of 25
His second consecutive batting title for which he did strive
It would be the only two batting titles he would win
But Joe D was still, without a doubt, the Yankees kingpin

The pitching was also disappointing except for a few
Especially the hurlers McCarthy counted on as the glue
Ruffing went from 21-7 to a shocking 15-12
While sore arm Gomez the Yankees did shelve

The Yankees turn around in **1941** was hard to believe
Finishing 17 games ahead of Boston they did achieve
Once again, the main attraction was Joltin' Joe
His 56-game hitting streak fanned the Yankees' glow

Let's pause a moment to relive The Streak
An event in time adding to Joe's mystique
From my book, *Baseball Memories*, it was taken
This poem of Joe's rare talent it will awaken

The Streak

It began innocently on May 15, 1941
No . . . it was not an exciting home run
Just a harmless single was the blow
By a guy nicknamed Joltin' Joe DiMaggio

The "Yankee Clipper" was another nickname
Over the years brought him well deserved fame
That harmless little single started it all
The greatest hitting streak in Major League Baseball

Against the Red Sox, the streak ran to ten
The sports media silent as Big Ben
By mid-June, the streak had reached 25
National coverage now came alive

As DiMaggio continued, the pressure mounted
Every at-bat, every pitch now counted
He singled on a 3-0 pitch in late June
Now the streak at 40, nothing picayune

Amongst all the media and fan ballyhoo
July 2, he set a new record at 42
In Cleveland, the record jumped to 56 without a hitch
As Joe slashed a single on Milnar's first pitch

> Over 67,000 fans came the next night
> To watch Joe extend the streak to their delight
> But sadly, it was not to be
> For Joltin' Joe went 0 for 3
>
> But the box score does not tell the true story
> Joe still went out in a blaze of glory
> 3rd baseman Ken Keltner, the player to blame
> Who robbed Joe of two hits, what a shame
>
> Joe was not finished, just more mystique
> The next day he began a 16-game hitting streak
> The summer of '41 Joe inspired a nation, it's true
> And help them forget oncoming World War II

DiMaggio was named the AL's Most Valuable Player
Over Boston's Ted Williams, a pitching slayer
All Williams did at 22, was hit .406 for the long season
Ted not chosen, no doubt, Boston's second place the reason

There were other reasons the **Yankees won their 12th flag**
One was a rookie you could fit in a duffel bag
A young shortstop named Phil Rizzuto
Who solidified the infield and replaced the Crow

DiMaggio was flanked by Keller in left and Henrich in right
Formed in '41, one of the best Yankee outfields, a fans delight
There was one sad moment for the Yankees, their fans and fun
The beloved "Iron Horse" passed away on June 2, 1941

Now on to the World Series against Brooklyn
Who hadn't won a pennant since 1920, what a sin
Durocher was their manager, brash and feisty, was he
A stark contrast to Joe McCarthy, silent and brainy

It was an "unmemorable" World Series until game four
Almost predicable, but certainly not a bore
Ruffing narrowly won the first game by a score of 3-2
Game two, Whit Wyatt beat Chandler 3-2 on a miscue

In game three, Yankee Marius Russo beat Hugh Casey
The score 2-1, the next contest impossible to foresee
Now on to game four, with Brooklyn barely leading 4-3
With two outs, in the ninth, a tied Series soon to be

Not so fast, Old Reliable Tommy Henrich is at bat
Casey's 3-2 pitch is anything but flat
Henrich swings and misses for the almost third out
But catcher Mickey Owen also misses, game in doubt

With the passed ball Henrich reaches safely at first
What happens next . . . clearly the Dodgers are cursed
Single, double, walk, another double, four runs scored
And just like that the Brooklyn Dodgers are floored

Murphy, in relief, set Brooklyn down, one, two, three
The final score Yankees 7 Dodgers 4, a stunning victory
The next day Bonham beats Brooklyn 3-1, a four-hit pip
New York Yankees win their ninth World Championship

It's time to segue into the season of **1942** and the battle fray
With the war blazing there was doubt MLB would even play
President Roosevelt gives a clear answer to the folks at home
Expressed in my book *Baseball Memories*, comes this poem

The Green Light Letter

In 1941 America was in love with baseball
A 56-game hitting streak by DiMag did enthrall
And Williams hit .406 as a 22-year-old
Then came Pearl Harbor a tragedy to behold

A Narrow Miss, another Winning Streak (1940-1943)

The U.S. was quickly drawn into the war
All, including ballplayers, volunteered galore
Leaving the 1942 baseball season in doubt
Prompting Commissioner Landis to ask **out**

Should baseball continue to operate?
For the answer, Landis didn't have long to wait
"It would be best for the country," said Roosevelt
A morale boost was clearly and emphatically dealt

With World War II on everyone's mind in full swing
Like others, Major League Baseball felt the sting
Hank Greenberg and Bob Feller among the first to volunteer
While other players were called to serve with good cheer

Initially, the Yankees lost only two players to the war
Johnny Sturm, a first baseman and Henrich, no more
The Yankees picked up Buddy Hassett to play first
A position in which he was well versed

Other than these changes, the Yankee club remained the same
Yet again, managed to control the Boston Red Sox and tame
Winning 103 games with the Sox in second, nine games back
It was their **13th AL pennant** with a dominating pitching attack

Bonham (21-5), Chandler (16-5), and Hank Borowy (15-4)
Along with Atley Donald (11-3) the key rotation corps
Plus, Ruffing, at 37, chipped in with a 14-7 mark
After the season to the draft board, he would embark

Controversy and shock dominated the 1942 season
The MVP award was hotly debated and for good reason
Shock perfectly described the Fall Classic this year
As the Yankee fans had little of which to cheer

Let's begin with the MVP award first
As it appeared Ted Williams was truly cursed
Yankee Joe Gordon was named MVP, to him a surprise
He hit .322 with 18 homers and 103 RBIs

For the second year in a row, Williams was denied
Some thought the voting of the writers cockeyed
Williams batted .356 with 36 home runs and 137 ribbies
Some writers did not like Ted and ignored his expertise

The World Series against St. Louis was the shocker of '42
Heavily favored, it would be the Series the Yankees would rue
The Cardinals were led by two very tough baseball outs
Rookie Stan Musial and Enos Slaughter, if any doubts

Mort Cooper (22-7) and Johnny Beazley (21-6) led the staff
With ERAs of 1.78 and 2.13 respectively and rarely a gaffe
The Cardinals were a young, hustling club who came to play
Winning 106 games, a franchise record that still stands today

The first game of the 1942 World Series was really weird
Ruffing, leading 7-0, close to a no-hitter, when all disappeared
The Cardinals fought back, scoring four runs in the eighth
Leaving the bases full, but giving the youngsters renewed faith

As the saying goes, the Cards lost the battle, but won the war
As they handily swept the New York Yankees the next four!
Next, Beazley beat Bonham 4-3, in game two
Then Ernie White blanked the "Bombers" 2-0, how do you do

Game four, the Yankees with a half empty bag of tricks
As the Cards surprisingly, outslugged New York 9-6
Both starters, Borowy and Cooper left the game early
As Cardinal pitcher, Max Lanier, stopped the hurly burly

A Narrow Miss, another Winning Streak (1940-1943)

The next day the Cards completed the embarrassing sweep
In the ninth, game tied 2-2, runner on, Kurowski went deep
The final score was Cardinals 4, Yankees 2
As shocked fans at the Stadium couldn't believe it was true

Before the **1943** season began military call ups steadily rose
As major leaguers changed baseball uniforms to military clothes
The Yankees lost DiMaggio, Rizzuto, Ruffing, Hassett, and Selkirk
Requiring McCarthy to put together a club that would work

In a trade, the Yankees obtained Nick Etten from the Phillies
Then searched their minor league system looking for Achilles
The Yankees brought up Billy Johnson to play third base
Bud Matheny and Johnny Lindell in the outfield to keep pace

The pitching rotation was close to full strength in '43
With Chandler, Bonham, and Borowy, still no guaranty
Although Chandler did step up and lead the rotation
Spud won 20, lost 4 with a 1.64 ERA, an AL leading sensation

Bonham won 15, Borowy 14, and each an ERA under three
Just what McCarthy hoped for . . . and few would disagree
But this season belonged to Chandler as he was named MVP
The third straight year a Yankee won the award, a rare reality

Keller had a big year, leading the club with 31 home runs
Etten drove in 107, Dickey batted .351, three big guns
The team finished 98-56, **winning pennant number 14**
The Senators finished 13½ behind the McCarthy machine

In the NL, St. Louis won the pennant by 18 games
Off to war were Slaughter and Terry Moore, key names
Also, the Yankees were seeking revenge from '42
It took the Yankees only five games the Cards to subdue

63

Due to the war, travel changed, Landis did remark
Three at the Stadium, the next four at Sportsman's Park
The Yankees won the first 4-2, Spud scattered seven hits
The Yankees ace walked one, using his arm as well as his wits

Hours before game two, Cooper was told his father died
Mort still pitched a courageous game with genuine pride
As did brother Walker, who caught the complete game
The 4-3 win carried with it mixed emotions just the same

The Yankees won game three, 6-2 behind Borowy
Just a solid pitching effort, nothing really showy
Murphy pitched the ninth to preserve the win
The Yanks left the Bronx for St. Louis, game four to begin

Game four, the Cardinals were nipped by a run
It was a tight game, but Russo out dueled Lanier, 2-1
The loss put St. Louis in a dangerous elimination spot
And now facing MVP Chandler just thickened the plot

21-game winner Cooper was called to stop the Yankees
But a two-run blast by Dickey, out came the Cards hankies
Chandler blanked the Cards with clutch pitching, 2-zip
As the **Yankees captured their 10th World Championship**

War Ends, New Ownership, another World Championship (1944–1948)

The **1944** season saw most of MLB's talent fighting a war
Eager to serve their country of which they did adore
Stripped of the most talented baseball players of the day
The game still provided an escape from horrors far away

Yet, it did provide an opportunity for some unable to fight
There was one player who inspired and overcame his plight
A poem from my book *Baseball Memories* relates this moving story
It's more about the man than the times, quite revelatory

One-Armed Wonder

His right arm was severed above the elbow
Most seven-year-olds could not handle the blow
But young Pete Gray was determined beyond belief
To put aside the accident and show little grief

Pete realized if he wanted to play baseball
His body and mind needed an overhaul
To bat and field one-handed . . . he learned
And became so accomplished he was rarely spurned

Pete played semi-pro in the minors,
And was often one of the headliners
With the Three Rivers Club, he achieved fame
By singling to right to win a game

>   The fans so ecstatic they threw money on the field
>   The amount totaled nearly a $700 yield
>   In '44 with Memphis, he stole 68 bases, batted .333
>   Winning for Pete the Southern Association MVP
>
>   The next year Pete joined the Browns in the AL
>   With a .217 batting average, he did not do well
>   For courage and desire, Pete Gray was a wonder
>   And throughout his career would not knuckle under
>
>   Pete Gray's legacy should not be judged by stats
>   Home runs, triples, doubles, stolen bases, or at-bats
>   By showing the disabled what he overcame
>   His glove is immortalized in the Hall of Fame

All the teams in 1944 were happy to be playing
While most of the country was working or praying
The Yankees finished third, attendance rose to 789,995
Proving Roosevelt's letter helped the country to survive

More Yankee players left in '44, as Uncle Sam wasn't picky
Gordon, Keller, Johnson, Chandler, and Bill Dickey
Leaving the Yankees with unfamiliar names, few knew
Mike Garbark, Mike Milosevich, and Bud Metheny are a few

However, all was not lost, there was sparkling play
Nick Etten led the league with 22 home runs by the way
George Sternweiss, nicknamed "Snuffy" performed well
Led the league in hits, runs, triples, and stolen bases, do tell

The 1944 World Series was an all-St. Louis affair
The AL Browns versus the NL Cardinals, indeed rare
All games were played in popular Sportsman's park
The Cards won in six, for the St. Louis fans, a lark

War Ends, New Ownership, another World Championship (1944–1948)

In **1945**, the Yankees finished in fourth place
As the Detroit Tigers won the pennant race
It was another ho-hum season except for Snuffy
Who won the batting title with .309, did he

On September 2, World War II finally came to an end
When Japan surrendered documents they penned
The U.S. joyously celebrated peace and more
Greeting brave men and women who fought the war

But the MLB story for the year was the Yankees sale
To a triumvirate headed by dynamic Larry MacPhail,
Dan Topping, and Dell Webb made up the owners three
With MacPhail visibly running the club for all to see

MacPhail had the experience and background
Flamboyant and unpredictable he could astound
He ran the Reds and Dodgers with success
But not without angst and accompanying stress

Topping was heir to a tin fortune, a millionaire
A reputation as a sportsman with playboy flair
Webb owned a lucrative construction business
Building retirement communities that did impress

Clearly, MacPhail would be running the team
A boisterous, innovative "genius" ready to scheme
While Barrow was named chairman of the board
Leaving McCarthy puzzled, at the moment ignored

But that moment didn't last very long
McCarthy's health was not strong
Gallbladder and drinking were two of his woes
So, a leave of absence to rest he did propose

While he was gone, MacPhail sold Borowy, his ace
To Chicago for $100,000, McCarthy did not embrace
This was the beginning of the end for Joe
At least with the Yankees, but not The Show

The following year **1946**, the first full season post war
DiMaggio, Keller, and Henrich were back . . . and more
Gordon and Rizzuto solidified the infield
Sadly, too late for winning results to yield

The Yankees finished third a distant 17 games back
Of the rival Boston Red Sox with a weak attack
Keller, Joe D, and Henrich tried to keep the offense alive
While most stats of the other returnees took a nosedive

But at the turnstiles the Yankees were first rate
Attendance skyrocketed to 2,265,512, absolutely great
Not everything was rosy as McCarthy resigned in May
More than one reason for Joe's sudden getaway

At age 39, Dickey was the new managing voice
The experienced veteran seemed the ideal choice
By season's end Dickey was dissatisfied and quit
As coach Johnny Neun finished the season, then split

Joe McCarthy left a legacy unmatched at the time
His managing style an ever-winning paradigm
In 16 seasons, eight pennants Joe did prevail
And seven World Championships, quite a tale

The New York Yankees put it all together in **1947**
Every move made seemed like Manna from Heaven
The experienced and outspoken Bucky Harris was hired
As a former winning manager, he was greatly admired

War Ends, New Ownership, another World Championship (1944-1948)

Harris in 1924, was named manager of Washington
And immediately made the Senators number one
At age 27, winning a World Championship, the story
Thus, named "The Boy Wonder" off of the glory

A year later, the Senators finished first once more
Lost the World Series, sadly no encore
After Washington, Bucky managed many other teams
Never winning a pennant, just chasing past dreams

With Murphy gone, Joe Page became a reliever
The fun-loving lefty turned into quite an achiever
He went 14-8 with a 2.48 ERA and 17 saves
Contributing mightily and deserving of the raves

Allie Reynolds for Gordon was a marvelous trade
As the "Chief's" record of 19-8 clearly displayed
From the PCL came right-hander Vic Raschi
Who, very soon a 20-game winner would be

George McQuinn signed as a free agent at 38
Batted .304 and drove in 80, never too late
Rookie Yogi Berra in 83 games made an impression
Batted .280 and drove in 54, a keeper no question

DiMaggio led the club, batting a worthy .315
With 97 ribbies and 20 homers, a familiar scene
Earning the Yankee Clipper his third and last MVP
Edging Triple Crown Winner Williams by one vote, you see

The Yankees finished the season 97-57 under Harris
The Detroit Tigers 12 games behind to embarrass
It was the **New York Yankees pennant number 15**
During the Highlander days who could have foreseen?

69

The Yankees' World Series opponent was Brooklyn
It was one exciting Series and that's no spin
The Yankees won in seven, not for the faint of heart
Especially in game four, you had to be tough like Bogart

The Yankees won the first two by scores of 5-3 and 10-3
At home, the Dodgers stung the Yankees 9-8 like a bee
Thus, game four and the Yanks' Bill Bevens' grief
Thousands of fans stood in total and utter disbelief

The Yankees scored off Harry Taylor in the first
And another run in a fourth-inning outburst
The Dodgers scored also but without a hit
But Bevens, on this day, would not quit

Bevens worked on a no-hitter entering the ninth inning
Leading 2-1, the Yankees on the verge of winning
Two out and Al Gionfriddo on first base
And Pete Reiser, a pinch-hitter for Bevens to face

Moments later Gionfriddo stole second base
The tying run now waiting and in place
Reiser was intentionally walked, a move that did stun
For it now put on base the potentially winning run

Reiser, with a bad ankle, was immediately replaced
With Eddie Miksis with all do haste
Pesky hitter Eddie Stanky was the next batter
Dodger manager Burt Shotton caused more crowd chatter

He replaced Stanky with "Cookie" Lavagetto
Who delivered for the Dodger faithful a mighty blow
Lavagetto lined a double off the right-field wall
Lost were the no-hitter and the game above all

The Yankees bounced back to win game five, 2-1
Another Yankee win and Brooklyn was done
The Dodgers met the challenge the very next day
Beating the Yankees 8-6 causing the final fatal fray

The hero of game seven was lefty Joe Page
Yankees leading 3-2 in the fifth, he took center stage
Blanking the Dodgers for five innings with only one hit
The final score 5-2, both clubs showing spirit and grit

It was the **Yankees 11th victorious World Series**
The excitement, thrill, and satisfaction never wearies
And while players celebrated and champagne flowed
A startling announcement MacPhail did unload

Larry was selling his one third interest in the team
To Topping and Webb, a logical move it would seem
Topping and Webb valued his talent for innovation
The co-owners were now looking for quiet emulation

They quickly announced the new GM, George Weiss
A shrewd baseball man, but colorless as white rice
But MacPhail, as an innovator, had few equals
In the future, the Yankees would experience no sequels

For the Yankees, **1948** was a roller-coaster year
With talent, a letdown, and even a tear
In February, Weiss made a very key trade
Obtaining lefty Eddie Lopat for rotation aid

Lopat teamed up with Reynolds and Raschi
To form a dependable mini staff of the three
The trio accounted for 52 of 94 wins by season's end
As Harris, on the three hurlers, did heavily depend

Even with Joe D and Henrich leading the offensive play
The Yankees lost the pennant on the next-to-last day
Di Mag hit .320 with 155 RBIs and 39 out of the park
Henrich hit .308/25/100 . . . still not enough spark

All season it was a tight and exciting three-way race
New York, Boston, with Cleveland capturing first place
But 1948 will also be remembered as a celebration
On June 13, marking the Stadium's 25th year of its creation

Also, on that day, Ruth's number was to be retired
Leaning on a bat cap in hand he was attired
On the back of his shirt was the number 3
The last time anyone would ever see

Two months later on August 16, the Babe passed away
He died of throat cancer at age 53, a sad, sad day
In the rotunda at Yankee Stadium his body was laid out
Thousands said farewell, and shed tears no doubt

Season over, then came an unexpected bombshell
For Harris, it was a message straight from hell
Weiss fired Harris over some vague fall out
From the PCL his replacement was in route

Stengel, Mantle Arrive, Joe D Retires, Five Championships (1949–1953)

Casey Stengel was his name, a true baseball lifer
The press found his words difficult to decipher
Fresh from winning the 1948 pennant in the PCL
Managing the Oakland Oaks, 114-74, his farewell

Thanks to his friend Weiss, Casey was back in The Show
Where he began his playing career many moons ago
The year was 1912, as a speedy and promising player
Ended his career five teams later as a noted stayer

Known to be somewhat of a clown during his playing career
Once releasing a bird from under his cap as fans did cheer
His lifetime BA was .284, no power, but loved the game
Never to be considered a candidate for the Hall of Fame

Although with McGraw's Giants he did hit .368 and .339
Both seasons performing during limited playing time
His managerial career in the majors was also lame
With inept teams, Casey was not entirely to blame

He managed Brooklyn from 1934 to 1936, no success
All three seasons in the second division he did possess
From 1938 to 1943 his Braves owned the second division
Boston firing Casey was an easy and painless decision

So why did the Yankees, an orderly, business-like team
Hire an unproven manager? Would seem quite extreme
Clown or jokester, Weiss and others saw much more
He knew baseball, strategy, and how to build rapport

Casey knew how to handle men, firm but sincere
There was more to Casey than would appear
Also, talent goes a long way to forming a reputation
In **1949,** the team would shine with some frustration

Casey was faced with several serious early woes
Injuries during the season repeatedly arose
Causing shuffling of players to different positions
Henrich from right to first caused by the conditions

With Dickey's instruction, Berra caught most of the time
Rizzuto played 153 games, the most inspiring and sublime
Needing a new outfield, most field bosses would cower
Casey chose Cliff Mapes, Gene Woodling, and Hank Bauer

But the big blow was the loss of DiMaggio until June 28
In time for a three-game series at Fenway, it was fate
Joe had been out for months with a bone spur in his heel
He woke up one morning and the pain was gone, totally surreal

Led by DiMaggio the Yankees swept the Red Sox
Dazzling fans and the old timers in the press box
Joe was a one-man hitting machine with power
Four homers, nine RBIs, the man of the hour

Throughout the season, pitching kept first place in sight
Raschi won 21, Reynolds 17, sharing the spotlight
The two lefties, Lopat and Tommy Byrne each won 15
Page with 27 saves, 13 wins, fanning batters, routine

The final two games of the season, Saturday and Sunday
Red Sox leading the Yankees by one game, two to play
At the Stadium all the Sox had to do was win one
And they would clinch the AL pennant and relish the fun

Stengel, Mantle Arrive, Joe D Retires, Five Championships (1949–1953)

Page and Lindell teamed up to win Saturday, 5-4
An exciting, dramatic, and nail-biting game and more
In relief of Allie, Page threw 6⅔ innings of shutout ball
Bottom of the eighth, tied at four, Lindell homered to enthrall

Sunday arrived, Ellis Kinder versus Vic Raschi
A marvelous pitching duel, ever so gutsy
Yankees leading 1-0 entering the bottom of the eighth
Boston fans had their fingers crossed, keeping the faith

The Yankees exploded for four huge runs, now five zip
But in the ninth, the Red Sox fought for the sinking ship
Boston scored three runs before Raschi got the final out
The **Yankees 16th pennant,** the hard way to come about

Across town, Brooklyn won their close pennant race
Beating St. Louis by a game, in an exciting chase
Brooklyn, looking for its first World Series crown
As was Casey . . . and to be the toast of the town

Reynolds versus Don Newcombe in the first game
A masterful job by both, but Reynolds did tame
The score 1-0, Allie allowing two measly hits
Henrich's ninth inning homer giving "Newk" fits

Game two saw another sparkling 1-0 shutout
As Preacher Roe returned the favor, no doubt
Raschi took the hard luck loss, as did Newk
It was all Yankees after the Dodger/Roe rebuke

Game three at Ebbets Field in Brooklyn
A wild game, don't know where to begin
A 1-1 tie entering the top of the ninth inning
Yankee fans were satisfied and grinning

As New York scored three times with two out
The score 4-1 of victory there was little doubt
Until Olmo and Campy homered in their half
Then Page settled down and avoided the gaffe

Game four, sixth inning, Yanks with a comfy 6-0 lead
Behind Lopat who gave up four runs, a singles stampede
Seven singles to be exact until Allie arrived in relief
Final score 6-4 New York, the save went to the Chief

Game five the Yankees won with ease 10-6
Raschi the win, Page the save in a quick fix
Young Bobby Brown, the Yankees' leading hitter
Batted .500, drove in five, and scored four, no quitter

It was the **Yankees 12th World Series title**, Stengel's first
And for many more the club and Casey would thirst
To the Yankees the next four seasons would be kind
Under Casey's leadership and the talent Weiss signed

In **1950**, the Yankees won the AL pennant once more
Nosing out Detroit by three games for an encore
It was the **Yankees pennant number seventeen**
With old and new players repeating the scene

Joe D led the club with 32 home runs at age 35
Showing no ill effects of the bone spur, he did survive
He also drove in 122 with a batting average of .301
But after next year, the great Di Mag would be done

Berra trailed DiMaggio in homers with 28
Bested him in RBIs (124) BA (.322), both first rate
But Rizzuto enjoyed his finest season of his career
In 155 games, most on the team, he did appear

There's more, he batted a team-leading .324
And the most hits on the club with 200, du jour
Defensively, Phil was all over the infield, the glue
No surprise, Rizzuto was named AL MVP, a coup

It was Billy Martin's first year at second, at age 22
His contribution minimal, a future few knew
He played in only 34 games, hitting a meager .250
From this, his impact, few could foresee

The experienced rotation held up just fine
Raschi (21-8) and Lopat (18-8) did shine
Byrne (15-9) and Allie (16-12) following suit
A very challenging combination to boot

Now add rookie Whitey Ford to the mix
Putting the opposition in a difficult fix
Ford was 9-1 with a nifty 2.81 ERA
Leaving batters two options, hope and pray

The 1950 Philadelphia Phillies won the NL flag
Nicknamed the "Whiz Kids" soon to hit a snag
In the upcoming World Series, over in four!
Facing tough Yankee pitching shutting the door

Raschi beat the Phillies 1-0, a two hitter, game one
Vic setting the pace as the sweep had begun
Game two, Allie pitched splendidly, a 1-1 tie after nine
Until Joe D homered off ace Robin Roberts, just in time

Now the Whiz Kids were in a serious mess
Needing a win in game three, nothing less
Phillies Ken Heintzelman (3-9) started game three
A lefty who won 17 the year before, no guarantee

Surprisingly, Ken led 2-1 entering the eighth
As the Philly fans had renewed their faith
Not for long, the Yankees tied the game
Then off Russ Meyer, a run in the final frame

Casey called on Ford to pitch game four
And the rookie brilliantly rose to the chore
He beat the Phillies 5-2, needing help for one out
Allie entered, averse to Casey's decision fans did shout

Another **Championship for the Yanks, number 13**
And the second for Casey Stengel, soon routine
In two seasons Stengel proved he could lead
Naysayers and clown callers had to concede

It was an exciting year for the Yankees in **1951**
Ditto the Giants with Thomson's famous home run
The Yankees would finish the season 98-56
From owners to fans getting their kicks

It would also be the final year for Joe DiMaggio
But a kid named Mickey would ease the blow
Joe finished the year batting an unlikely .263
The lowest of his career, a sad sight to see

Joe D announced his retirement the following year
At 37, the aches and pains ending a brilliant career
The Yankee brass wanted him to stay for big bucks
Said no, his pride of performance was the crux

Plus, the Yankee farm system was at its peak
Producing players like a talent boutique
The gem was Mantle, a 19-year-old switch-hitter
That had veteran baseball scouts all aglitter

Stengel, Mantle Arrive, Joe D Retires, Five Championships (1949–1953)

Early on he was touted as the successor to Joe
He could hit, he could run, and he could throw
Plus, he had power from both sides of the plate
And in the era of TV, superstardom was his fate

In '51 there was other Yankee talent to come out
With fame and stardom on the way to sprout
Gil McDougal and Billy Martin come to mind
Solid players ready to contribute once they unwind

Stengel looking for a third straight World Series win
Now a genius, no longer a clown or has been
But the **1951 AL pennant race** was far from a breeze
The competition from Cleveland caused much unease

The Cleveland pitching staff was simply awesome
Bob Feller led the club with 22 wins, hard to overcome
Twenty games, each won by Mike Garcia and Early Wynn
Bob Lemon with 17, yet Cleveland lost, what a sin!

The Yanks, Raschi, Lopat, and Reynolds held their own
With Allie throwing two no-hitters, quite a milestone
Yogi led the club with 27 homers and 88 RBIs
To win **AL pennant number 18**, always the goal and prize

Because of Thomson's pennant-winning home run
For the New York Giants' fans, baseball again was fun
The Giants, not in a Series since '37, led by Bill Terry
And ironically, the New York Yankees their adversary

Two rookies were featured in the Series, Mantle and Mays
Both potential HOF'ers received enormous praise
The Giants, riding momentum from Thomson's home run
Behind Dave Koslo's stellar pitching took the opener 5-1

The Yankees bounced back in game two, 3-1 behind Lopat
"Steady Eddie" spread five hits and was a pesky gnat
The story of the game was Mantle's freak accident
Catching his spikes in a sprinkler head, a Series ending event

Game three saw the Giants beat up Vic Raschi, 6-2
Giving Giant fans hope what the future would ensue
Game four the Yankees tied the Series behind Allie, 6-2
Game five, the Yanks clobbered the Giants, 13-1, who knew

McDougal, Rizzuto, and Joe D drove in 10 of the 13
Gil four, Phil and Joe three each, oh so obscene
Now on to game six and a real thriller
A diving catch in the ninth by Bauer the killer

Hank's catch saved a run that would have tied the score
Ironically, he was Mickey's fill-in, adding to baseball lore
The Yankees won 4-3 for their **14th World Championship**
It was their third consecutive opponent they did whip

In **1952,** the Yankees lost some talented players
This brought out the many Yankee naysayers
Jerry Coleman was tapped for military duty in Korea
So, Casey called on Martin as the second base panacea

The versatile Gil McDougal held down third base
While Dr. Bobby Brown went to Korea, his new workplace
The outfield was solid with Mantle, Woodling, and Bauer
Plus, Yogi's 30 homers and 98 ribbies, clutch power

Reynolds led the rotation (20-8) with a 2.06 ERA
While Raschi, Lopat, and Sain were more than okay
As the Yankees finished the season in first place, 95-59
Cleveland, a mere two games back, went home to pine

Stengel, Mantle Arrive, Joe D Retires, Five Championships (1949–1953)

It was the Yankees **19th American League flag**
Giving fans more reason to smile and brag
At this point in time no other AL team was close
The Philadelphia A's with nine AL flags had the most

The 1952 World Series was a nail-biter to the end
A heads-up play by Martin the fans did commend
But this is getting ahead of the full seven-game Series
As to a specific hero there are plenty of theories

The Brooklyn Dodgers had a very powerful team
Finished the season 96-57, held in high esteem
They were *The Boys of Summer*, penned Roger Kahn
Avid Dodger fans no doubt thought: bring it on

At Ebbets Field, the Dodgers won the first game, 4-2
As Joe Black outpitched Reynolds, a six-hitter he threw
The Yankees came right back the following day
As Raschi spun a three-hitter (7-1), fan fears to allay

Taking turns the Dodgers won game three, 5-3
Yogi's passed ball scoring two, Dodger runs the key
Now the Yankees turn, winning game four, 2-0, amen
As Reynolds fired a nifty four-hitter, fanning a cool 10

The Dodgers won game five in 11 by a score of 6-5
This meant the Yankees had to win again to survive
They did (3-2), as Reynolds stopped Brooklyn cold
In relief of Raschi for 1⅓ innings, pitching to behold

Now on to game seven, and the ultimate thriller
The Dodgers, bottom of the seventh, looking for a killer
They were trailing 4-2, when Raschi in the game did arrive
Relieving Allie who spelled Lopat, the Yanks trying to survive

Raschi quickly loaded the bases with only one out
As thousands of Dodger fans did yell and shout
Casey called for Bob Kuzava, for years moved around
In a 10-year career with eight teams, it did astound

Was it a gutsy move by Casey or dumb? We'll see
Kuzava faced Snyder as Dodger fans roared with glee
Kuzava went 8-8 during the season with a 3.45 ERA
He also racked up three saves, Yankee fans began to pray

Hope restored as Duke popped up for out number two
The fearsome Jackie Robinson was next, what to do?
All assumed Casey would replace Kuzava with a righty
Not so fast when dealing with a decision so mighty

Kuzava stayed, induced Jackie to pop up to the infield
An easy out as the Dodger's fate was now sealed
But everyone in the infield froze, as the ball did roam
And the wind slowly carried the ball toward home

An alert Martin raced toward home lunging for the ball
Catching it two feet off the ground, cap going AWOL
All three runners were on their way to score
Billy's heads-up play will be remembered evermore

Kuzava blanked the Dodgers the last two innings
As the Yankees began counting their Series winnings
It was the **Yankees fourth consecutive World Series** title
And a mind-boggling **fifteenth overall**, everyone vital

Casey's **1953** Yankees won the AL flag once more
It was their **fifth in a row** and never done before
The Yankees finished with a record of 99-52
Once again, Cleveland with a second-place view

Stengel, Mantle Arrive, Joe D Retires, Five Championships (1949-1953)

It was the Yankees **AL pennant number twenty**
Many, many more to come just wait and see
Back from military service was pitcher Whitey Ford
Who led the rotation with an impressive 18-6 record

And Raschi, Reynolds, and Sain, always reliable so true
But Lopat at age 35 went 16-4 with an ERA of 2.42
Berra led the club with 27 homers, 108 ribbies
But Yogi was only one of the many important keys

The '53 Yankees led the AL in batting average at .273
Woodling at .306 led the club, a solid season all did agree
Mantle with 21 dingers was second on the Yankees
One homer traveled 565 feet without a strong breeze

It was measured by scribe Arthur "Red" Patterson
The Yankees PR director having some fun
It came off Chuck Stobbs of Washington, so forlorn
"As the tape-measure home run was born"

In the NL, the Brooklyn Dodgers finished 105-49
Leaving Milwaukee 13 games back on the sideline
Brooklyn and New York, a subway World Series repeat
In the five boroughs and beyond a guaranteed treat

In six exciting games the Yankees won the Series
The talented Dodgers lost again, despite the theories
The unlikely hero of the World Series was Billy Martin
And rightly so, but oh my gosh, where do I begin?

For the Series Billy batted 12 for 24, a cool .500
As Brooklyn simply shook their heads and wondered
Game one, Billy walloped a three-run triple, first inning
Creating the positive mindset it's all about winning

The final score was Yankees 9, Brooklyn 5
Joe Collins' key hits put the Yanks in overdrive
Johnny Sain, the winner, coming on in relief
Of Allie Reynolds, the now aging Chief

Game two, in the seventh, Billy hit a game-tying homer
For the moment, making a no power hitter a misnomer
The Yankees won the game by a score of 4-2
When Mantle hit a two-run homer, his pal to outdo

Brooklyn not quitting, won games three and four
By scores of 3-2 and 7-3, the Yankees said, no more
Game five another homer by Billy in a Yankee rout
The score 11-7, the victory never in doubt

In game six, the Yankees were leading 3-1
Top of the ninth, were the Dodgers done?
Reynolds on the mound, Duke Snider drew a pass
Furillo homered, tying the game, another impasse

Now to the bottom of the ninth, Yankees at bat
Runner on second, Billy nicknamed "The Brat"
Drilled a Clem Labine pitch for the game winning hit
Then named Series MVP, a most deserving fit

It was the **Yankees fifth World Championship in a row**
And **16th overall** that left an historic baseball afterglow
A record that still proudly stands in 2024
And Yankees fans can recall and adore

A Pause, Four Pennants, and Two Championships (1954–1958)

Cleveland no longer the bridesmaid, now the bride
With a record of 111-43, in **1954** they took pride
And rightfully so, beating the Yankees by eight games
With a pitching rotation stacked with famous names

Lemon (23-7), Wynn (23-11), and Garcia (19-8)
Houtteman (15-7), Feller (13-3), all pitched great
Plus, Mossi and Narleski at the ready in the pen
The reason the Indians won time and time again

Cleveland heavily favored over the Giants, no surprise
As bookies, sports writers, and fans did agonize
The 1954 World Series is now part of baseball history
How the Giants swept the Indians is still a mystery

It was a disappointing season for the Yankees in '54
Despite winning 103, an aging rotation hard to ignore
Reynolds, Sain, and Lopat were age 36 or plus
While Raschi was surprisingly sold, no fuss

Wait . . . Vic Raschi was sold in 1954?
Yes, to the Cardinals in a mild uproar
He refused to take a 20 percent pay cut
To his peers it came as a blow to the gut

Ford (16-8) and rookie Bob Grim (20-6) did their best
No match for Cleveland's pitchers who were blessed
The Yankees led the AL in hitting once more
Batting three hundred or better there were four

Not including Bill Skowron who shared first base
With Joe Collins who he would eventually replace
Berra played in 151 games the most on the team
Hitting .307/22/125 . . . and never out of steam

His excellent season earned him the AL MVP
It was his second MVP, and given deservedly
Mantle led the club with 27 homers at age 22
Plus 102 RBIs and hit .300, an exciting preview

Young Andy Carey hit a respectable .302
And would anchor third base, his glove like glue
Irv Noren batted .319, his Yankee career high
But traded in 1957 as New York said, bye, bye

By seasons end, pitching was the Yankees headache
So, a blockbuster trade with Baltimore they did make
It involved 17 players and took two weeks to complete
The biggest trade in MLB history, how sweet

Key pitchers obtained were Don Larsen and Bob Turley
Both young right-handers, the latter muscular and burly
Shortstop Billy Hunter was also part of the deal
As Rizzuto, an aging 37, no longer the big wheel

The incredible World Series streak was no more
While it lasted a marvelous reality to love and adore
Casey and the Yankees were now looking to **1955**
To start a new winning streak after the '54 dive

It was **pennant number 21**, Cleveland back three games
Yankees aided by two rookies soon to be cheered names
One was Bill "Moose" Skowron a force at first base
And Elston Howard, the Yankees first of his race

A Pause, Four Pennants, and Two Championships (1954–1958)

Both would have solid careers and be loved by fans
And an integral part of the future Yankee plans
Also, Howard was the Yankees first black player
A long time since Robinson, racism getting grayer

In 1955, the Yankees finished with a mark of 96-58
With Yogi and Mickey tough outs at the plate
Berra, another strong season, voted MVP, his third
While Mantle belted 37 homers leading the AL herd

Ford had a marvelous season (18-7) with an ERA of 2.63
Clearly the lefty was the staff leader, yet so carefree
Turley, his first season in pinstripes, went 17-13
But led the AL with 177 walks, not a manager's dream

At 35, Tommy Byrne (16-5) had a comeback year
Led the AL with a .762 WPCT, a mark to revere
In a limited starting role, Larsen went 9-2
And would make baseball history in '56, who knew?

Again, the Yankees foe in the World Series was Brooklyn
Determined to throw off the shackles of defeat and win
Brooklyn opened with Don Newcombe (20-5), staff ace
Ford for the Yankees and a 6-5 win to set the pace

Game two, Byrne went the distance in a 4-2 Yankee win
As the Dodgers' Billy Loes took it on the chin
"It seemed like old times", now down two games to zero
What Brooklyn needed was a genuine hero

His name was Johnny Podres (9-10), a struggling lefty
To beat the Yankees, an assignment quite hefty
But the youngster came through in the clutch
Defeating New York 8-3, clearly, he had the touch

In game four, with renewed hope, Brooklyn won 8-5
On homers by Campy, Hodges, and Snider they did thrive
In game five, Brooklyn won 5-3 behind Roger Craig
Giving the Dodgers an important one-game nest-egg

In game six, the Yankees won 5-1 with Whitey Ford
Who spun a brilliant 4-hitter as "Chairman of the Board"
Now on to game seven, with Podres emerging once more
As the mighty hero all Dodger fans will always adore

Young Johnny pitched a brilliant 4-hit, 2-0 shutout!
Ending a shaky Brooklyn start with the final turnabout
The Dodgers first and only **World Championship** in Brooklyn
Today, Dodger fans recall the '55 Series with an adoring grin

Despite the '55 Series loss, the Yankees came back
In **1956**, with a potent offensive attack
And what a season Mickey had, joining MLB's elite
An awesome and astonishing baseball feat

Mickey won the rare and coveted Triple Crown
And was repeatedly, in New York, the talk of the town
A .353 average, 52 homers, and 130 RBIs
The award, the flag were his and the Yankees' prize

But it wasn't all Mickey Mantle in 1956
It was a powerful and steady offensive mix
Berra with 30 homers and 105 RBIs
Another great season, no surprise

Bauer with 26 homers and Moose 23
In winning the long ball often the key
As a team they hit 190 four baggers
First in the AL, the number stagers

A Pause, Four Pennants, and Two Championships (1954–1958)

Yankee pitching was equal to the hitting, so great
Ford (19-6), Kucks (18-9), and Sturdivant (16-8)
Plus, Larsen (11-5) and a slumping Turley (8-4)
Burying Cleveland in second place, an eyesore

The **Yankees twenty-second AL flag,** effortless
In first place all season, very little stress
Brooklyn narrowly won the National League
Setting up a repeat World Series filled with intrigue

To everyone's surprise or perhaps astonishment
Brooklyn won the first two games, now content
But the Yankees, undaunted, came roaring back
Winning games three and four to get on track

Oddly, Casey chose Larsen in game five to throw
The results best described in my poem below
From my book *Baseball Memories,* it appeared
A game millions watched and revered

27 Up 27 Down

He played 14 years in the major leagues
Not including 2 years in military fatigues
He bounced around with 7 different teams
Never quite fulfilling his boyhood dreams

He would never be accused of being a parson
The night life he enjoyed did Don Larsen
With a losing major league record of 81-91
Clearly, Larsen was not any team's big gun

But in 1956 Don Larsen made baseball history
Pitching a perfect game and truly a mystery
Looking at the circumstances in retrospect
Larsen would not be the guy you would expect

The Yankees and Dodgers met in the '56 World Series
Who would win the rivalry created unlimited theories
The Dodgers won the first game at Ebbets Field
Larsen would start game two Casey revealed

The Yankees quickly handed Larsen a 6-0 lead
But he blew it with the help from others, indeed
According to Larsen: "I was mad at myself"
He believed he was finished and put on the shelf

At the Stadium the Yankees won the next two
While Casey's pitching selection came out of the blue
Yes, it was Larsen like a jailbird given a stay
Handed the fifth game with Casey's okay

Brooklyn's lineup was awesome from top to bottom
As his early departure in game two had taught him
The first inning for Larsen was somewhat breezy
Except for the 3-2 count on Reese, it was easy

In the second Robinson smashed a grounder to third
That bounced off Carey to McDougald . . . how absurd
Gil fired to first nabbing Jackie by an eyelash
A fortunate play that happened in a flash

In the fourth inning Mantle homered to right
Giving over 64,000 fans a thrilling delight
In the fifth Mantle saved a hit with his glove
When a blast to left center, he disposed of

A Pause, Four Pennants, and Two Championships (1954–1958)

In the sixth, the Yankees added an insurance run
Now led the Dodgers 2-0 . . . but they were done
The next several innings Larsen had scary situations
But the Yankees infield caused Brooklyn frustrations

In the ninth Larsen walked slowly to the mound
Thousands at the Stadium did not utter a sound
Larsen admitted he was "weak in the knees"
To himself, he said, "Someone help me please"

Carl Furillo up first easily flied out
Campy grounded to second . . . no doubt
Pitcher Maglie was the next batter
Larsen knew it really didn't matter

Manager Alston sent Mitchell to the plate
One of the great contact hitters, first-rate
Larsen ran the count to 1 and 2
The next pitch a fast ball he threw

Mitchell fouled it into the left field seats
Imagine the crowd with racing heartbeats
The next pitch nicked the plate just fine
Ump Pinelli raised his arm, the out sign!

Don Larsen had pitched a perfect game
A World Series first and well-deserved fame
He said it's a record that will never be broken
"The best they can do is tie it," well spoken

Perfecto or not, the Series was far from over
Game six, Clem Labine won 1-0, Dodgers in clover
Kucks in game seven, pitched a clutch three-hit shutout
Newcombe lost 9-0, the game never in doubt

The **Yankees World Series title number seventeen**
With more to come, a familiar and expected scene
The Yankees were the most winning franchise in baseball
And would continue their many loyal fans to enthrall

Lots happened in **1957** on and off the field
Never boring once, the facts were revealed
Let's begin with the trade with Kansas City
From the Yanks, Morgan, Hunter, Noren, not pretty

In return Shantz, Boyer, and Art Ditmar
Others involved made the deal quite bizarre
However, the trading of players was far from over
And Martin's Yankee future no longer in clover

Prior to the Copa incident, a tragedy took place
In Cleveland, pitching ace Herb Score hit in the face
Specifically in the eye by a Gil McDougald line drive
Never to be the same and lucky to be alive

At the Copacabana night club, Billy's demise did begin
Celebrating Yogi and Martin's birthdays within
Several Yankee players and wives attended the party
As drinks and entertainment were plenty and hearty

Sammy Davis Jr. was the star performer that night
He was heckled by a table of bowlers, a racial slight
Bauer asked the bowlers in profane terms for silence
The exchange of words ended in ugly violence

It happened in the men's room away from all view
A bowler was found out cold on the floor, who knew?
The next day Bauer was charged with felonious assault
Charges were dropped as he claimed it was not his fault

A Pause, Four Pennants, and Two Championships (1954–1958)

The Yankees fined each player at the Copa that night
Sadly, it would eventually determine Martin's plight
GM Weiss, as all knew, was not a big fan of Billy
His relationship with the outspoken young man was chilly

So, it came as no surprise Martin was traded to KC
With Ralph Terry for reliever Ryne Duren, a spirt free
Martin's departure was a blow to Mantle and Ford
Both of whom, Alfred Manuel Martin Jr., they adored

No matter the Yankees continued their winning ways
If you are counting, **pennant number 23,** fans to amaze
The Yankees finished the season 98-56
Beating out Chicago, a very talented mix

The "Mick" batted .365 . . . a career high
Lost the batting title to the "Splendid Splinter" guy
Ted Williams at age 38 batted a cool .388
His fifth batting title, next year another would await

Mantle, Berra, and Skowron were the offense
This meant the pitching had to be immense
And clearly it was the reason for winning the flag
With a league-leading 3.00 ERA, a reason to brag

Bobby Shantz (11-5) led the AL with a nifty 2.45 ERA
Gaining him Comeback Player of the Year for his play
While Sturdivant, Turley, Larsen, Grim, and Ford
Turned in winning seasons, another pennant the reward

Now to the World Series to meet the Milwaukee Braves
The Yankees itching to, metaphorically, put them in graves
Ford won the first game beating Warren Spahn 3-1
Burdette beat Shantz the next day 4-2 not to be outdone

In game three, the Yankees clobbered the Braves 12-3
Led by Kubek who drove in four, two homers the key
Game four Hank Aaron and Frank Torre hit the long ball
Driving in four runs, and a temporary cure-all

Top of the ninth inning Yankees trailing 4-1
Two runners on, and Howard hits a home run
Game tied; Braves failed to score in their half
Time for the Yankees to write the Braves epitaph

Top of the tenth, Spahn allows a single by Kubek
Hank Bauer promptly triples, the former Leatherneck
Mantle flies to right for the final out of the inning
Yankees led 5-4, bottom of the tenth, plan on winning

Tommy Byrne hit the first Braves batter
A disputed call and lots of umpire chatter
Mantilla now running for Nippy Jones who was hit
And is quickly sacrificed to second, lickety split

Johnny Logan then doubles to tie the game at 5-5
The Braves, once again, are well and alive
Followed by Eddie Matthew's towering home run!
The final score 7-5, the Braves not to be outdone

That man Burdette beat Ford 1-0 in Game Five
Turley won Game Six, 3-2, to keep the Yankees alive
Lou Burdette started Game Seven on two days rest!
And blanked the Yankees 5-0, he was at his best

Burdette was named the World Series MVP
Lou won three games which no one could foresee
Pitching all three complete games, needing no relief
Yankee fans are still harboring a nagging disbelief

A Pause, Four Pennants, and Two Championships (1954–1958)

So, World Series victory number 18 was not to be
New York fans had to wait 'til next season, how beastly
And during this short hiatus changes were made
In June acquiring Virgil Trucks and Duke Maas in a trade

First base coach Bill Dickey left the field of play
Now a securities dealer to earn a living another way
Joe Collins was sold to the Phillies but quit
While Jerry Coleman to the front office he did split

'58 was noted for Casey's unforgettable appearance
Before a Senate Subcommittee and his incoherence
It was widely known to the baseball world as Stengelese
An hour at the U. N. with Casey could bring world peace

The Yankees (92-62) easily won **AL pennant #24**
An opportunity to play the Braves, even the score
It was a well-balanced Yankee offensive season
Eight players hit 11 or more homers the reason

Mantle led with 42 homers and 97 runs batted in
Plus, the other power categories, the team's linchpin
Turley was the star on the mound in 1958
He was red hot right out of the gate

Turley went 21-7 with a marvelous 2.97 ERA
Earning the Cy Young Award, the team's mainstay
Ford was solid as ever (14-7) with an ERA of 2.01
Duren, the erratic closer, won six, saved 19, all in fun

The World Series, Braves vs Yankees once more
Yankee fans looking for revenge to be sure
At County Stadium Spahn beat the Yanks 4-3 in 10
Game two that man Burdette won 13-5, again

At the Stadium, Larsen blanked the Braves 4-0
Bauer driving in all four runs, clearly the day's hero
Game four Spahn pitched a two-hit, 3-0 shut out
Beating Ford who had little support, Series in doubt

Game five Turley threw a 7-0 shutout besting Burdette
Keeping the Series alive and a positive Yankee mindset
Game six went 10 innings as the Yankees won 4-3
To game seven and who owns the ultimate victory

Burdette, Yankee killer in the Series only one year ago
Took the mound for Milwaukee to instill the final blow
Larsen was chosen in hopes of an outing like game three
For both hurlers a victory was not to be

With the game tied 2-2 entering the eighth frame
Skowron blasted a three-run homer icing the game
Final score 6-2, Turley in relief New York did whip
It was the **Yankees eighteenth World Championship**

For Casey it was World Championship number seven
Tying him with Joe McCarthy in baseball heaven
Casey had the opportunity to win one more
But lost in 1960, a Series now part of MLB lore

Five Pennants, Two Championships, Casey Fired, CBS New Owners (1959–1964)

The **1959** season was almost a total mess
Why? It's anyone's educated guess
Key players who played brilliantly the year before
Lacked what fans were eagerly seeking, an encore

In late May, the Yankees dropped to last place!
Mighty New York in the basement, a disgrace
Valiantly they fought back, finishing a poor third
It was the fault of a few Yankees, that was the word

Turley most of the season seemed not to have a clue
He dropped to 8-11 with an earned run average of 4.32
Compared to '58, the righty was 21-7 with a 2.97 ERA
One of the primary reasons the Yankees went all the way

Mantle had an off season with only 75 RBIs
Batting a poor (for him) .285 and what it implies
Bauer at age 36 (soon to be gone) hit a mere .238
Young Siebern at .271 failed to carry his weight

The '59 season wasn't a total loss for New York
A couple of significant trades they did uncork
Sturdivant, Kucks, and Lumpe went to the A's
For Terry and Héctor López, a deal deserving praise

But the Yankees were far from finished trading
In December with KC, they continued invading
Sending Marv Throneberry, Siebern, Larsen, and Bauer
For two others and Roger Maris, the man with power

In **1960**, the Yankees began another five-pennant streak
A season challenged by Baltimore; a team no longer meek
Although the Yankees finished 97-57, eight games in front
The second-place Orioles were always in the hunt

Unaware, Mantle and Maris setting the stage for 1961
By their 1960 performances while all were having fun
Mantle belted 40 homers, and Maris 39, a blitzkrieg
Mantle drove in 94, Maris 112 . . . and led the league

For the MVP Award Maris received 225 votes
Beating Mantle's 222, a close race it denotes
Also, Howard began catching more than Berra
As Yogi played left, ushering in a new era

The pitching was good enough to win 97 games
With Art Ditmar (15-9) leading all the names
Coates (13-3), Ford (12-9), and Terry 10-8
More than enough, the opposition to eliminate

With 11 saves Shantz was a very solid reliever
The nearsighted Duren a frightening deceiver
Combined, it gave the **Yankees pennant number 25**
And Casey's 10th the most of any manager dead or alive

The 1960 World Series the Yankees should have won
Sorry Pittsburgh, it should have been a 1927 rerun
Seven games later, the city of Pittsburgh was rocking
To all loyal Yankee fanatics, it was simply shocking

My book *Baseball Memories* tells of the Series briefly
As Pittsburgh recalls "Maz" and the exciting victory
In the poem there have been minor changes made
Rendering the content a last-minute upgrade

Five Pennants, Two Championships, Casey Fired, CBS New Owners (1959–1964)

The Miracle in Pittsburgh

The New York Yankees were back
In the World Series and ready to attack
The Pittsburgh Pirates were their foes
A solid team but with very few dynamos

The 1960 World Series opened at Forbes Field
With a Yankee victory all signed and sealed
Shockingly, the Pirates knocked out Ditmar in the first
Won the game 6-4 as if the Yankees were cursed

Not so fast said the Yankees in game two
Winning 16-3, driving Pirate pitching cuckoo
On to Yankee Stadium and game three
Where some 70,000 fans cheered ace Whitey

The Bombers won 10-0, the final score
Richardson slammed; Ford shut the door
The Yankees feeling superior at this point
As the widely partisan crowd rocked the joint

In game four, Law and Face did pitch
A magnificent game with hardly a hitch
Final score: Pittsburgh 3, New York 2
Had fans wondering how the Series would ensue

Haddix with help from Face won game five
The score 5-2, the Yankees needed a win to stay alive
Back at Forbes Field, the Pirates crashed into a Ford
Who blanked them 12-0 did the Chairman of the Board

Some 36,680 fans attended the do or die game seven
A matchup made by the baseball gods in heaven
The Yankees sent game two winner Turley to the mound
For Pittsburgh, Law, winner of two games, was crowned

Surprisingly, Pittsburgh took an early 4-0 lead
But much too early for the Yankees to concede
In the sixth New York jumped ahead 5-4
Capped by Yogi Berra's three-run blast du jour

The Yankees were not finished by a long shot
Adding two more runs in the 8th to thicken the plot
Forbes Field was quiet with six outs to go
It was time for the Pirates to quicken the tempo

And that's exactly what Pittsburgh needed, a quick fix
Four singles, one a bad hop, quickly made the score 7-6
Then with two on Smith jacked one over the brick wall
Now Pittsburgh in front 9-7 . . . what a windfall!

Wait, the Yankees tied the game in the 9th with two
Entering the bottom half tied at 9, the game a lulu
First batter Bill Mazeroski stepped to the plate
Ralph Terry on the mound he did patiently wait

Terry's first pitch was taken by Maz, ball one
His next pitch Maz did hit, Terry was done
It was a huge blast traveling 430 feet or so
The **first World Series game seven walk-off blow**

Maz circled second waving his helmet over his head
While the Pirates' fans screamed as joy did spread
The entire team waited for Maz at home plate
To greet the hero and the victory to celebrate

Five Pennants, Two Championships, Casey Fired, CBS New Owners (1959–1964)

The irony of the '60 Fall Classic is hard to believe
As the Yankee fans certainly still do grieve
For all of you too young or not paying attention
The incredible stats are here to mention

New York out-scored Pittsburgh 55-27
Out-pitched them with an ERA of 3.54 to 7.11
And there is much more to enumerate
But what's the point . . . it's far too late

But there is one more fact you must know
The first time the Series MVP did not go
To a player from the team that won
It went to the Yankees Bobby Richardson!

After the Series, the Yankees gathered the press
The conference turned out to be a genuine mess
Dan Topping and Del Webb tried to soften the blow
That Stengel in 1961 was not returning to The Show

Was he fired or retired? The press wanted to know
The two owners, around the question did tiptoe
Then finally Casey had his time at bat
And told the press, "I was fired", take that

But Casey, as usual, was far from finished
Voicing a memorable line undiminished
"I'll never make the mistake of being 70 again",
A brilliant quote that appears now and then

Soon after, the Yankees named one-time catcher
As their new manager and a man of great stature
Ralph Houk was a major in World War II
Fought in the Battle of the Bulge, everyone knew

He earned Bronze and Silver Stars, and a Purple Heart
And having managed in Denver not an arrogant upstart
Houk over time won the respect of those who knew him
So, the decision was not made on a sudden whim

There was another change, GM Weiss resigned
Given a lucrative consulting deal he quickly signed
Replaced by Roy Hamey, who Weiss had hired
For his business experience, a man he admired

In **1961** the AL expanded to 10 teams, not through
And increased the total games from 154 to 162
But '61 was all about the exciting "M & M Boys"
As the press and Yankee fans created lots of noise

From *Baseball Memories*, a poem about the '61 chase
Of Ruth's 60 homer record, the Boys wanted to erase

"M & M Boys" and the Asterisk

They were affectionately called the M & M Boys
In 1961 they made lots of baseball noise
With their bats aimed at Ruth's home run mark
Mickey Mantle and Roger Maris did embark

Besting Ruth's record of 60 home runs the goal
During the season the pressure took its toll
Early in the season manager Houk made a switch
Maris batted third, Mantle fourth the lineup to enrich

By the end of June Maris had 27 homers, the lead
Mantle with 26 made it a tight race all agreed
On July 17 Commissioner Frick entered the race
And gave a new outlook on the home run chase

Five Pennants, Two Championships, Casey Fired, CBS New Owners (1959-1964)

You must exceed 60 homers in 154 games, Frick ruled
His edict was controversial, unexpected and ridiculed
Frick argued if homer 61 came after the 154th game
A "distinctive mark" be added to the record, his proclaim

In 1961 the MLB season was upped to 162
Who thought it would cause such a fuss and stew
It was 154 games when Babe Ruth played
And set the record . . . and now this charade

With Frick's ruling the pressure now intensified
While Maris pulled ahead, Mantle did backslide
Beginning September Maris with 56 had the lead
Mantle trailed with 53, way too early to concede

Then shocking news was announced to the press
Bringing Mantle fans to a new level of distress
Mickey developed an abscess in his hip joint
Maris now alone became the focal point

By game 154 Maris had a home run total of 58
According to Ford Frick, it was much too late
In game 159 he hit number 60 off Fisher of Baltimore
It tied Ruth and now evened the score

As the season drew to a close, Maris hit a drought
And left baseball fans, Frick aside, with some doubt
Only three games on the schedule to play
Young Roger Maris fans began to pray

Roger failed to hit a homer in games 160 and 161
Now only one game remained to hit a home run
Tracy Stallard pitching for Boston at Yankee Stadium
Who knew what was bouncing inside Roger's cranium

On his first at-bat, Maris flied to left field
As the small crowd yelled and squealed
Roger came up in the fourth with one out
The fans all tense-looking for **THE CLOUT**

On a 2-0 count, Roger swung at a fastball waist high
The ball headed for the right field stands . . . bye-bye
Babe Ruth's mighty 34-year-old record was no more
While Frick and others the record-breaker did ignore

But Roger Maris had the last laugh
For Frick had made a huge gaffe
It was suggested an asterisk be used
In the record books so fans would not be confused

Frick agreed and many took him at his word
But he did not have the authority all heard
It was learned MLB had no "official" record book
So, an asterisk never appeared, by hook or crook

And now for one final remark
It is important, no lark
The asterisk never, never ever appeared
In any record book official or not as feared

As much as the '61 homer race excited fanatics
There was much more, a plethora of dramatics
The Yankees won **AL pennant number 26**
They won 109 and lost 53, pure talent, no tricks

It was Houk's first pennant, but not his last
His managing style vs Casey, a noticeable contrast
The Yankee players responded to his authority
An understanding leader, but far from carefree

Five Pennants, Two Championships, Casey Fired, CBS New Owners (1959-1964)

The '61 Yankee season aside, the homer race was unreal
From the owners to the avid fans, it did appeal
Six players hit 20 or more homers, a long ball machine
Maris with 61 and Mantle 54, it was enough to demean

And Blanchard and Howard each hit 21
Berra smacked 22 and Skowron 28, having fun
Plus, Roger drove in 141, Mickey 128
These guys were swinging right out of the gate

No surprise, Maris won the MVP award
Still the baseball writers were narrowly on board
With so much chatter about the Yankee power
One might think the pitching went sour

Au contraire, Ford led the league in wins, 25-4
Also, in WPCT and innings pitched, there's more
Throwing a career high 283 innings, praises sung
To the tune of a well-deserved award called Cy Young

Ford had help from Stafford (14-9) and Terry (16-3)
And Sheldon and Coates, both 11-5, who did foresee
Don't forget Luis Arroyo with a record of 15-5
And 29 saves making it easy for New York to thrive

"The World Series against Cincinnati, a piece of cake",
Said author Donald Honig or more like a wake
In game one Ford blanked the Reds on two hits
Giving Cincinnati hitters uncontrollable fits

In game two, the Reds bounced back behind ace Joey Jay
The final score 6-2 as Jay pretty much had his way
Maris won game three on a ninth inning home run
The score 3-2, Arroyo the winner, the Reds about done

The Yankees won game four, 7-0, behind Ford
The pitcher New York fans most adored
While winning his second game in four days
Once again, the baseball world he did amaze

Whitey broke Ruth's 29⅔ scoreless innings streak
When he pitched five scoreless for 32, a new peak
The next year the streak ended in Candlestick Park
When Ford got five outs, it ended at 33⅔ a new mark

The Yankees won game five 13-5 and the World Series
They were simply a better club so skip all the theories
It was **New York's nineteenth Fall Classic win**
This time their dominance in baseball needs no spin

The New York Yankees won **pennant number 27 in 1962**
With less excitement and new stars that came through
While Maris' home run production dropped from 61 to 33
Mantle fell to 30, but still was voted the American League MVP

Ford won eight less games (17-8) than the year before
Terry won 23 but lost 12, which is hard to ignore
Bobby Richardson, age 26, at second base batted .302
And led the American League with 209 hits, hard to outdo

But four young "kids" helped Houk win once more
With a record of 96-66 the "Major" became a mentor
At short, Tom Tresh hit .286, 20 homers, and 93 RBIs
This earned him a spot on the All-Star Team, his prize

The Yankees had other young future stars
One even wrote his tell-tale memoir
His name is Jim Bouton who wrote *Ball Four*
Which Yankee management and players did abhor

Five Pennants, Two Championships, Casey Fired, CBS New Owners (1959–1964)

Phil Linz, later on talked about harmonica fame
Was a utility infielder of little acclaim
And then there was first baseman Joe Pepitone
Blessed with talent but needed a chaperone

The San Francisco Giants were the Yanks World Series foe
Recently beating the Dodgers in an exciting playoff show
Both clubs in 1958 moving to the lucrative west coast
Looking for more bucks while alienating loyal fans the most

Whitey Ford beat the Giants 6-2 in game one
Ending his scoreless inning streak on an earned run
The player scoring the run? The great Willie Mays
A neat trivia question to use with friends to amaze

The Giants bounced back to win 2-0 in game two
Jack Sanford pitched a three-hit shutout, a lulu
The Yankees won game three, 3-2, on Maris' bat
And Bill Stafford's pitching, taking the Giants to the mat

Now it was the Giants turn, winning game four 7-3
On the strength of Chuck Hiller's grand slam, the key
Ralph Terry took the win (5-3) in game five
On Tresh's three-run blast, can the Giants survive?

The Giants were now against that old brick wall
They need a victory, the Series to forestall
And that's what they got from Billy Pierce
Who outdueled Ford (5-2), ever so fierce

Now the Series was down to game seven at last
Fans at Candlestick were nervous but held steadfast
Ralph Terry and Jack Sanford took to the mound
Who would become the winner and duly crowned?

In the top of the fifth the Yankees scored a run
It wasn't pretty, but Kubek got the job done
Tony hit into a double play, Skowron scoring from third
The one-run lead held into the ninth, Terry undeterred

Was Terry thinking about 1960 and Maz's home run
And the World Series Terry lost and the Pirates won?
It had to enter Terry's mind, but would he let it?
As pinch-hitter Matty Alou led off with a bunt hit

Terry kept his composure and that's what matters
For he struck out the next two Giant batters
Willie Mays doubled down the right field line
Alou raced to third, Mays to second, not a good sign

Terry elected to pitch to Willie McCovey up next
Rather than pitch to Cepeda, a situation so vexed
On Terry's second pitch, Willie swung with all his might
And hit a bullet to the Giant fans' delight

Sadly for them, it was right at Bobby Richardson
For the third and final out, the Giants were done
If the line drive was a foot either way, left or right
Terry would have been in for many a sleepless night

It was the **Yankees twentieth World Championship**
Time for another celebration and deserved ego trip
Little did anyone in baseball know in October of 1962
The next World Series title would take 15 years to accrue!

In **1963**, the Yankees won **AL pennant number twenty-eight**
Houk's third and seemed, each year, the Yankees mandate
The Yankees finished 104-57 with pitching the key
Ford (24-7), Bouton (21-7), and Downing (13-5), the top three

Five Pennants, Two Championships, Casey Fired, CBS New Owners (1959-1964)

Terry won 17 but lost 15, not much of a net plus
As age caught up Berra became superfluous
Howard did the catching and won the AL MVP
He led the club with 28 home runs, a new reality

Injuries caused the M&M Boys to be off their game
Total home runs 38, far from their '61 fame
Young Pepitone and Tresh gave it their best shot
Joe from the left side, Tom from both could swat

At age 22, Pepitone hit 27 home runs with 89 RBIs
Tresh, at 24, drove in 71, clouted 25, no surprise
Pepitone a character, not in the staid Yankee way
He was a free spirit using a worn-out cliché

The Yankees Series foe were the Dodgers from LA
Pitching their strength and for the Yanks doomsday
Sandy Koufax was 25-5 with an ERA of 1.88
Don Drysdale (19-17, 2.63 ERA), a worthy teammate

Johnny Podres and Bob Miller added to the LA clout
Closer Ron Perranoski (16-3, 1.67 ERA), the knockout
Dodger Tommy Davis had the most RBIs at 88
Big Frank Howard hit 28 homers, his outfield mate

Foreseen or not, the Dodgers the Series did sweep
As the Yankee bats due to LA pitching went to sleep
Koufax beat Ford in game one (5-2), fanning 15
Played at Yankee Stadium it was an ugly scene

Game two, manager Walter Alston chose Podres to start
Instead of Drysdale, a righty, a strategic move so smart
The Stadium with a short right field fence favored southpaws
As Podres beat the Yankees 4-1 helping the Dodgers' cause

At home, the Dodgers with a 2-0 lead and ready to prevail
Were anxious to pitch their number two starter, Drysdale
The righty answered the call with a brilliant 1-0 three-hitter
Looking for the sweep, the city of Los Angeles was all aglitter

And why wouldn't they be with Koufax on the mound
As the Yankees sent their ace Ford looking to rebound
But it was not to be as Sandy out dueled Whitey
The final score 2-1 and a sweep few could foresee

Yankee fans still recovering from the Series loss
When the front office made Yogi the new field boss
Houk the general manager, not happy with the change
More comfortable on the field, the new position strange

It all started when Roy Hamey decided to retire
In time the sudden and surprising moves did backfire
Many doubted Berra could handle the new position
Disciplining former teammates, a delicate transition

The Yankees gave Yogi only a one-yearcontract
A lack of confidence in his leadership ability, a fact
By mid-August the Yankees were in third place
Battling Chicago and Baltimore to keep pace

About this time in August, a startling event occurred
It was announced that CBS bought the Yankees, how absurd!
Quickly approved by AL clubs in an 8-2 vote
With Topping and Webb keeping 20% share, please note

The 20% would give them operational control
Topping was named Yankee president the key role
$11.2 million, the reported final price
In hindsight it was plainly a fool's paradise

Five Pennants, Two Championships, Casey Fired, CBS New Owners (1959-1964)

Getting back to Yogi and his challenges on the field
Veteran players losing respect for Yogi revealed
Two of his problems were Mantle and Ford
Others complaining to Houk who they adored

The Phil Linz "harmonica incident" hurt Yogi's image
After losing four to Chicago and the bus scrimmage
Some say a turning point, Berra showed he could lead
And a wake-up call to the team as they agreed

Suddenly, the Yankees went on a winning rampage
Berra, overnight turned from a buffoon to a sage
The team pulled through behind Yogi by season's end
Winning 31 of 40 games the club did not bend

It was the Yankees **AL pennant number 29**
And a record fifth in a row, all seemed divine
In the NL, St. Louis was in a tight pennant race
Winning on the last day, the Phillies a sad case

During the season, Cardinal boss Keane heard hearsay
Of his dismissal much to his anger and dismay
But Johnny Keane led his club to the bitter end
His players and his steady leadership never did bend

Ken Boyer and Bill White, the Cards offensive clout
Boyer drove in 119 with 24 homers he hit out
White not far behind with 21 and 102 runs batted in
Lou Brock hit .348, stole 33 bases to help the Cards win

Pitchers Bob Gibson, Curt Simmons, and Ray Sadecki,
Won 57 of the 93 games for St. Louis and the key
Sadecki was 20-11, Gibson 19-12, and Simmons 18-9
It was Gibson who rose to the occasion to shine

Mantle led the Yanks with 35 home runs and 111 RBIs
Pepitone drove in 100; Howard hit .313, no surprise
Maris hit 26 home runs, continuing his slide from 1961
And the pressure to top the Babe no longer fun

Ford had another great season (17-6) and a 2.13 ERA
Bouton (18-13) and Downing (13-8) helped lead the way
It was the rookie right-hander Mel Stottlemyre's first year
At 22 he went 9-3 with a 2.06 ERA, a bright future did appear

The Yanks and Cards, '64 pennant winners, put on a show
Until the fatal seventh game it was touch-and-go
Ford lost game one by a score of 9-5
The Yankees won game two 8-3 to revive

Bouton won next, 2-1, on Mantle's ninth inning home run
In game four, New York led 3-0 until Downing came undone
Sixth inning, bases loaded Ken Boyer hits a home run
Cardinals eventually win 4-3, and the action has just begun

Gibson won next (5-2), St. Louis needing one game
But Bouton won the crucial game six (8-3) to tame
With help from a grand slam by Joe Pepitone
To game seven where St. Louis would atone

The Cardinals won game seven on the arm of Gibson
The great right-hander a gutsy complete game he spun
Final score: 7-5, the Yankees second Series loss in a row
For Yankee owners, players, and fans a devastating blow

For the next 11 seasons the Yankees could not win
Close at times . . . and that comment has a lot of spin
Until along came a former Yankee named Billy
Who restored winning and excitement until it turned silly

Yankee Dynasty Crumbles, Steinbrenner New Owner (1965-1975)

Yankee fans had hardly gotten over the Series loss
When news broke that Yogi was no longer field boss
Mostly communicating with players his downfall
His replacement shocked most fans of baseball

As the new manager, the Yankees named Keane
That startling announcement few could have seen
If you recall, Keane, during the season was upset
Over talk of his possible firing, he obviously did fret

So, after his World Series victory he quit
Signed with the Yankees not giving a wit
For the Yankees future did not look bright
Or to embarrass St. Louis just out of spite

Keane now a member of a winning organization
That earned respect, praise, and adulation
Sadly, for Keane Yankee domination was over
Ending a glorious rein, now no longer in clover

In **1965**, the New York Yankees finished in sixth place!
The start of a long stretch Yankee haters would embrace
Keane was now stuck with an aging team
The recent glory days seemed like a pipe dream

The Yankees record was 77-85, not impressive
Trailing the Twins by 25 games, quite regressive
No Yankee regular hit close to .300
Avid fans around the country simply wondered

Maris and Howard suffered injuries that hurt the team
Maris batted .239; Howard .233, the long ball a dream
Mantle hit 19 homers, drove in 46, a poor season for him
And the outlook for the Mick was nothing but grim

Except for Stottlemyre, nothing to brag about
Mel went 20-9 with a 2.63 ERA, a lonely standout
At 36, Ford won 16, lost 13, Downing 12-14
Bouton at 4-15, a career soon ending, so byzantine

The players not the only ones to blame for the fall
Keane too strict with veterans, which did not enthrall
He was much better with younger players to teach
Eager to learn, they were much easier to reach

Despite aging players and tension, Keane stayed in **'66**
Until they went 4-16 and needed a quick fix
Keane was fired, Houk back as the Yankees field boss
With Topping as acting GM, helpful or an albatross?

In 1966, the Yankees were never in the race
They finished 70-89 in an unfamiliar 10th place
Going down to the basement in glowing flames
Trailing AL winning Baltimore by 26½ games

Another miserable season without a .300 hitter
Attendance down and fans now bitter
Rookie pitcher Fritz Peterson went 12-11, 3.31 ERA
The only starter with a winning record, by the way

In September, Topping departed, enter Mike Burke
From CBS as president, the dapper Young Turk
Who owned a magnificent and unbeaten resume
But knew little to nothing about baseball per se

Yankee Dynasty Crumbles, Steinbrenner New Owner (1965–1975)

Credit Burke with upgrading the Yankees ballpark
Among improving events he made his mark
Hiring Lee MacPhail as GM, who knew the game
And would solely run baseball operations his aim

Trades were made before the **1967** season began
Maris and Boyer were traded as some kind of plan
Roger went to the Cardinals for Charlie Smith
Clete to the Braves for Bill Robinson forthwith

In 1967, mediocrity once again, the fans worst fear
The team was going nowhere it did appear
Aging players, some traded like Howard, others retired
No adequate upgrades, in the second division to be mired

The Yankees finished the season in ninth place
Scored 522 runs, lowest in the AL, a disgrace
Ford retired, leaving pitching records galore
In time an easy selection for the HOF for sure

On the brighter side, Mickey hit an historic home run
It was number 500 and he was still not done
Red Ruffing was inducted into the Hall of Fame
Shined most when pitching in a big game

In **1968** and **1969** the Yankees finished in fifth place
An improvement, but neither year ever in the race
The once great dynasty was slowing crumbling
For the players and fans, it was quite humbling

Pepitone never lived up to his predicted potential
Placed in the outfield and soon to be nonessential
While Tresh began a very promising and bright career
Saw his batting average drop, could not get back in gear

Pitcher Stan Bahnsen was Rookie of the Year in '68
With a record (17-12, 2.05 ERA), he owned the plate
Three years later he was traded to Chicago
For Rick McKinney, straight up, no dough

Stottlemyre had two 20-win seasons in '68 and '69
With a club wallowing in fifth place, he did shine
Plus, an ERA below 3.00 in each year
Giving Yankee fans something to cheer

Mantle, after a glorious career, retired in '69
The sad news came in March as fans did opine
Age and injuries finally caught up with him
A day all knew was coming, yet still grim

Hope shined in **1970;** the Yankees finished second
With a record of 93-69 as first place did beckon
But let's take a closer look at the so-called race
New York trailed Baltimore by 15, a serious chase?

Houk and MacPhail doing their best to bring a winner
But the talent seemed to be getting thinner and thinner
An infield of Cater, Clarke, Michael, and Kenney
Delivered little offensive spark, if any

Bobby Murcer and Roy White gave the Yankees power
While Munson at .302, soon to be the man of the hour
The grumpy catcher was voted Rookie of the Year
Began a marvelous, but tragically shortened career

Peterson, Stottlemyre, and Bahnsen led the pitching staff
Peterson winning 20, but later unveiling a social gaffe
While Lindy McDaniel saved a lofty 29 games
A career high pitching in over 111 frames

Yankee Dynasty Crumbles, Steinbrenner New Owner (1965-1975)

The Yankees finished fourth in **1971, 1972, and 1973**
New faces, old faces, the same result . . . sadly
Although one of the new faces in '72 was Sparky Lyle
Who led the AL with 35 saves and a certain style

In 1972, the sale of Cleveland hit a brick wall
Discussions between Steinbrenner and GM Gabe Paul
It seemed Cleveland owner Vernon Stouffer backed out
The change of heart for good reason, no doubt

After the 1972 season the Yankees made a key trade
Getting Greg Nettles from Cleveland, a hot corner upgrade
Nettles would remain a Yankee for 11 productive years
A player highly respected by the fans and his peers

A few lines back the word "gaffe" was linked to Peterson
Unexplained, but serious and not just done for fun
It's another poem from *Baseball Memories*, my book
The story is hard to believe, but true, take a look

The Craziest Trade Ever

> They never entered the Hall of Fame
> So you might not know either name
> In spring training 1973 they decreed
> We are **trading families** with all due speed
>
> Lefty hurlers are noted for their quirkiness
> But this revelation was bizarre, God bless
> From the front office out came the hankies
> These two were from the New York Yankees

Fritz Peterson and Mike Kekich, the two bad boys
Who created in the media scandalous noise
The Yankees gave the announcement a dandy spin
But still, the two bad boys couldn't win

Peterson won 8 lost 15 . . . what a swoon
Kekich won and lost 1, was gone by June
The Yankees finished 17 back for the '73 season
Fritz and Mike were part of the reason

The wife swapping was only half the deal
Which included the kids, please get real
It also included a Terrier and Poodle
Both of which the kids could canoodle

Fritz and Susanne married, had four kids of their own
Mike and Marilyn flamed out, whereabouts unknown
GM Lee MacPhail playfully had this to say:
"We may have to call off Family Day"

In '73 it was rumored the Yankees were up for sale
A group headed by Steinbrenner bought the club without fail
A cool $10 million dollars was the reported sale price
A nasty $4 million dollar loss for CBS based on poor advice

Post '73 season the Yankees traded for a guy named Lou
His last name Piniella, a clutch hitter like very few
His first season (.305, 70 RBIs) with the Yanks was '74
A fan favorite and an emotional guy, never a bore

The effective date for the new owners was **January 2, 1974**
Burke and Steinbrenner leading the group, an oddity for sure
But George wisely kept his ties with Gabe Paul
An experienced operative who knew baseball

Yankee Dynasty Crumbles, Steinbrenner New Owner (1965–1975)

Several more changes were made in 1974, you know
Lee MacPhail resigned, replaced by a duo
There were two GM's now running the show
Tal Smith and Gabe Paul, an oddity the combo

The dual arrangement didn't last; in 1975 Smith resigned
Despite the second-place finish in '74, it was a grind
Houk resigned after the '73 season, he had enough
Bill Virdon was hired and finished second, showing his stuff

In April 1974, Paul made another great swap
The GM negotiated a four for three flip-flop
The key acquisition for the Yanks was Chris Chambliss
A first sacker who helped the Yankees out of the abyss

The Yankees signed free agent Jim Hunter in late '74
The 25-game winner created a serious bidding war
Catfish signed for over $3 million, unheard of at the time
Steinbrenner sending a message, a new spending paradigm

The other news in '74 was Bowie Kuhn's harsh action
Suspending George for two years for his infraction
A federal conviction violating campaign contribution laws
Yankee haters greeted Commish Kuhn's edict with applause

Which brings us to **1975**, the Yankees finished third
Virdon was gone after 104 games, fired the word
The Texas Rangers fired their manager as well
It was Billy Martin, the firing not much of a bombshell

Martin had been let go a few times previously
By the Twins and Tigers and once again now free
Not for long as Paul signed Billy with George's okay
Soon, both Billy and George would rue the day

Yes, '75 was the season the Yankees bounced back
They built the nucleus of a club in the past they did lack
Granted, they finished 12 games behind the Red Sox
Strengthening the '75 club was no longer a paradox

Jim Hunter (23-14, 2.58 ERA) the new star in town
His mates, however, were not of the same renown
Plus, Lyle had an off year out of the pen, saving six
The lefty also won five and lost seven, not a good mix

Bobby Bonds led the club in home runs with 32
Acquired from the Giants for Murcer, quite a debut
Munson led in runs batted in with 102
And a .318 batting average his mates he did outdo

The Yankees infield appeared solid once again
With Chambliss and Nettles at the corners, amen
Sandy Alomar at second and Jim Mason at short
Added a sound double play combo for strong support

The Yankees it appeared had all the pieces in place
To make a serious drive during the next pennant race
From Steinbrenner to the bat boy, all wanted to win
And 1976 would be the ideal season to begin

Four Pennants, Two Championships, Managerial Madness (1976–1981)

The New York Yankees were back to the glory days
A scrappy manager, a shrewd GM, new players, no malaise
The Yankees won the **1976 AL East** with a record of 97-62
West winners, Kansas City, looking to subdue

Thurman Munson was voted the AL's MVP
With a stat line of .302/17/105, he won deservedly
He was also named captain of the team
A position of leadership and high esteem

Thirty-two home runs did Nettles crack
To help the long-waited New York comeback
And the first time a Yankee won the home run crown
Since Roger Maris in 1961, electrifying the town

The Yankees drew over two million avid fans in 1976
With exciting leaders, talented players, the right mix
The anticipation and thrills would be hard to forget
As the Yankees were headed to KC and George Brett

The ALCS went the full five exciting games
Many heroes and soon to be talked about names
Hunter won game one, 4-1, going the distance
With White's two-run double for early assistance

Pitcher Ed Figueroa lost game two, 7-3, as KC did revive
He and Mickey Rivers traded for Bonds in late '75
Dock Ellis won game three, 5-3, with a save from Lyle
One more save to the 23 during the season he did compile

Martin chose Catfish for game four on three days' rest
Hoping his 17-game ace and the Yankees were blessed
Hunter and the Yankees lost the game, 7-4
The fans were now treated to one more

At Yankee Stadium a sell-out crowd of 56,821
Came for excitement and an ending of fun
Top of the eighth, the Yankees leading 6-3
Two runners on base, who would the batter be?

KC fans couldn't ask for a better hitter, George Brett
With a .333 season's average and a long ball threat
Brett hit Grant Jackson's second pitch . . . home run
Tying the game at 6-6 was KC's favorite son

Now to the bottom of the ninth, Chambliss at the plate
Hit Mark Littell's first pitch over the fence, checkmate
Yankees win their **30th AL pennant** dramatically
For Yankee fans it was an unforgettable sight to see

Next to meet Cincinnati, Sparky Anderson's mighty team
The "Big Red Machine," loaded with talent to the extreme
Joe Morgan, Johnny Bench, and Pete Rose to mention a few
With seven hurlers winning 11 or more, a talented crew

Thus, the Reds swept the Yankees in four straight
Bench hit .533, drove in six runs, simply great
No contest, he was named the World Series MVP
One could hardly in good faith disagree

The Yankees lost by scores of 5-1, 4-3, 6-2, and 7-2
Hard to believe as an avid Yankee fan, but true
Cincinnati outscored the Yankees 22-8
And outhit them 42-30, a sad, sad state

Four Pennants, Two Championships, Managerial Madness (1976-1981)

Steinbrenner was embarrassed over the Series sweep
Jumped into the free agent market knee-deep
Signed the Reds' 11-game winner Don Gullett, a lefty
For a reported $2 million for six years, quite hefty

The trade market was still alive and brisk
The Yankees traded Ellis for Mike Torrez, small risk
Plus, traded LaMarr Hoyt for Bucky Dent
In the '78 playoff game, the Red Sox would lament

Then Steinbrenner began pursuing Reggie Jackson
Wildly courted the free agent, not to be outdone
While Reggie's huge ego was enjoying the chase
Avid fans waited for him to sign so they could embrace

Finally, the courtship came to an agreeable end
For $2.96 million for five years George did spend
During spring training Jackson took his ego for a dry run
In an interview he questioned the leadership of Munson

"I'm the straw that stirs the drink," ye gad
Adding, "Munson can only stir in bad"
Obviously, Thurman was angry and upset
Voiced his opinion and would never forget

George and Billy added fuel to the fire
Martin didn't want, nor need, George's new hire
Next came the now famous incident in Fenway
When Martin yanked Jackson out of the game of play

Martin accused Reggie of loafing on a ball his way
Jackson disagreed then began an ugly melee
Martin and Jackson had to be separated, all agree
George was furious, it was on national TV

The creative press tagged the club with a new name
Now called the "Bronx Zoo" . . . what a shame
The Yankees were now the talk of "basebrawl"
Dominating the sports world, the fans it did enthrall

Despite the zoo, the Yankees won the **1977 AL East**
Attendance soared to over 2.3 million, a love feast
Nettles 37 homers and 107 RBIs, both career highs
Reggie and Thurman drove in 100 or more, no surprise

After two seasons of scant work, Guidry arrived
The young lefty, out of sorts, was finally revived
Guidry won 16, lost 7 with a low 2.82 ERA
Laying the groundwork for future play

But the 1977 pitching honors went to Sparky Lyle
With incredible stats in 72 games, he did compile
He won 13, lost 5 with 26 saves, and a 2.17 ERA
And a Cy Young Award for his outstanding play

In **1977**, the Yankees again faced KC in the ALCS
And another exciting final game loaded with stress
The Yankees were trailing 3-2, top of the ninth, game five
And needed one measly run to keep the series alive

Paul Blair, first up the count goes to 2-2
He singles, Yankee hopes to renew
Roy White walks, Blair to second base
A scoring opportunity now in place

Mickey Rivers promptly singles to tie the game
White to third, Herzog to change pitchers his aim
Finally, he brings in the closer, Mark Littell
Who retired Randolph on a deep fly, the death knell

Four Pennants, Two Championships, Managerial Madness (1976–1981)

White scored the go-ahead run, Yankees lead 4-3
Brett's error scored another run, still no guarantee
Until Sparky entered to close out the game
The Cy Young winner adding to his fame

The **Yankees thirty-first AL pennant**, two in a row
For the KC Royals another heartbreaking blow
Now to the World Series to meet the Dodgers from LA
Yankee fans recall the '63 sweep and want to repay

The Yankees won the World Series in six games
As the Lasorda losing Dodgers went up in flames
It was the **Yankees World Series title twenty-one**
But the first since 1962, a depressing and long run

The MVP of the Series was clearly Reggie Jackson
He batted a cool .450 and I have just begun
He hit five home runs, drove in eight, and scored 10
From *Baseball Memories,* a replay of the homers again

"Mr. October"

After losing in 1976 the New York Yankees returned
To the 1977 World Series, they had dearly earned
The Los Angeles Dodgers was their mighty foes
But the Bronx Bombers won in six so the story goes

This poem is not about the Series per se
It's about a player and his home run display
Reginald Martinez Jackson is his name
A talented player always seeking fame

He earned the name "Mr. October" from heroics
In game six he woke up all those baseball critics
The Yanks were leading the Series three games to two
A win in game six would bring a Championship overdue

The Yankees were losing 3-2 as Reggie came to the plate
On Burt Hooten's **first pitch** hit a homer scoring a mate
In the fifth belting Elias Sosa's **first pitch** duplicating the feat
Another home run, another pitcher he did mistreat

In the eighth on the mound for LA was Charley Hough
His dancing knuckleball to hit was extremely tough
On the **first pitch** Reggie sent it flying 450 feet
Into the centerfield bleachers . . . his day complete

Three swings three home runs . . . simply amazing
The stage now set for Yankee fans hell-raising
Oh, by the way, New York won the game 8-4
Their 21st World Series title and looking for more

Jackson not noted for his humility
Expressed in words rare gentility
"Babe Ruth was great," said he
"I'm just lucky," he added with glee

After the Series, George was again on the loose
Seeking more talent, this time the "Goose"
Gossage signed despite having Lyle in the pen
Prompting quick-witted Nettles to turn comedian

Lyle at 33, Gossage at 26, didn't make Sparky pleased
"He went from Cy Young to Sayonara," Nettles teased
In **1978** Gossage had 27 saves, Lyle only 9
The next season Sparky was with Texas, bottom line

Four Pennants, Two Championships, Managerial Madness (1976–1981)

Changes occurred in the Yankees front office too
President Gabe Paul sold his interest in the Bronx Zoo
He returned to the Cleveland Indians as president
While Cedric Tallis replaced Paul, that's how it went

In Yankee history the **1978** season was unparalleled
Except for several individual performances, it smelled
Guidry won the Cy Young Award, hands down
With a 25-3 and a 1.74 ERA he earned the crown

Ed Figueroa won 20, lost 9 with a 2.99 ERA
While Catfish added another 12 wins along the way
Lyle and Gossage combined won 19 and saved 36
Despite team hitting, the Yankees were still in a fix

During the summer, the bickering was infantile
Among George, Billy, and Reggie it turned vile
Hurting the team and almost out of the race
As the Red Sox had a tight grip on first place

Over a bunting incident Martin suspended Reggie
The atmosphere surrounding the team turned edgy
Billy, probably aided by drink, opened to the press
Claiming it was all on the record, what a mess!

About Reggie and George, here's the line Billy inflicted
"One's a born liar, the other convicted"
Shortly after, Billy resigned and spoke to the press
He apologized to George, left in tears from the stress

Third-base coach, Dick Howser, managed one day
Then Bob Lemon took over the rest of the way
Bob let go early in the season by the White Sox
So available to manage the Yankees, the hot box

Lemon, in contrast to Martin, was easygoing
What happened soon after was mind blowing
It was the annual fun-filled Old-Timers Day
And announced Billy would return in '80, hooray

The jam-packed crowd went absolutely wild
As Billy ran on the field waving so beguiled
Day over, Lemon was now faced with reality
Then quietly led the Yankees on a winning spree

Of the last 68 games the Yankees won 48
While Boston could not match this rate
In September, the Yanks and Boston played for
The series at Fenway, nothing like it before

The Yankees swept, their confidence to restore
Whipping Boston15-3, 13-2, 7-0, and 7-4
Called "The Boston Massacre" a crushing display
Of baseball dominance, Boston to forget someway

The Boston Massacre was accurately named
For the Sox in four games were clearly shamed
The Yankees compiled 42 runs and 67 hits
Boston 9 runs, 21 hits, 12 errors, a blitz

But by season's end, both clubs were tied
Once again both teams would collide
In a one-game playoff at Fenway
Winner takes all . . . an old cliché

Guidry versus Mike Torrez on the mound
After six, Boston led 2-0 playing sound
Top of the seventh, two on, two out
A key moment beyond any doubt

Four Pennants, Two Championships, Managerial Madness (1976–1981)

Light-hitting Bucky Dent steps to the plate
Ninth in the order, Torrez couldn't wait
Dent hit a long, long fly ball to left
Over the Green Monster leaving locals bereft

The Yankees added another insurance run
Making the score 4-2 when the inning was done
In their half of the seventh, the Sox failed to score
As Gossage, in relief, gave them nothing more

In the eighth, Reggie hit a crucial blast
To pad the lead now 5-2 . . . at last
"It was an insurance run," Reggie explained
"So, I hit it to the Prudential Building," he ordained

Now to the bottom of the eighth
RBIs by "Yaz" and Lynn gave Boston faith
But in the ninth, Boston failed to score
As the Yankees won the game 5-4

One final word about the home run by Dent
It was a highly unusual and dramatic event
The second pitch was fouled off the foot of Bucky
And attended to by the trainer . . . ever so lucky

Rivers, on deck, pointed to a crack in Dent's bat
So, he borrowed one from Mickey . . . just like that
On the next pitch, the ball over the Monster it went
In New England, he is called Bucky (%#@&%) Dent

In the ALCS the Yankees, again, beat Kansas City
This time in only four games, what a pity
Jackson hit .462 with two homers and six RBIs
The **Yankees thirty-second AL pennant**, the prize

The Yankees and Dodgers in the Series, a repeat
LA won the first two games, Yanks still upbeat
As they roared back winning the next four
Guidry winning game three, 5-1, the score

In game three, Nettles' defense was amazing
Saving numerous runs deserves unusual praising
Game four went into extra innings tied at three
White scored on Piniella's single for the victory

Game five was a total Yankee runaway
The score 12-2, the Dodgers close to doomsday
Rivers and Munson had three hits each, also Dent
Plus, Munson drove in five to LA's lament

The Yankees put an end to the Series in game six
Catfish and the Goose, a dominating mix
Dent had another great day at the plate
Going 3 for 4 with three RBIs, time to celebrate

The final score was New York 7, Los Angeles 2
The **Yankees 22nd World Series,** not yet through
Dent was named the Series MVP, hitting .417
Along with seven runs batted in, quite a scene

Brian Doyle had a good World Series too
Hitting .438 while Jackson hit .391, not through
Including two home runs and eight RBI's
To the occasion, once again, Reggie did rise

In early November, Sparky was traded to Texas
No doubt, it felt like a punch in the solar plexus
Dave Righetti came to New York in a ten-player deal
And the two players that gave the trade appeal

Four Pennants, Two Championships, Managerial Madness (1976-1981)

Steinbrenner always looking to improve the team
Picked up two free agents both held in high esteem
Right-hander Luis Tiant and lefty Tommy John
Both veterans seeking a winner in hopes to catch on

With three pennants and two World Series in a row
The **1979** Yankees wanted to keep the winning tempo
Until a silly accident occurred on that fatal April day
Goose and Cliff Johnson had words that led to horseplay

And sadly, to Gossage injuring his right thumb
The Goose sidelined for three months the outcome
His loss hurt the Yankees chances to repeat
Despite John's 21-9, 2.96 ERA stunning feat

Absence of a hitter who drove in 100 runs or more
Or bat .300, the Yankees were done for
New York was never really in the race
So, George made a managerial change to save face

He fired Bob Lemon after a 34-31 mark
And brought back Billy for that inspirational spark
Not good, the Yankees finished in fourth place
Thirteen and a half back of Baltimore, a futile chase

Then tragedy struck, the August 2 Munson plane crash
His death causing the team a shocking backlash
Just when the loss of Thurman began to fade
Martin was involved in a hotel bar charade

Billy and a "marshmallow salesman" got into a fight
The salesman was decked, Billy back in the limelight
When George heard of the incident, Martin was fired
Finley of the A's called and Billy was quickly hired

Howser, former Yankee coach was named field boss
At the time, coach of Florida State, now their loss
In November, the Yankees sent Chambliss to Toronto
For catcher Cerone and lefty Underwood, a trade so-so

The Yankees to free agency for **1980** did roam
Brought Rudy May back to his previous home
Signed veteran Bob Watson to play first base
Led the club in hitting with a .307 pace

In 1980, the Yankees won the East with 103-59
The pitching of John, Guidry, and May did shine
Underwood and Ron Davis helped in a major way
As Gossage nailed down wins with a fastball display

May also led the AL with a low ERA of 2.46
His curve, fastball, and change-up, a fine mix
Jackson hit .300/41/111, quite a season indeed
His 41 home runs tied for the league lead

In the ALCS the Yankees met Kansas City
For the Yankees fans it was not very pretty
The Royals swept the Yankees, 7-2, 3-2, and 4-2
Followed by a tirade of anger George did spew

"I was never so disappointed," said he
And "It's embarrassing as hell to me,"
Steinbrenner continued acting quite bratty
"It was even more embarrassing than Cincinnati"

Officially, Howser resigned, enough said about that
GM Gene Michael, now named the new doormat
Again, George went looking for a star that appealed
He signed his man 6'6" 220 pound Dave Winfield

Four Pennants, Two Championships, Managerial Madness (1976–1981)

The price estimated at $20 million over 10 years
His peers, no doubt, had nothing for Dave but cheers
The **1981** team looking for revenge for the KC sweep
With the help of Dave Winfield, it didn't come cheap

June 12, the 1981 season was in a state of confusion
As the players strike caused a major intrusion
Losing free agents, the owners wanted compensation
Among the fans the strike caused enormous frustration

On August 10, the dastardly strike finally ended
Wiping out over 700 games, leaving fans offended
MLB had to come up with a season saving solution
Their criticized idea, a split season the resolution

About the split season, there was plenty of doubt
But in the end, there was very little fallout
The Yankees won the first season with a 34-22 mark
Milwaukee (31-22), the second season ready to embark

Before the two teams met George made a change
Since it was days before the playoffs it was strange
He fired Gene Michael and hired Bob Lemon anew
It was George's "ninth managerial switch" at the Bronx Zoo

On October 7, the ALDS finally began in the best-of-five
Under pressure, Gossage and Righetti did thrive
Gossage saved three games, Righetti won two
Plus being named Rookie of the Year, thank you

It took five games to beat Milwaukee, so true
As Oakland swept Kansas City 2-1, 4-1, and 10-2
Up next for the ALCS title, the Yankees and the A's
Led by Martin and "Billy Ball," his winning ways

The five-game series was over in a quick sweep
The Yankees used the broom, from Billy not a peep
John won the first game 3-1 with a Gossage save
While George Frazier, the winner of a 13-3 shock wave

Game three "Rags" threw a six inning 4-0 shutout
The Yankees the better team left little doubt
Nettles drove in nine runs, voted series MVP
It was the **Yankees AL pennant number 33**

A Yankees/Dodgers World Series for the 11th time
With the Yankees winning eight of ten, so divine
At the Stadium, the Yankees won game one 5-3
Watson's three-run homer in the first was the key

Guidry earned the win, Gossage another save
John won game two, 3-0, for LA it looked grave
But Tommy needed late help from the Goose
And one more save as he turned the heater loose

In game three at Dodger Stadium, Rags was hit hard
The Dodgers won 5-4 as Fernando Valenzuela starred
LA won next, 8-7, in a wild and wooly game
Each team using five pitchers, the lead to reclaim

Game five, the score 1-0, the Yankees barely leading
Bottom of the seventh the Dodgers not conceding
Guidry facing Pedro Guerrero whose homers tied game
Next up, Steve Yeager who caught the bug, did the same

The Dodgers led 2-1 and that's how the game ended
Steinbrenner was upset and personally offended
Now comes a Steinbrenner believe it or not tale
He fought two drunks in the hotel elevator, both male

They insulted his team and NYC, so the story goes
Fists flew and beer bottles were used, nobody knows
It was reported George had a "broken thumb"
After all the lies and hyperbole that was the outcome

Now back to Yankee Stadium for game six
Before over 56,000 fans the Yankees need a fix
Sadly, the Dodgers won in a romp, 9-2
Now the fun began as Steinbrenner went cuckoo

In the *Times* he issued an apology, indeed rare
". . . to the fans of the New York Yankees everywhere"
For the performance in the World Series of the team
And immediately begin work for 1982 the theme

And the start of his disenchantment with Winfield
The "$20 million man" and his poor Series revealed
Dave went 1 for 22 against the pitching of LA
Years later George would refer to him as "Mr. May"

Fourteen-year Dry Spell, Managerial Madness Continues (1982–1995)

In **1982**, the Yankees finished in fifth place
Sixteen games back, not even a race
It was a season of unparalleled reshaping
Moving players, managers, and holes gaping

In '81 when Jackson became a free agent it began
He signed with California for a five-year span
They also traded for the senior Ken Griffey
His performance over five years, somewhat iffy

The Yankees added new players galore
At best their performances were a bore
Doyle Alexander, 1-7 with a 6.08 ERA
As opposing hitters were having a field day

During the season, players were coming and going
For Yankee fans it was nothing but mind-blowing
Traded were Bob Watson and Bucky Dent
As the Yankees tried the infield to reinvent

Ron Davis and Tommy John also traded
The latter unhappy and somewhat jaded
Catcher Butch Wynegar was another new face
Along with John Maybury at first base

I'm getting tired, I don't know about you
The good news: a few more and we're through
Roy Smalley came to replace Dent at short
The teenage girls probably now hate the sport

Fourteen-year Dry Spell, Managerial Madness Continues (1982–1995)

To help buttress the outfield came Lee Mazzilli
Now managerial changes if you think this was silly
It began with Lemon fired after going 6-8
Ending his managerial career since nothing did wait

Gene Michael was back in the dugout for another try
But with a 44-42 record, it was soon bye-bye
Next came a baseball lifer, current scout Clyde King
Who finished 29-33, ending the managerial string

But there were moments in '82 that were bright
Winfield's numbers (.280/37/106) that did delight
Nettles appointed captain, Mattingly his debut
The start of a sterling career would quickly ensue

In **1983**, Martin was back managing for the third time
To his credit the Yankees in the standings did climb
With a good record of 91-71, they finished third
And Billy finishing the season the good word

Don Baylor and Steve Kemp were signed
Baylor to fill the DH spot as previously outlined
Kemp would move to the right-field position
As Griffey moved to first completing the transition

With a solid everyday club, first place still a wait
Despite Guidry's 21-9 record and Righetti's 14-8
Plus, Gossage's 13-5 mark and a 2.27 ERA
A first-place finish was still many seasons away

Three moments in 1983 Yankee fans will recall
A no-hitter, a killing, and a near brawl
On July 4, George's birthday, he was given a gift
When he and the Yankees needed a positive lift

Righetti pitched a no-hitter beating the Red Sox
The temp was in the 90's, the Stadium a hot box
Rags fanned Wade Boggs to end the game
And a future place in Yankee lore to proclaim

The most haunting moment, the "Pine Tar Game"
When it was finally over both teams it did inflame
Top of the ninth, the Yankees were leading 4-3
The Royals with a runner on base the key

Goose on the mound and George Brett at the plate
On the next pitch a mighty debate Brett would create
He lined Goose's fastball for a two-run homer
That turned out for many days to be a misnomer

The home run put the Royals in front, 5-4
Billy claimed Brett's bat was illegal, now the war
The pine tar too far up on the handle Billy claimed
The umps agreed as Brett ran on the field inflamed

Calm restored, KC protested the game pronto
Later, AL president Lee MacPhail delivered the blow
He upheld the protest forcing the Yankees to play
So, the game continued on another scheduled day

Top of the ninth ended when Hal McRae struck out
Now the Yankees looking for a gem saving clout
It was not to be, three up, three down
KC won the game 5-4, New York was not a happy town

The third memorable moment involved a seagull
From Winfield's view point it wasn't dull
In Toronto, Dave accidently killed the bird
After warmups with Baylor, bottom of the third

Fourteen-year Dry Spell, Managerial Madness Continues (1982–1995)

Dave hit the seagull, throwing to the bat boy
The dead seagull screaming fans did not enjoy
After the game, the police took Dave to the station
Bail was set at $500 . . . plus the aggravation

The bail was paid and Dave was released
The next day the case dropped; the idiocy ceased
But not before Dave took more heat on the road
It's still discussed as a rare and unique episode

After the '83 season, Martin was fired once more
Fans unhappy as this charade was now a bore
Yogi was brought back, who managed in 1964
And the Yankee fans and the world did adore

The Yankees made changes before the 1984 season
Most, if not all, for a very good reason
Nettles was traded to the Padres after 11 years
And many great moments to applause and cheers

Gossage, as a free agent went to San Diego too
Now the Yankees had two positions to pursue
From Cleveland they acquired Toby Harrah for third
And sent Righetti to the pen, a move rarely heard

The Yankees were not finished improving quite yet
Signed free agent Phil Niekro, 45, still a threat
Plus, other changes they still finished third in **1984**
The Tigers, almost unbeatable, their year to adore

Despite the poor finish there were players who starred
Righetti with 31 saves as a closer held in high regard
Knuckleballer Niekro led the club (16-8) and a 3.09 ERA
As the slumping Guidry went 10-11 to his fan's dismay

Mattingly and Winfield created the most fan elation
Rooting for their choice through loud ovation
As they fought all season for the AL batting crown
Who would get hot or who would breakdown?

Mattingly won the title on the very last day
Going 4 for 5 in the game and pulling away
"Donnie Baseball" finished with an awesome .343
Winfield finished at .340; it was not meant to be

With 1984 history, the Yankees began looking ahead
Steinbrenner wanted Rickey Henderson it was said
So, the Yankees sent five players to the Oakland A's
For Rickey, the speedster with power who could amaze

The Yankees also went for a free agency pitcher
Righty Ed Whitson who became instantly richer
A four-year contract for a reported $900,000 per year
Seriously disliked he often received the Bronx cheer

In **1985**, the Yankees finished in second place
With a 97-64 record and another nutty race
Yogi fired after only 16 games with a 6-10 mark
GM Clyde King broke the news, it was not a lark

Yogi was replaced by guess who? Billy Martin
Quite a few players it served to dishearten
Mattingly, Baylor, and others were quite upset
For the craziness Billy and George would beget

After an initial slump the team got red hot
". . . 30 wins in 36 games," to thicken the plot
In the fall, the Yankees tried to overtake Toronto
But failed, the Jays won three of four, a final blow

Fourteen-year Dry Spell, Managerial Madness Continues (1982–1995)

Martin was fired for the fourth time, how bizarre
But not before he fought Whitson in a Baltimore bar
Despite the loony season, some players performed well
Mattingly, Henderson, and Guidry did excel

Don Mattingly, was a consistent clutch hitter
Led the AL with 145 RBIs, 48 doubles, no glitter
Along with 211 hits and an average of .324
A slick fielder and with the fans a great rapport

He also hit 35 home runs, most on the team
Named AL MVP, a season others can only dream
Henderson's first season was quite splendid
Stole 80 bases, the old Yankee record amended

Leading off, Rickey batted a respectable .314
And scored 146 runs showing off his speed gene
Guidry and Righetti combined to earn raves
Ron led the league with 22 wins; Rags 29 saves

In October, Piniella was named the manager for **1986**
Lou, who never managed, handed the mess to fix
Since '82, Lemon, Michael, and King all failed
As did Martin and Berra twice then derailed

Pitching was the problem and needed change
Not easy for a rookie manager to rearrange
Lefty Britt Burns acquired from Chicago in a trade
Wound up with a degenerative hip, never played

Phil Niekro was released, another stunning move
The unhappy 46-year-old pitcher did not approve
His brother Joe was affected by Phil's quick exit
He went 9-10 with a 4.87 ERA, brothers close-knit

Guidry (9-12) not the same pitcher as the prior year
The beginning of the end of a marvelous career
By July, Whitson was gone along with his ERA of 7.54
And with him a Yankee experience he would deplore

Despite Rasmussen's 18-6 mark deserving raves
And Righetti's record setting 46 timely saves
The Yankees managed to post a miserable team ERA
It was a wretched 4.11, a stat that will often betray

The Yankees ended the 1986 season 90-72
A second-place finish, leaving an unhappy crew
Some were traded and Wynegar left for home jaded
With a mysterious condition and eventually traded

Don Mattingly again led the Yankees at the plate
Leading the majors in hits with a whopping 238
He also collected 53 doubles and batted a cool .352
Plus 31 homers and 113 RBIs with no personal ballyhoo

The **1987** season for the Yanks was another bummer
For the fans, an up-and-down frustrating summer
New York finished 89-73 and in fourth place
Leading at the All-Star break, then blew the race

As in '86 the pitching was the conundrum
With a team ERA of 4.39, the season was glum
Rick Rhoden led the team with a record of 16-10
And returnee Tommy John 13-6 and a hot bullpen

Of the 47 saves, Rags racked up a solid 31
Three other relievers the remaining they spun
The Yankees made a pitching trade with Chicago
New York getting Steve Trout for Tewksbury, a kayo

Fourteen-year Dry Spell, Managerial Madness Continues (1982–1995)

Trout went 0-4 with an inflated ERA of 6.60
Another unneeded and damaging blow
What would the Bronx Zoo be minus controversy?
Enter Henderson; Piniella showing no mercy

Rickey spent 55 days on the injured list
Claiming a hamstring problem did exist
This hurt the club just more than a bit
Lou not buying the story, said he was "jaking it"

Of course, Steinbrenner had to get into the act
Supporting Rickey and raising another irritating fact
An unhappy Lou was not available for a George call
This set the stage for Piniella's managerial downfall

Mattingly another great season, fourth in a row
Setting a record with six grand slams, quite a show
Also, in eight consecutive games he hit a home run
Tying the Pirates, Dale Long, now not the only one

Donnie missed 18 games, his back the suspect
Years later he admitted it was a "congenital defect"
He had two more seasons of strong hitting
Until he decided it was time for quitting

Season over, George moved Lou to the GM's spot
To fill the manager's job, out did Martin trot
If you're counting, it was an unheard-of **number 5!**
The question is: how long will Billy survive?

In **1988**, the Yankees signed free agent Jack Clark
To help the offense, the long ball his trademark
He led the club with 27 homers, then was gone
Probably the 141 K's the reason he didn't catch on

Jay Buhner for Ken Phelps also didn't work out
While Buhner's home run power began to sprout
But signing free agent John Candelaria was fine
With a 13-7 record, the staff he did outshine

The pitching rotation was once again lacking
Age and injuries would soon have some packing
John at 45, Guidry 37, and others too old
Some knew when to quit; others had to be told

Winfield had a superb season batting .322
With 25 homers and 107 RBI's, quite a coup
Mattingly had a fine season, power stats behind
His back situation not better so keep this in mind

The long ball the back did encumber
But Donnie batted .311, a solid number
And a nifty on-base percentage of .353
He was still a tough out most would agree

Mike Pagliarulo and Claudell Washington lent power
Not enough to offset the pitching that went sour
It was surprising in May Billy had the club in first place!
By June, only a few games behind but still in the race

On June 23, with a record of 40-28, Billy was fired
Replaced by Piniella, recently from the job retired
Lou ended the season 45-48, in fifth place
Three and a half back of Boston, ending the chase

Billy gave George plenty of off-field firing ammo
His brutal fight in a Dallas strip club quite a show
Two ump encounters caused a three-game suspension
Elevating Steinbrenner's angst and tension

Fourteen-year Dry Spell, Managerial Madness Continues (1982–1995)

It was Martin's final firing and Yankee connection
The last time he suffered a self-imposed rejection
In December 1989, Billy died in an auto accident
A controversial individual and malcontent

The **1989** Yankees repeated their fifth-place finish
As their past dynasty days continued to diminish
Even under their outspoken manager Dallas Green
Who led the 1980 Phillies to a World Champion scene

It turned out to be a year of constant change
Some of the moves made sense, others strange
Clark, Henderson, and "Pags" were traded, not done
Plus, Rick Rhoden, Al Leiter, and Richard Dotson

Free agent Willie Randolph signed with LA
Replaced by Steve Sax, second to play
Sax had an outstanding season in 1989
With 205 hits, a .315 average he did shine

Tommy John was released and Ron Guidry retired
So far none of the changes left anyone inspired
Andy Hawkins and Dave LaPoint were signed
Both finished with ugly ERA's, their season defined

Candelaria pitched in 10 games, an injured knee
Winfield was the big loss, no one could foresee
Surgery for a herniated disk, Dave did undergo
Missed the entire season which was quite a blow

Mattingly led the club with 113 RBIs
Bad back and all to the occasion he did arise
Donnie also batted .303 with 191 hits
A consistent threat giving pitcher's fits

The Yankees poor play got Dallas Green fired
The '78 playoff hero, Bucky Dent, was hired
With an 18-22 record lasted to the season's end
Attendance down, fans unhappy, what did it portend?

Before leaving 1989 and starting a new decade
It's time for the Dave and George ugly charade
It involved the charitable Winfield Foundation
This caused, between the two, anger and frustration

When Steinbrenner did not pay the foundation
As stipulated in the contract, it resulted in litigation
Then Steinbrenner made a very foolish mistake
He hired Howard Spira, a gambler and flake

Spira's job was to uncover dirt about Dave
This was found later to be deadly grave
Commissioner Fay Vincent issued a daily ban
On George's Yankee activities for a two-year span

The **1990** season had Yankee fans aghast
The once dominating franchise finished **dead last**
With a 67-95 record, 21 games back of the Red Sox
After many changes and millions spent, a paradox

Now that Steinbrenner was no longer in charge
GM Gene Michael's decisions loomed extra large
To the Angels, Dave Winfield was the first to go
Where his star once more would shine and glow

Not long after, went manager Bucky Dent
With an 18-31 record, not an unexpected event
Replaced by "Stump" Merrill, a minor league lifer
A decision difficult to grasp and decipher

Fourteen-year Dry Spell, Managerial Madness Continues (1982–1995)

Barfield led the club with 25 home runs
And 78 RBIs, one of the team's big guns
Mattingly missed 60 games, again the back
Hit five home runs, the ball he could not attack

Kevin Maas at 25, was a bright spot
He hit 21 homers showing he could swat
Within a few years the lefty swinger flared out
By 1995 gone from baseball, losing his clout

The pitching was really, really, really bad
They ranked 12 of 14 AL teams, how sad
There were 19 losses by veteran Tim Leary
Relievers, no doubt, were tired and weary

Righetti saved 36 games, his second highest sum
Next year pitching for the Giants as a Yankee alum
Lee Guetterman won the most games, a pathetic 11
With no complete games, he lost seven

There's more to the 1990 story that could be told
But enough is enough, it's time to fold
Can't forget Stump, who had a poor record of 49-64
Ending the season and another Yankee eyesore

In **1991**, the Yankees did manage fifth place
Scott Sanderson (16-10, 3.81 ERA) was the ace
No other hurler had more than eight wins
Pitching again is where their sad story begins

The everyday regulars were average as well
Except for a few, the rest did not excel
With 24 homers, catcher Matt Nokes led the team
While Mel Hall, with 80 runs batted in, was supreme

Steve Sax had the highest batting average .304
These stats in the dynasty days, a total bore
The obvious question: who is to blame?
At Steinbrenner the vocal fans took aim

Before leaving 1991, hear this anecdote
It is true, but what did it denote?
It involved Mattingly, a Yankee great
And the benching it did create

Prior to the new season a captain was named
Donnie Baseball it was happily proclaimed
Then in August, Don was given a strange choice
Trim your hair or you're benched, said the voice

Now competitively aroused, Donnie said "no"
And he was benched by Stump, a low blow
It's embarrassing to even repeat this event
What were Stick and Stump thinking or their intent?

In **1992**, the Yankees had a new field boss, his name?
William "Buck" Showalter, with scant fame
At 36, he was a knowledgeable baseball man
Managing in the Yankee minors where it all began

And for five years with impressive success
Finishing first four times, he did impress
It would take time to turn the Yankee ship around
Eventually it would have to start on the mound

But not in '92, the pitching was severely lacking
Improvements long overdue, time to get cracking
Mélido Pérez (13-16), the victim of little support
With an ERA of 2.87 his won/lost record did distort

Fourteen-year Dry Spell, Managerial Madness Continues (1982–1995)

After Pérez the starting rotation fell apart
Except for the closer, needed was a fresh start
At age 35, Steve Farr saved 30 games
In Yankee history, not one of the known names

Danny Tartabull signed a $25.5 million contract
For that Tartabull hit .266/25/85, a sad fact
The Yankees acquired free agent Mike Stanley
And replaced Sax at second with Pat Kelly

It didn't take a baseball genius or thinker
Even with minor changes, Buck could only tinker
The talent was lacking as the Yankees finished 76-86
Tied for fourth and fans looking for a quick fix

Steinbrenner was okay to return to baseball
From his nasty two-year ban if you recall
He had to wait until March of 1993
To resume his day-to-day activities, you see

So, fans were not quite so upbeat or delighted
Recalling the 80's and the distractions he ignited
The question: would George and Buck get along?
Or would Showalter soon be singing his swan song

Four new faces showed up for the Yankees in **1993**
Wade Boggs at third and left-hander Jimmy Key
Along with pitcher Jim Abbott and Paul O'Neill
The latter in a trade with the Reds was a steal

The Yankees finished the season in second place
With a record of 88-74, seven games off the pace
The last time New York was in second was 1986
Soon the Yankees would have a winning mix

With Key the Yankees finally had a stopper
And with an 18-6 record quite a whopper
Abbott, born without a right hand!
A miracle to be on the mound with command

Jim won 11 games to help the team
But on September 4, he uncorked a dream
Against Cleveland he pitched a no-hitter!
Today, it would have been all over Twitter

O'Neill batted .311 with some power
Boggs .302, ground balls he would devour
Tartabull led the club with 102 RBIs
And 31 homers, the team to energize

Showalter accomplished a lot in two years
Normalcy, fan support, and loud cheers
Over 2.4 million attended in 1993
The most since 1988, stability the key

Showalter began the **1994** season, third in a row
Houk did it in 1969, a long, long time ago
Of course, Houk stayed until 1973 when he quit
Saying, "The fans constant booing . . ." caused his split

The Yankees got off to a fast start
With very little controversy a big part
By May, the Yankees were in first place
And in control of the East Division race

The Yankees (70-43) led Baltimore by 6½
Then on August 12, baseball made a huge gaffe
The players all went on strike
In essence, they told the fans to take a hike

Fourteen-year Dry Spell, Managerial Madness Continues (1982–1995)

And what was the strike all about?
MONEY, there never was any doubt
The owners wanted to impose a salary cap
Among other issues, it was the major flap

All of the upcoming playoffs were scrapped
It felt like MLB had been kidnapped
This included the '94 World Series too
While animosity among fans quickly grew

League attendance fell as owners did vent
While fans in both leagues did lament
Yankee attendance was down over 30%
A message from unhappy fans emphatically sent

Leading the hitters in his second year was O'Neill
To the Yankee fans he quickly did appeal
He led the AL with an average of .359
And on the Yankees (21 HRs, 83 RBIs) he did shine

Jim Leyritz and Stanley shared the catcher's role
Combined for 34 homers and 115 RBIs to extol
Add Matt Nokes and his 28 games behind the plate
You now have 41 homers and 134 RBIs, first rate

Jimmy Key led the Yankee pitchers by far
With a dandy 17-4 record, a 3.27 ERA, the star
Jim Abbott and Pérez each won nine
Yankee improved pitching, an encouraging sign

Players and owners each hardened their positions
It appeared they were on destructive missions
Sadly, the players strike extended into **1995**
Games were lost, animosity still alive

The strike ceased on April 2, ending a mess
The regular season reduced to 144 games, 18 less
The Yankees finished 79-65 in the East Division
Earning a wild-card slot based on the playoff revision

It was the first season of the three-division alignment
East, Central, West, plus the wild-card refinement
As the Yankees clinched the wild-card slot
With a .549 winning percentage, still a long shot

In the ALDS, the Yankees faced Seattle
In a best-of-five series, it was quite a battle
The Yankees won the first two at home
Seattle the next two at the Kingdome

Game five, bottom of the eighth, Yanks leading 4-2
David Cone still on the mound, a win to pursue
Ken Griffey Jr. homers, Yankees lead by only one
Two outs later, Cone still far from done

Seattle loads the bases, two walks and a hit
Pitch count mounting, Cone won't quit
Doug Strange at the plate, full count
The number of pitches 147, the amount!

It was his last as it hit the dirt, game tied
Rivera enters, fans the batter, big inning denied
Yankees score in the 11th, now lead 5-4
McDowell on the mound to shut the door

But Jack was quickly in a very deep hole
Runners on first and third, need self-control
The dangerous Edgar Martínez at the plate
Took a strike with the patience to wait

On the next pitch, Martínez doubles to left field
Clearing the bases, a Mariners victory it did yield
The final score was Seattle 6, New York 5
Despite the loss, Yankee dominance soon to arrive

Losing game five in 11 innings was a tough loss
This upset everyone including George "The Boss"
Shortly after, in October, Showalter was fired
Some say he resigned; either was not admired

The Yankees were building and destined to win
O'Neill was tops: 22 homers, 96 runs batted in
Boggs, Williams, and O'Neill hit .300 or higher
But four rookies would soon set the team on fire

Andy Pettitte in his rookie season was 12-9
Of future greatness it was clearly a sign
A call up came late in the season for Derek Jeter
Played 15 games, soon to be a world-beater

Jorge Posada and Mariano Rivera sat on the bench
Not for long, key positions they would soon entrench
The four were part of the late 90's World Series lore
They would eventually be known as the "Core Four"

Torre, Jeter Arrive, Six Pennants, Four Championships (1996–2003)

The hunt was on for a new **1996** field boss
Showalter's firing or quitting, a tough loss
GM Michael's assistant Brian Cashman did object
On Steinbrenner it had little to no effect

Eventually Michael recommended Joe Torre
Who led the Mets, Braves, and Cardinals did he
His total record with all three clubs was 894-1003
Not very encouraging, but who could foresee?

As it turned out, Torre would stay for 12 years
Through the ups and downs, boos and cheers
In Joe's first season, the Yankees acquired
Tino Martinez and Jeff Nelson, both greatly admired

With Mattingly retired, Tino took over first base
Replacing Donnie Baseball with class and grace
Nelson added another strong arm in relief
Called on anytime giving tough batters grief

In late 1995, the Yankees traded for Joe Girardi
A solid receiver, pre-Posada, in four years set free
Dwight Gooden signed with New York in '96
George hoped something was left in his bag of tricks

In **1996**, the Yankees finished first in the AL East
An excellent start for Torre to say the least
The Yankees (92-70) faced Texas, tops in the West
New York won three of four, fans were impressed

In game one, Texas won easily 6-2
David Cone took the loss, Yanks overdo
Game two, the Yankees won 5-4
In twelve innings and looking for a lot more

Game three in Texas, another close call
As the Yankees won 3-2, wanting to end it all
Nelson got the win, Wetteland the save
One more victory the Yankees did crave

The Yankees won game four 6-4 in a comeback
Behind Williams' two homers he did whack
The Yankees now moved on to the ALCS
Facing Baltimore and a great deal more stress

The Yankees won game one 5-4
It went on 11 innings and ended in a mighty roar
As Williams belted a walk-off home run
Off Randy Myers, Bernie now the favorite son

But in the bottom of the 8th, Jeter tied the game
On a disputed homer, Jeffrey Maier to blame
He caught the ball before Tarasco had a chance
Orioles called interference; umps another stance

Unfazed, Baltimore won the second game 5-3
Offensively the Yankees were simply crappy
Stranding 11 runners throughout the game
As David Wells, the Yankees he did tame

Game three, the Yankees were trailing 2-1
Scored four in the top of the eighth to stun
Key pitched a marvelous game, final score 5-2
Wetteland the save, a hitless frame he threw

The Yankees kept the pressure on in game four
Hitting four homers, winning 8-4, the score
Williams and O'Neill hit homers, one each
Strawberry two times, the stands he did reach

The Yankees scored six runs in the third, game five
Then held on with Pettitte pitching to stay alive
The final score was 6-4, with Andy getting the win
The **Yankees thirty-fourth pennant,** now no has-been

Bernie Williams was named the ALCS MVP
With clutch hits and a .474 average, easy to agree
And the Yankees first World Series since 1981
Torre's first after 32 years in the game, a long run

Fielder said, "This team worked hard, never quit"
Closer John Wetteland said, "Wow, this is really it"
The 1996 champs were joyous, hopeful, and merry
"This is a special group," said Darryl Strawberry

The Yankees to face the pitching of the Braves
Superb hurlers who deserve nothing but raves
John Smoltz (24-8, 2.94 ERA) their ace
Greg Maddux (15-11, 2.72 ERA) tough to face

And Tom Glavine, 15-10 with a 2.98 ERA
Three times a 20-game winner, a mainstay
The big three pitched almost half of the innings
Accounting for 56% of the team's winnings

The '96 Series began with New York whipped
That was not part of the Yankees' script
The final score 12-1, Pettitte lost, Smoltz won
A dashed Yankee beginning, but far from done

Game two all Maddux, blanking the Yanks on six hits
With help from Mark Wohlers, causing New York fits
Final score 4-0, putting the Bombers in a huge hole
Key the loss, now to Atlanta, a must win their goal

In game three, David Cone picked up the win
Wetteland the save, halting the Yankee tailspin
The final score was 5-2, with three in the eighth
Led by Williams' two-run homer restoring faith

Game four was a hitter's paradise by far
Total pitchers used: 13, quite bizarre
The Braves jumped out to a 6-0 lead
But the Yankees, unsurprisingly, would not concede

The Yankees scored three in the sixth inning
Beginning their comeback and final winning
But, pathetically, cut the lead only in half
Soon a sub would write the Braves' epitaph

In the sixth, Jim Leyritz entered the game
Replacing Joe Girardi, later to enjoy lasting fame
Top of the eighth, two Yanks on base
On the mound Mark Wohlers, a relief ace

Leyritz tirelessly worked the count to 2-2
Then fouled "off two blistering fastballs," phew!
The next became a three-run clout
Said Leyritz, "He hung a slider and I hit it out"

The Yankees went on to win the game 8-6
The victory suddenly caused Atlanta to transfix
The Series tied; Atlanta appeared subdued
Game five expected to be quite a feud

Pettitte out for revenge for the game-one loss
Around his neck, it was like an Albatross
Facing Smoltz, who beat Andy badly
With the Series tied, Pettitte faced reality

Andy rose to the occasion like a true pro
Throwing a five-hit shutout, wouldn't you know
The score 1-0, the Yankees took the Series lead
Back to the Stadium, off the fans they would feed

The matchup in game six, Maddux verses Key
In the third, New York scored a big three
Getting RBIs from Williams, Jeter, and Girardi
The Yankees soon to begin a new dynasty

The final score was 3-2 with plenty of tension
It came in the ninth with nervous apprehension
Wetteland already giving up the second run
Braves on the corners, two out, standing everyone

Mark Lemke at the plate, a base hit needed to tie
He popped a foul fly . . . the crowd did sigh
Wetteland delivered, this time the ball stayed fair
As Hayes made the catch, ending the Braves despair

It was the **Yankees twenty-third World Championship**
And the first for Torre, a 32-year long trip
It was the first Yankee World Series victory since 1978
The 56,000 plus couldn't wait to celebrate

Who will ever forget the ticker tape parade
Down Broadway's Canyon of Heroes crusade
The Yankees come-from-behind World Series win
A new dynasty led by Cashman and Torre to begin

In **1997**, the Yankees did not stand pat
Looking to improve on the mound and at bat
From Japan, the Yankees signed Hideki Irabu
It was a bad choice and The Boss would stew

In '97, Irabu was 5-4 with an ERA of 7.09
A complicated man and hard to define
Hideki Irabu at the young age of 42 died
Determined cause of death: suicide

The Yanks also signed David Wells, age 34
A veteran pitcher who was never a bore
David won 16, but lost 10 with a 4.21 ERA
A bit of a flake, attitude and actions did convey

Free agent Wetteland signed with Texas
A devastating blow to the solar plexus
But, opened for Mariano Rivera the closer role
In the future to be the team's heart and soul

Martinez, at first, had an outstanding year
Giving Yankees fans much to appreciate and cheer
He led the club with 44 homers and 141 RBIs
Both of these exceptional stats and career highs

Despite the rest of the team playing solid baseball
And a 96-66 mark, they faced a Baltimore brick wall
The Yankees ended two games back, that's no canard
In the AL making them the embarrassing wild card

The Yankees and Cleveland met in the ALDS
Game one was a see-saw battle causing fan stress
In the first inning, Cleveland scored five
As the Yankees pecked away to keep alive

By the sixth, the Yankees took the lead
With five runs of their own with all due speed
Including three straight homers, a bit surreal
By Tim Raines, Derek Jeter, and Paul O'Neill

The Yankees finally won the battle, 8-6 the score
The Indians won game two, 7-5, looking for more
But stymied by Wells' pitching in the third game
Allowing five hits, one run, the Indians he did tame

The final score was 6-1, O'Neill driving in five
Four of the RBIs, a grand-slam drive
But Cleveland won the next two, 3-2 and 4-3
Sending the Yankees home to face reality

In early February **1998**, GM Bob Watson quit
Replaced by young Brian Cashman, a better fit
Cashman joined the Yankees as an intern in 1986
Gaining knowledge, know-how, and viewing conflicts

In 1989, he joined the Yankees full-time
Advancing to the GM position, his final climb
Soon after his appointment, Cashman made a trade
Acquiring Chuck Knoblauch, second base he played

In 1997, free agent Boggs signed with Tampa Bay
The Yanks acquired Scott Brosius, third to play
However, the key acquisition was a young pitcher
Who fled Cuba and soon would become richer

Orlando Hernández, nicknamed "El Duque"
Who was given a four-year $6.6 million payday
In 1998, with a 3.13 ERA, he won 12 and lost four
Helping the Yankees to a 114-48 record and more

Chili Davis, a veteran free agent happily signed
As a DH with "Straw" and Raines, it was designed
Hitting honors went to Martinez leading the team
With 28 homers and 123 ribbies, a season supreme

O'Neill had a superb season of which to be proud
Displaying talents of which he was endowed
Paul hit .317/24/116 and patrolling right with style
The other starters were solid, causing Torre to smile

The pitching staff was simply amazing
And fans could not be faulted for praising
A 20-7 and 3.55 ERA registered by Cone
But Cone was far, far from alone

Wells won 18, lost 4 with a 3.49 ERA as well
With a .818 winning percentage, he led the AL
Wells also threw a 4-0 rare perfect game
On May 17 against the Twins, earning lasting fame

Four other Yanks won at least 10 games or more
Let's not forget Rivera, with 36 saves more to adore
Now to the 1998 ALDS as it doth wait
The Yankees vs. Texas to determine their fate

It was not a surprise Yankee pitching dominated
As Texas hitters joined the ranks of the ill-fated
The winning trio . . . Wells, Pettitte, and Cone
That's all it took, the Rangers to dethrone

Wells blanked Texas 2-0 in game one
With help from Rivera, the Yanks having fun
Pettitte won game two, 3-1, "Mo" another save
The situation for Texas quickly turning grave

The series ended with a shutout by Cone
The score 4-0 as Texas fans did moan
David was yanked after a rain delay
The bullpen keeping the Rangers at bay

After Texas, the Yankees flew back to New York
Before Cleveland in the ALCS, the bubbly to uncork
With the celebration over, it was time to play ball
In game one, Wells' 7-2-win, Cleveland's downfall

Cleveland won game two, 4-1 the score
With three runs in the 12th, now wanting more
Game three was all Cleveland's, Bartolo Colón
The hard-throwing righty was in a zone

He allowed four hits in a 6-1 complete game
Hats off to Colón, the Yankees he did tame
The win put Cleveland in the driver's seat
The Yankees needed to match Colón's pitching feat

El Duque quietly answered the needed call
Pitching seven clutch shutout innings of ball
While Stanton and Rivera blanked the Tribe
The last two innings as Torre did prescribe

The 4-0 win by El Duque tied the series after four
The Yankee's confidence, the victory did restore
New York won game five, a relatively easy win
Behind Wells, 5-3, much to Cleveland's chagrin

Game six of the ALCS looked like it was over
The Yanks led 6-0, Cone pitching, Yanks in clover
Then Cone came apart in the fifth, giving up one run
Until Thome hit a grand slam, Indians down by one

Torre, Jeter Arrive, Six Pennants, Four Championships (1996–2003)

Cleveland's euphoria didn't last but a short while
In the sixth, the Yankees scored three to stockpile
Led by Jeter's timely hitting, 9-5 the final score
The **Yankees thirty-fifth AL flag**, still wanting more

The New York Yankees 1998 World Series foe
The San Diego Padres put on a gallant show
In the end, the Padres were no match
As the Yankees swept the Series with dispatch

The Yanks won game one, behind Wells, 9-6
Sound pitching, timely hitting, a winning mix
Wells credited with the win, the save went to Mo
Chuck and Tino drove in seven, the death blow

Game two the Yankees won easily 9-3
Behind El Duque with support the key
With home runs from Williams and Posada
Members of the Bombers home run armada

On to Qualcomm Stadium for game three
The Padres needing to change their strategy
Cone started, Sterling Hitchcock for San Diego
Neither finished the game; Brosius the show

The Yankees came from behind to win 5-4
Brosius drove in four; Padres left with one more
The end came for San Diego in a humbling way
Andy, Jeff, and Mo making it look like child's play

Andy the winner, Mo the save; final score 3 zip
The **Yankees twenty-fourth World Championship**
Brosius was named World Series MVP, deservedly so
Batting .471, six RBIs, and two homers, quite a show

Back at the clubhouse players sprayed champagne
Even George Steinbrenner failed to complain
He announced for all to hear, as if gone mad
"This is as good as any team I've ever had"

Cashman's first season as GM was a huge success
No doubt, looking to repeat despite the stress
Over the winter, Williams signed a new contract
Seven years, $87.5 million, worth the money a fact

Then Cashman, in a bold move, made a daring trade
Acquiring Roger Clemens, the rotation to upgrade
It sparked Yankee fans, recalling his Red Sox days
When Roger was the enemy and heard little praise

The trade turned out well, despite negative theories
With Roger, New York won four AL flags and two World Series
In six seasons his record was a solid 83-42
As Roger was more than an aging player passing through

In the spring, Torre disclosed he had prostate cancer
Surgery, according to doctors, clearly the answer
The procedure was performed successfully
Torre back with the club in May, few did foresee

The Yankees finished the **1999** season 98-64
Not close to the previous year, but not a bore
Attested to the fact over 3.2 million attended
An unmatched record with ovations so splendid

One of the highlights was a perfect game
By David Cone on Yogi Berra's Day, it came
Against the Expos with Don Larsen present
Game over, "Coney" on his knees, totally spent

Torre, Jeter Arrive, Six Pennants, Four Championships (1996–2003)

There were lowlights in 1999 to grieve
In March, the great DiMaggio this earth he did leave
Six months later, Catfish followed suit
Leaving Yankee fans sad and emotionally destitute

Through it all, the 1999 Yankees played well
Jeter, at 25, single handily did raise lots of hell
Derek hit .349, and led the AL with 219 hits
And drove in 102 runs, giving the opposition fits

Williams batted .342 and led the club with 115 RBIs
Tino hit 28 homers, the club leader, no surprise
Hernández led the staff with 17 wins, the workhorse
Throwing over 214 innings, he was a vital force

Rivera, once again brilliant in the closer role
Saving 45 with a super cutter and pinpoint control
Resulting in an unheard of 1.83 ERA
Even though hitters knew the pitch was on the way

The Yankees' foe in the ALDS were no strangers
Led by power hitter Rafael Palmeiro of the Rangers
Along with right-hander Aaron Sele who won 18
Plus, Wetteland with 43 saves, truly mean

The Yankees swept the Rangers with relative ease
Game one, El Duque shutout Texas 8-0, a breeze
Pettitte won game two, 3-1, Mo the routine save
Game three, the Yanks continued to misbehave

Strawberry hit a three-run homer in the first
That's all Clemens needed as Texas was cursed
Mariano mopped up for save number two
Next? The Boston Red Sox to happily subdue

On to meet the Boston Red Sox in the ALCS
When these two teams meet, nothing but stress
The two clubs always put on a great show
Win or lose, fans of each team will crow

The Yankees beat Boston 4-3 in game one
When Bernie hit a 10th-inning walk-off home run
Yankee fans went absolutely daffy and wild
Filled with wonder and delight, simply beguiled

Torre chose Cone to start game two
To many, a surprise choice who came through
New York behind after six and a half, 2-1 the score
Plated two in the seventh, the victory to restore

Clemens started game three, it was a route
The winner was never, ever in doubt
The final score: Boston 13, New York 1
The Sox had 21 hits having payback fun

Boston's fun didn't last too long
As the Yankees came back very strong
They won game four, 9-2 the score
Pettitte the winner, Yanks need one more

In game five, New York scored two in the first frame
When Jeter homered one on, that was the game
The final score was 6-1, El Duque got the win
Let the **thirty-six AL pennant** celebration begin

But a World Series victory, the ultimate feat
The Yankees had one more team to defeat
The Atlanta Braves finished their season 103-59
Then beat the Mets and Astros, a positive sign

Torre, Jeter Arrive, Six Pennants, Four Championships (1996–2003)

Many believed pitching would dominate
It was an interesting and worthy debate
But few thought the Yanks would sweep!
As Atlanta folded with hardly a peep

Game one El Duque beat Maddux 4-1, a late rally
Rivera with a save holding Atlanta to the one tally
Game two, Cone was handed a seven-run lead
Final score 7-2, Kevin Millwood hit hard all agreed

Game three came to be the closest of the four
Atlanta leading 5-3, Yanks going after more
Scored two in the 8th to tie the game at five all
Until Chad Curtis' walk-off, the Braves downfall

Game four the Yankees scored three in the third
When Tino drove in two, Jorge one, sweep the word
The Yankees had one more in the eighth, the Braves too
Clemens the win (4-1), Mo the save, a dynasty to renew

The **Yankees twenty-fifth World Championship**
No other franchise close; time for another ego trip
It was Torre's third World Series in four seasons
The next would be a dandy for obvious reasons

Before leaving 20th Century Baseball let's agree
Mariano deserved to be the World Series MVP
Threw 4⅔ scoreless innings often with men on base
Winning one game, saving two, with a poker face

The 2000 New York Yankees finished 87-74
Not an exciting team but not a total bore
At least compared to the two previous years
When the Yanks dominated their peers

In fact, the Yankees backed into first place
And damn near lost their division race
Losing thirteen games of their last fifteen
Narrowly beating out Boston, an ugly scene

It was clear during the season the 2000 team
Compared to the '98/'99 clubs lacked steam
Were some of the key players getting on in age?
Always a difficult assessment to gage

The idea of winning three Series in a row
May prey on the minds of players and Joe
At second, Knoblauch suddenly lacked a spark
Coney, at 37 was ineffective with a 4-14 mark

The Yankees were struggling by the end of June
Something had to be done and very soon
So Cashman made an impactful trade
He acquired David Justice and his hitting tirade

Cashman made other moves, Justice the key
In hindsight, most baseball experts did agree
In 78 games David batted a cool .305/20/60
Helping to raise the low team esprit

New York at Oakland, the 2000 ALDS began
The Yankees losing 5-3, clearly not the plan
Game two Pettitte pitched seven plus for the 4-0 win
Rivera mopped up for the save, always the kingpin

The Yankees won game three, 4-2, a nail biter
El Duque proving he was a clutch pitcher and fighter
Rivera pitched the ninth for save number two
The Yankees a win away from a playoff round anew

Torre, Jeter Arrive, Six Pennants, Four Championships (1996–2003)

The pace shifted in game four, Oakland dominated
Winning 11-1 tying the series, A's fans briefly sated
Game five New York came out swinging, a new attack
Scoring six runs in the first, winning 7-5, a comeback

Now to face the Mariners (91-71) from Seattle
In the ALCS, which should be an interesting battle
Seattle's manager, Lou Piniella, popular in the city
A tough competitor, often explosive and gritty

Freddy Garcia beat the Yankees 2-0 in game one
At the Stadium, the Yankees clearly out done
For Torre and the Yankees, it was a wakeup call
They won the next three games, a windfall

Game two, El Duque won 7-1 but had to wait
For the Yankees to score all seven in inning eight!
Andy Pettitte easily won game three, 8-2
Rivera with another save, Seattle almost through

Game four heroics to Clemens' one-hit shutout
Striking out 15, the outcome never in doubt
The final score was 5-0, Jeter a three-run blast
And Justice a two-run homer, support so steadfast

Facing elimination, Seattle never quit
They won game five 6-2 with desire and grit
Back to NYC and their fans the game to help sway
At the Stadium a screaming crowd on every play

Game six, Seattle jumped out to an early lead
Score 4-3, El Duque not sharp some did concede
Then came the fatal seventh inning for Seattle
No longer a game, it now was a battle

José Paniagua put runners on first and third base
Replaced by Arthur Rhodes, justice to face
David promptly smacked a timely home run
Yankees now led 6-4, and still not done

The Yankees loaded the bases, O'Neill at the plate
Paul singled scoring two, opening the floodgate
José Mesa relieved Rhodes and walked one more
Then José Vizcaíno's sac fly made it 9-4

Seattle did not quit, scoring three in the eighth
The Yankee lead now 9-7, fans turned to faith
Rivera getting roughed up the previous inning
Closed out the ninth, the first Yankee grinning

The **Yankees thirty-seventh AL pennant** wasn't easy
And the fans at times, no doubt, felt kind of queasy
Looking back at tense moments, but no regrets
For now, it was to the World Series to meet the Mets

The Mets 94-68 record was a very good sign
Led by the "outspoken" Bobby Valentine
In the NLDS they were deemed the wild card
Facing the Giants of San Francisco with disregard

The Giants had the best record, a challenging scene
In game one, whipped the Mets 5-1, quite routine
Then the Giant fans became suddenly appalled
The Mets won the next three, their fans enthralled

In the NLCS, the Mets continued their winning ways
Defeating St. Louis four games to one with praise
To the World Series and the ill will of the two teams
In a "Subway Series," chasing championship dreams

Torre, Jeter Arrive, Six Pennants, Four Championships (1996–2003)

Game one featured veterans Pettitte and Al Leiter
Neither went the distance, the game never tighter
The Yankees won in inning 12, the score 4-3
On Vizcaino's winning RBI, the Bronx went wacky

Clemens, in game two, shutout the Mets for eight
As the Yankees were leading 6-0, a loss did await
Jeff Nelson pitched the ninth, allowed three tallies
Before bringing in Rivera, the killer of rallies

With a runner on, Mo allowed a single and home run
The blast, cutting the lead to 6-5, by Jay Payton
But then Mo fanned Kurt Abbott to end the game
A 2-0 Series lead, the Yankees did now proclaim

But first a word about the Clemens and Piazza spat
In game two, a Clemens' pitch shattered Piazza's bat
The foul ball splintered the bat towards the mound
Clemens threw the bat towards Mike, hitting the ground

Clemens' recall about throwing the bat, his pitfall
He thought the bat fragment was the ball!
Whatever was going through Roger's mind
Was regretfully voiced and clearly ill-defined

The Mets down by two games, credit now due
In game three, they regrouped and came through
Beating the Yankees with two in the eighth
Final score: 4-2, giving Met fans renewed faith

The Mets momentum was crushed the next game
The Yankees winning 3-2, the edge to reclaim
Now the Mets were in quite a dreadful mess
But with Leiter pitching, at Shea, to ease the stress

Williams homered in the second, the Yanks lead
The Mets scored two, their half, with all do speed
Derek Jeter homered in the sixth, now two all
It remained that way until the ninth, if you recall

The Yankees plated two and now led 4-2
The Mets had the ninth to tie, believers few
With Mo on the mound, two out, runner on third
Piazza at the plate, home run was the byword

On a 0-1 count, he hits a very long fly ball at Shea
One could imagine 55,000 would collectively pray
In the dugout it was said Torre screamed "no"
Seconds later Williams caught the mighty blow

It was the **Yankees twenty-sixth Championship**
And since '96, Joe Torre's fourth winning trip
Jeter was named MVP of the Series, batting .409
In July also named the All-Star MVP, a season divine

Before **2001**, the Yankees made a pitching addition
Signing free agent Mike Mussina, a star acquisition
The NYT reported he signed for $87 million, six years
Cheers came from the fans and his now Yankee peers

For 10 years Mussina had been with Baltimore
Compiling a record of 147-81, hard to ignore
Now strengthening the Yankees strong rotation
Their fourth straight World Series, their fixation

The other change, moving Knoblauch to left field
His throwing problem at second, his fate sealed
Alfonso Soriano replaced him at second base
His power and speed, the Yanks would showcase

Torre, Jeter Arrive, Six Pennants, Four Championships (1996-2003)

By early September, the Yanks thinking post season
And the playoffs for a very logical reason
They had a strong lead over Boston in their division
Then September 11 struck and changed the vision

MLB forgotten and the nation refocused attention
As the Twin Towers crumbled, sadly to mention
Almost 3,000 lives lost, a terrible calamity
For those directly affected and the extended family

While the nation and New York City mourned
Osama Bin Laden and his ilk were scorned
Finally, on May 2, 2011, Osama was shot and killed
By the United States Navy Seals, warriors so skilled

The nation and those who lost family and friends
Always to remember that day tearfully, it never ends
It was a tragedy that should never have taken place
A horrifying time in our history, an indelible disgrace

Six days later, Major League Baseball resumed play
Even with 9/11 still fresh in the minds everyday
The Yankees clinched the AL East September 25
With a 95-65 record as the team came alive

The Yankees, led by Clemens with a record of 20-3
At thirty-eight, a performance hard to foresee
Roger won his sixth Cy Young Award for his success
Selected by the BBWAA he did impress

Clemens would win Cy Young number seven in 2004
With Houston (18-4, 2.98 ERA) his last encore
With the Yankees in 2001, Clemens had support
Mussina (17-11, 3.15 ERA), the opposition to thwart

Plus, Pettitte went 15-10 with a 3.99 ERA
Rivera with 50 saves, the Yanks had their way
Five Yankees hit 20 homers or more
Martinez with 34, the big leader of the corps

Tino also led the club with 113 RBIs
Soriano, his first full season, a pleasant surprise
He hit .268, but had 18 homers and drove in 73
Alfonso also led the club with 43 steals, did he

Season over, the Yankees looking for another trip
To the World Series and another championship
Under Torre it would be their fourth in a row
But first, two very tough opponents to kayo

What's needed is to win the ALDS against the A's
And win the division handily, the goal to amaze
Then on to the ALCS and the Mariners from Seattle
Beating them soundly in the line of battle

On to the World Series to face the Diamondbacks
The Yankees winning in a swift and ugly climax
If all of what has been written would come true
For Torre and his gang, a monumental coup

Only Casey can boast of five World Series in a row
From 1949–1953, ending in 1954, a Cleveland blow
The Indians won the pennant with a 111-43 mark
Then the New York Giants swept the Series, no lark

McCarthy's Yankees won four in a row, 1936-1939
Lost the pennant in '40 by two, the bottom line
McCarthy's team won the Series in 1941, you know
Playing "what if", it would have been six in a row

Torre, Jeter Arrive, Six Pennants, Four Championships (1996–2003)

In 2000, the Yankees faced Oakland in the ALDS
The first two games at the Stadium, no success
Oakland won both 5-3 and 2-0, Yanks in a hole
Back to Oakland, Yankees need to take control

The Yankees woke up by winning game three
Behind Mussina and Rivera's pitching, the key
The score 1-0, Posada's fifth inning home run
And Jeter's incredible defensive play did stun

Game three was the turning point of the ALDS
Shifting momentum and easing Yankee distress
And was further demonstrated in game four
The Yankees took a 7-2 early lead, added more

Final score, 9-2, El Duque picking up the win
With help from the pen, series tied to A's chagrin
Singles, doubles, and triples was the order of the day
The long ball not needed against Oakland to slay

Game five at the Stadium, Oakland an early lead
Yankees tied 2-2, then ahead with all due speed
To the end, Oakland put up a strong battle
But lost 5-3, now the Yankees to face Seattle

Game one of the ALCS was played at Safeco Field
Pitching and timely hitting the Yanks revealed
Final score 4-2, thanks to O'Neill's two-run blast
Plus, Pettitte and Rivera's pitching, unsurpassed

The Yankees won the next game 3-2
Mussina the win and Rivera in a redo
Now back to the Bronx to finish the task
Shockingly, Seattle their offense did unmask

The Mariners whipped the Yanks, 14-3 the score
For Yankees fans a game to forget, an eyesore
But game four was a thriller to the very end
In the eighth, game tied at 1-1, no one would bend

Top of the ninth Rivera quickly retired the side
Bottom half, Yankee fans were not to be denied
With one out, Brosius on an infield single at first
From the over 56,000 fans, a thundering outburst

Rookie Alfonso Soriano walked to the plate
Was it a poor pitch, skill, or just plain fate?
Soriano smacked a walk-off home run
Final score: New York 3, Seattle 1

Game five turned out to be an early rout
The Yankees won 12-3, the win never in doubt
By the end of three innings, the Yanks led 4-zip
Then piled on and tightened the grip

It was the fourth straight AL pennant for Torre
And **38** for New York, an enviable record and story
Arizona finished the season 92-70, and in the NLDS
Beat St. Louis three games to two, they did impress

After St. Louis, the D-backs went on a rampage
Defeating Atlanta in five games, setting the stage
Between an inexperienced four-year old franchise
Against the mighty Yankees, World Series the prize

Was the young franchise underestimated?
Plus, only four players will have you captivated
They had two great pitchers, Johnson and Schilling
For hitters facing either, it was quite chilling

Torre, Jeter Arrive, Six Pennants, Four Championships (1996–2003)

Randy (21-6, 2.49 ERA), intimidating on the mound
At 6'10 destined for the HOF, he was bound
Curt (22-6, 2.98 ERA), a veteran of the game
A tough competitor that brought him fame

The D-backs had two potent hitters in the outfield
Luis Gonzales and Reggie Sanders, stats revealed
Luis hit .325/57/142, Reggie .263/33/90, very telling
Ninety homers between the two, quite compelling

The 2001 World Series began at Bank One Ballpark
With the Yankees losing 9-1, lacking any spark
Schilling pitched seven innings of three-hit ball
With relief help as the Yankee bats went AWOL

Game two, Johnson pitched a three-hit shutout
The score 4-0, the Yankees now fighting self-doubt
On to NYC with President Bush on the mound
With 9/11 in the air, he threw a strike to astound

Prompting thousands to shout "USA, USA, USA"
Yanks won 2-1 this soulful night, the Clemens way
In seven, Roger allowed three hits, fanned nine
Of the six Mo faced, he fanned four, a good sign

Game four was a nail biter from beginning to end
Tied at 3-3 after nine, neither team willing to bend
Rivera retired the side in the 10th frame
Kim, the D-backs closer, stayed in the game

It was the 22-year-old's third inning in relief
With two out and a 3-2 pitch, Kim met grief
As Derek Jeter homered to win the game
Tie the Series, two each, adding to his fame

Game five was another nerve-wracking contest
Again, the Yankees in extra innings were blessed
Arizona leading 2-0 in the ninth, Kim got the call
Two out, Posada doubled, now the downfall

Scott Brosius hit a 1-0 pitch over the left field wall
Kim replaced by Mike Morgan, the right call
Until the bottom of inning 12, the game held at 2-2
Now comes the fatal inning . . . it was a lulu

Chuck Knoblauch led off with a base hit
Brosius bunted him to second lickety split
Soriano promptly singled in the winning run
But the Series was far, far from done

On to game six at Bank One Ballpark
Where Arizona beat the Yanks 15-2, no lark
Twenty-two hits and 15 runs by inning four
D-back fans were joyous, the game a bore

Johnson went seven innings for his second win
Pettitte gave up six runs in two innings, a sin
Game seven of the World Series finally did arrive
The question on everyone's lips: who will survive?

Clemens and Schilling, clutch winners head-to-head
Competitors on the mound, not to break bread
Clemens in six and a third, gave up only one run
In seven and a third, Curt gave up two, then he was done

Bottom of the eighth, the score Yanks 2, Arizona 1
Torre called on Rivera to get the job done
Mo answered the call, striking out the side
In the ninth, the Yankee bats also denied

Torre, Jeter Arrive, Six Pennants, Four Championships (1996–2003)

To the bottom of the ninth, Mo still on the mound
Defensive lapses, an error, and hits did abound
The score now 2-2, Rivera also hit a batter
Bases full, one out, Yankee dreams soon to shatter

Infield and outfield moved in to cut off the run
Now Rivera facing Gonzalez, the dangerous one
Mo threw a cutter, Luis a blooper over Jeter's head
Yankee fans watching on TV were seeing red

Schilling and Johnson named Co-MVP's
The veteran hurlers were the two main keys
Memories of the 2001 World Series will disappear
The loss of loved ones in 9/11 will forever persevere

The Yankees acquired two players before **2002**
One was a Yankee before, the other brand new
Free agent David Wells was back at age 39
A few pounds heavier but pitching just fine

The player they nicknamed "Boomer"
With a unique sense of humor
Finished 19-7 with a WPCT of .731
Best of the Yankee starters, bar none

In December, the Yankees made an unusual trade
With the Mets, both players of high grade
The Yanks obtained Robin Ventura for third base
In exchange for Justice to help in the Mets race

Ventura had a solid season, 27 homers, 93 RBIs
Traded him in 2003 to the LA Dodgers, a surprise
But the big deal was the signing of Jason Giambi
For $120 million, seven-year contract, quite gutsy

Giambi's first season turned out to be his best
He hit .314/41/122, with talent he was blessed
However, PED rumors constantly haunted him
Until he admitted use in 2007, a story so grim

Soriano, his second full season led the AL in hits
With 209, he scored 128, and stole 41, a blitz
He hit .300/39/102, and made the All-Star team
Many major League players admitted dream

Behind Wells, Mike Mussina was 18-10
Clemens 13-6, needing help from the pen
Pettitte with an ERA of 3.27 was 13-5
Often on the IL Mo's saves (28) did dive

The Yankees still managed to finish 103-58
First in the AL East, for Torre five straight
In the ALDS, the Angels were the adversary
The wild card the Yankees should easily bury

Although the Yankees won the first game 8-5
The Angels fought hard, a propensity to survive
It took a Williams three-run homer to win
The Angels not awed by the Yankees' fame herein

To prove the point the Angels won the next three
They battled fiercely until it was a reality
The scores were: 8-6, 9-6, and 9-5
The never give up approach kept them alive

"No team has played better against us," Jeter said
Spoiling a fifth straight pennant for Torre instead
As Brooklyn often said, "wait 'til next year"
And the Yankees would be back and in high gear

Torre, Jeter Arrive, Six Pennants, Four Championships (1996–2003)

In **2003,** the Yankees were right back on top
Winning **pennant 39** in a drastic flip-flop
Finishing first in the AL East with a 101-61 mark
Led by Giambi with 107 RBIs, 41 out of the park

Jason was backed by Posada who hit .281/30/101
And Soriano .290/38/91, plus Japan's favorite son
His name Hideki Matsui, played 10 years in Japan
Signed for $21 million over a three-year span

Matsui an instant success on and off the field
To the media and Yankee fans he appealed
In 2003, Matsui played in every Yankee game
Hitting .287/16/106 . . . and lasting fame

To put it bluntly, the Yankee rotation was old
Still pitching well, perhaps time to remold
At age 40 Wells (15-7), Clemens (17-9) were fine
And Pettitte, 21-8, with a 4.02 ERA, he did shine

Mussina another good season, 17-8, 3.40 ERA
Mo a 1.66 ERA, 40 saves a closer gourmet
There were several notable events during 2003
Jeter named captain, the retirement of Mattingly

Also, Roger Clemens won his 300th baseball game
Plus getting his 4,000 strikeouts to wide acclaim
From the Reds the Yankees acquired Aaron Boone
Who would become famous . . . and very soon

The 2003 ALDS opened in New York vs The Twins
Who finished the season with 72 losses, 90 wins
On paper not a threat with a team ERA of 4.41
Tori Hunter who hit .250/26/102, their power gun

A Brief History of the New York Yankees

The only thing that counts is on the field of play
As the Twins won 3-1, the inevitable to delay
As Pettitte, Clemens, and Wells won the next three
By scores of 4-1, 3-1, and 8-1 to meet their rivalry

Yes, the Yankees and the Red Sox in the ALCS!
The series went seven with plenty of stress
Boston won game one 5-2, Mussina the loss
The Yanks bounced back 6-2, happy was The Boss

Game three at Fenway and still recalled today
Between Clemens and Pedro Martínez, a nasty fray
After Matsui drove in a run with a double
Karim García was hit by a Pedro pitch, now trouble

Ground ball by Soriano scored another run
Yankees now led 4-2, stay tuned more fun
Enrique Wilson popped up to end the inning
Leaving the field, Martínez and García not grinning

In fact, their remarks were ugly no doubt
That resulted in teammates joining the shout
Now to the bottom of the fourth, Ramirez to bat
Clemens on the mound all business no chitchat

And with the ugly tension between the clubs high
Roger on his first pitch became the bad guy
Intentional or not, it was high and tight
Bothe benches emptied, thus began the real fight

72-year-old coach Don Zimmer, on the Yankee team
Charged on to the field, this did seem extreme
"Zim" went directly for Pedro, an obvious mismatch
Pedro pushed Zim to the ground with dispatch

Torre, Jeter Arrive, Six Pennants, Four Championships (1996–2003)

Zim was taken to the hospital, a safeguard
Not hurt, perhaps his reputation a tad scarred
The Yankees won the game 4-3 setting the scene
For exciting game seven, an ending unforeseen

Boston won game four 3-2, the winner Wakefield
The loser Mussina, but the Yanks would not yield
Winning game five 4-2, Wells and Mo did tame
Boston won next 9-6, now to the famous last game

Game seven, Martínez and Clemens in a replay
In a see-saw battle, the Yankees held sway
Boston jumped to a 4-0 lead by the end of four
Giambi homered in the fifth and wanting more

Giambi did it again in the seventh inning
The Yankees comeback was just beginning
Ortiz homered in the eighth to extend the lead
The Yanks in their half down 5-2, did not concede

The Yankees scored three runs to tie the game
The critics on manager Grady Little laid the blame
For leaving a tired Martínez to continue to pitch
With rested relievers he could have made a switch

Jeter doubled, Williams singled, Pedro remained
Then Matsui and Posada doubled as if ordained
The game now tied at 5-5, Rivera in the game
Pitched three scoreless innings to great acclaim

The bottom of the 11th Wakefield on the mound
The first batter he faced the results did astound
Aaron Boone hit a walk-off into the left-field seats
Now the celebration on the field and in the streets

It was the **Yankees thirty-ninth AL flag**
The most in both leagues and the right to brag
The MVP of the ALCS was Rivera, the mainstay
In eight frames, won one and saved two with a 1.13 era

But the 2003 season was far from complete
The Florida Marlins, in the World Series, to meet
The Marlins were overmatched it appeared
And by the Yankees, they certainly weren't feared

The Marlins were not an exceptional team
Ending the season as a wild card, clearly a dream
Finishing 10 games in back of the Atlanta Braves
Not a team that could make serious waves

Yet in the NLDS, they beat the Giants three straight
After losing the opener 2-0 as Chicago did wait
Game one of the NLCS, the Marlins continued to win
Beating the Cubs 9-8, no thought of giving in

Then the roof fell in and the Cubs took control
Won the next three, one away from their goal
But it was not to be, never part of the Cubs destiny
As the Marlins regrouped and won the next three!

Now on to the 2003 World Series, the big stage
Where the Yankees and Marlins will engage
Despite Wells' solid pitching in game one
The Marlins prevailed surprising everyone

The Yankees bounced back the next day 6-1
In eight plus innings Pettitte allowed one run
Matsui hit a three-run homer in the first inning
In hindsight, all the Yankees needed in winning

Mussina won game three, Rivera a save
The score was 1-1 until the Marlins did cave
The final score: Yankees 6, Marlins 1
Looking back, the last game the Yankees had fun

Florida won game four, 4-3, a walk-off home run
Not expected by many, actually probably none
Hit by Álex González in a 5-for-53 slump
Perfect timing to get over the nasty hump

Series now tied at two games each
An upset victory still within their reach
As the Marlins won the next game 6-4
Behind Brad Penny, now looking for one more

Game six, Marlins manager McKeon rolled the dice
Picking Josh Beckett, three day's rest to be precise
Josh answered the call, a brilliant complete game
A five-hit shutout (2-0), a World Series to proclaim

A-Rod Arrives, Boston Comeback, Three More East Titles (2004-2007)

Series over, the Yankees looked to next year
Losing Pettitte, now a free agent, a definite fear
He signed with Houston a three-year contract
After winning 21 with the Yanks, it had an impact

As a free agent Clemens signed with Houston too
Wells was another free-agent the Padres did woo
Among the three they won 53 games in 2003
To replace them you would need the Almighty

Acquired Javier Vázquez, Jon Lieber, and Kevin Brown
With all due respect, they were a huge let down
Thus, New York went looking for consistent power
For free agents the field they did vigorously scour

Signed three players in December they revealed
Miguel Cairo, Rubén Sierra, and Gary Sheffield
In January signed first baseman Tony Clark
A switch hitter who loved the game, his hallmark

In February, Alex Rodriguez was big baseball news
Texas agreed to a trade, New York did not refuse
The Rangers sent Alex, plus cash for Soriano
And a player to be named later, who could say no

Early in February, Boone tore a ligament in his knee
Playing basketball, out for the season, a reality
Ergo, A-Rod agreed to play third base
His new position he did quickly embrace

A-Rod Arrives, Boston Comeback, Three More East Titles (2004-2007)

The Yankees won the AL East once more
With a record of 101-61, and a playoff encore
Sheffield led the offensive hitting .290/36/121
Matsui hit .298/31/108, not to be outdone

A-Rod hit .286/36/106, completing the big three
The remaining six were solid hitters, no hyperbole
The team ERA of 4.69 . . . deserves few raves
Except for Rivera with an ERA of 1.94 and 53 saves

In the ALDS the Yankees faced the Twins
Winning the AL Central Division with 92 wins
The Twins had a solid club but not frightening
They had a 20-game winner, quite enlightening

Johan Santana (20-6, 2.61 ERA) was his name
And won the Twins only playoff game
Beating Mussina 2-0 at the Stadium, no less
But that was the Twins only moment to impress

The next three games the Yankees did take
As Minnesota couldn't catch a break
Scores of 7-6, 8-4, and 6-5, all very tight
As the Twins lost, but not without a fight

Now the matchup fans were waiting for
Yankees versus Red Sox, guaranteed not to bore
Especially after beating the Sox last year
On Boone's homer, and Series hopes to disappear

The 2004 ALCS began with Boston dazed
The Yankees won the first three games unfazed
Mussina won game one 10-7, Rivera the save
Both teams were orderly and did not misbehave

Jon Lieber pitched seven strong innings in game two
Winning 3-1 with Mo, another save, the tension grew
The series now moving to friendly Fenway Park
Where Boston was hoping to ignite a spark

At Fenway, game three, the Yankees won 19-8!
The embarrassing loss should have sealed their fate
No, Boston won game four, 6-4 in 12 innings, no less
Thanks to David Ortiz's walk-off, it brought success

Game five, another extra inning feud, this time 14
Boston winning 5-4, Ortiz, again a hero on the scene
It was a clutch single, scoring the winning run
Ortiz gave the Sox renewed hope, not to be outdone

Game six was all about the pitching of Curt Schilling
Pitching with a repaired torn tendon sheath, chilling
Bleeding visible through his white sanitary sock
But Curt labored on through seven, solid as a rock

The final score was 4-2, Schilling the win
The series now tied, Yanks in a tailspin
Said Torre, "Everybody was as tight as a drum"
The players were gloomy, baffled, and numb

In game seven, Torre reluctantly chose Kevin Brown
Not an upbeat guy and capable of a meltdown
As in game three he was hit hard, a bust
Brown was also a guy his teammates didn't trust

Game seven was a complete blowout
The score was 10-3, if there was any doubt
Boston was ahead 6-0 after the second inning
Ortiz's two-run homer just the beginning

A-Rod Arrives, Boston Comeback, Three More East Titles (2004-2007)

Second inning Brown loaded the bases, one out
Torre chose a new pitcher wanting a turnabout
He chose Javier Vázquez, the game now in his hands
Damon hit his first pitch into the right-field stands

The 2004 ALCS was a very, very painful loss
To players and fans, especially The Boss
It would take five seasons before a return to glory
And led by another Joe, not named Torre

In **2005** New York aimed to help their pitching
And to sign Carl Pavano they were itching
He was 18-8 with the Marlins the year before
For the Yankees (4-6, 4.77 ERA), no '04 encore

Another signing was free agent Jaret Wright
Who was 5-5 with a lofty 6.08 ERA, out of sight
The key was Arizona's Randy Johnson in a trade
Three players and cash, the Yankees did persuade

"A nine-time strikeout champion," at age 41
And a "five-time Cy Young winner," not yet done
Randy led the club with a record of 17-8 and a 3.79 ERA
His value would come in post-season play

Chien-Ming Wang, a pitcher from Taiwan
Up from the minors he quickly caught on
The right-hander won only 8, lost 5
But the next two seasons he would come alive

Tino Martinez signed in January for another year
His last, ending a noteworthy 16-year career
Rookie Robinson Cano took over at second base
And for the next eight seasons a welcome face

A-Rod was named the AL MVP and rightly so
Hitting .321/48/130 . . . quite a show
Backed by heavy hitters Matsui and Sheffield
The eighth straight AL East title it did yield

The Yankees record was 95-67, down from 2004
It didn't affect attendance as it did soar
Over four million fans went through the gates
Proof that winning . . . attendance it generates

In the ALDS the Yanks faced the Angels from LA
For Yankee fans, the series was a painful fray
The Yankees won the opener at LA 4-2
The combo of Mussina and Mo came through

LA won game two, 5-3, on Yankees sloppy play
And game three 11-7 with 19 hits, a hitting display
The Yankees now with their backs against the wall
Won game four 3-2, a very, very close call

So, the series came down to a single game five
And what team would ultimately survive
The Angels won 5-3, Mussina had an off game
In 2⅔ innings he allowed all five runs, what a shame

But Mussina shouldn't be given all the blame
One even admitted, Rodriguez his last name
"I just had a bad series," said A-Rod
And could be said of others on the Yankee squad

Aside, the Yankees lost and the season ended
And certainly not as the front office intended
It was never too early to begin planning for 2006
The Yankees looking for quality, not a quick fix

A-Rod Arrives, Boston Comeback, Three More East Titles (2004-2007)

In January **2006**, Damon signed a Yankee contract
A free agent as Boston lost interest, a fact
The Yanks called up Melky Cabrera, his name
Played left most of the season to some acclaim

In July, the Yankees traded for Bobby Abreu
A veteran outfielder and solid hitter, age 32
The additions turned out to be a good move
Despite injuries to players the team did improve

With a 97-65 record, 10 games ahead of the Jays
And **ninth straight AL East title** deserving praise
Under the leadership skills of Cashman and Torre
Brought winning back to New York and due glory

The top Yankee hitters were Jeter and Cano
Derek at .343 and Robbie .342, quite a combo
Giambi had a good season: 37 homers, 113 RBIs
And A-Rod with 35 and 121, the Yanks power guys

Detroit (95-67) was the Central Division wild card
In game one, playing in the Yankees own backyard
New York scored five in the third to take the lead
Won the game 8-4 behind Wang (19-6), take heed!

Shockingly, a sweep was to quickly proceed
The **Tigers won the next three** with due speed
Game two, the Yankees blew a 3-1 lead
Pecking away at Mussina the Tigers did succeed

In the fifth, Detroit scored on a sac fly
In the sixth, Carlos Guillén homered for a tie
In the seventh, Granderson tripled a man on base
Making the final score 4-3, Tigers to set the pace

Tigers won game three 6-0 behind Kenny Rogers
As the pathetic Yankees played like old codgers
No surprise, the Yankees lost 8-3 the final game
Behind Jeremy Bonderman the Tigers did tame

In **2007,** the nine straight East titles was snapped
Despite changes to improve the club and adapt
The Yanks finished second (94-68) a wild card spot
Ready for the playoffs and hoping to get hot

For the 2007 season, the focus was on pitching
Two newcomers and two old timers switching
The Yankees were high on rookie Phil Hughes
Despite an injury, he went 5-3, the good news

The other pitcher was another 21-year-old rookie
Named Joba Chamberlin . . . and slightly kookie
A Native American and an "immediate sensation"
With Joba and Mo, a rally-ending creation

The other two pitchers were former Yankee aces
Roger Clemens and Andy Pettitte, familiar faces
Both leaving Houston and into the Yankee rotation
Roger at age 44 was 6-6, ERA 4.18, not a sensation

Andy did better, 15-9, with a high ERA of 4.05
At 35, it was more of a challenge to simply survive
Chien-Ming Wang was the ace, 19-7, 3.70 ERA
The most dependable hurler, the Yankees mainstay

A-Rod was named the AL MVP for the third time
And deservedly so for a season so prime
He led the league with 54 homers and 156 RBIs
Plus, 143 runs scored, a season to eulogize

A-Rod Arrives, Boston Comeback, Three More East Titles (2004-2007)

Matsui hit .285/25/103, healthy once more
While Abreu hit .283/16/101, both hard to ignore
Plus, consistent hitters Posada, Cano, and Jeter
Still the Yanks were not the East title repeater

The Cleveland Indians at 96-66 finished first
And for a World Series title they did thirst
Now to face New York in the ALDS, the best of five
In a short series, pitching can help to survive

CC Sabathia (19-7) faced Wang (19-7) in a rout
As the Indians won 12-3, an unlikely blow out
By the sixth inning, Cleveland led 11-3
Wang had an off day, all would agree

Game two was a tough loss to swallow
Leaving the Yankees frustrated and hollow
A nail biting 2-1, 11 inning Cleveland win
Despite Pettitte's pitching, margin of error thin

Before leaving game two, it must be noted
It was called "the bug game," accurately quoted
For in the seventh inning, a swarm of insects
Invaded Jacob Field, annoying little objects

Players had trouble concentrating on the game
Interrupted by causal spraying, a solution lame
Joba was affected by the invaders the most
Control not the same with the bugs engrossed

At the Stadium for game three, Yanks losing 3-1
If Cleveland could hold on, the Yankees were done
But New York rallied, four runs in the fifth
And three more in the sixth forthwith

The game ended 8-4, Hughes the winner in relief
Yankee fans looking to win the next two, a belief
Wang, the Yanks' ace, got the call, three day's rest
But Chien-Ming was far, far from his season's best

By the end of five, Cleveland led the game 6-1
Off Wang and Mussina, the scoring was done
It was enough as the Yankees pecked away in vain
Game and series over, 6-4, Torre left to explain

The Cleveland defeat was the end of Torre's rein
A World Series win was badly wanted, that's plain
But Torre was offered a new $5 million contract
Containing a pay cut, an insult to Joe in fact

Torre was offered the contract at a Tampa meeting
The Boss and the top brass did the greeting
No room, however, for any negotiations
A one-year deal ending in parting relations

A New Joe and Stadium, A Pennant and Championship (2008–2017)

To hire a manager was the immediate concern
Joe Girardi was chosen, open and willing to learn
The value of analytics in managing a team
With Cashman's agreeing, but not to the extreme

In 2006, Joe managed the Marlins finishing 78-84
With a $15 million payroll, it was a frustrating chore
Yet Girardi was named NL Manager of the Year
The Yankees made a wise choice, it would appear

The **2008** Yankee season on the field, was a bore
Finishing third, with fans looking for much more
The 89-73 record, not enough for post season play
The first time since 1993, but only for a short delay

Also, '08 was the last season of the old ballpark
With farewell celebrations at this great landmark
In 2009, a new Stadium would be up and running
New amenities and fan comforts, simply stunning

One of the features was the All-Star game
And attended by many a popular name
But none bigger than Steinbrenner, The Boss
In a golf cart, fans cheering, love came across

The ride to home plate would be his last
His health was deteriorating quite fast
After the 2008 season, Hal, the younger son
Approved by MLB owners, the Yankees to run

One highlight on the 2008 field of play
Mussina won 20 games, yet would not stay
He called it quits after the season of 2008
The Cooperstown HOF call, at age 39 to wait

Cashman and Girardi focused quickly on **2009**
To strengthen the club . . . the bottom line
They signed pitchers CC Sabathia and A. J. Burnett
Both had the potential to win 20, a real threat

In fact, CC was now the Yankee's new ace
A Cy Young winner the fans would embrace
He weighed 300 pounds, 6 feet 6 inches tall
This didn't affect how he threw the ball

In 2008 Burnett went 18-10 with Toronto
Prompting the Yankees to shell out the dough
$82.5 million for five years, not a good signing
Three years later traded with a World Series ring

Another signing was Mark Teixeira for first base
Since Giambi was a free agent, he took his place
"Tex" signed for $180 million for eight years
His stadium swing would bring fan cheers

The final addition came in a multi-player trade
It was Nick Swisher, for the Stadium tailor-made
A switch-hitting outfielder and a clutch hitter
An instant favorite, upbeat, outgoing, no quitter

The Yankees finished 103-59, and an AL East title
For confidence and World Series hopes it was vital
So how did the four additions help in 2009?
Some more than others, collectively just fine

A New Joe and Stadium, A Pennant and Championship (2008–2017)

Sabathia went 19-8 with a .337 ERA
He was outstanding in post season play
Burnett a disappointment, not much to say
Won 13, lost 9, with a high 4.04 ERA

Teixeira hit .292/39/122 with no downside
His 122 RBIs led the AL, his 39 homers tied
Swisher hit 29 homers, third best on the team
Never a super star, but living his dream

A-Rod had a fine season despite surgery to his hip
His runs batted in production did not slip
The twelfth straight season of 100 or more
Despite admitting steroid use in 2001 before

In the ALDS, the Yankees faced the Twins
A quick clean sweep and three straight wins
There were plenty of Yankee stars to go around
Some with the bat, some on the mound

The new Stadium hosted its first postseason game
With New York down 2-0, the lead to claim
A two-run blast by Jeter and Swisher's timely hit
Matsui's two-run homer, A-Rod's single, that's it

Sabathia got the win; the final score was 7-2
As Girardi used four from the pen to make due
Game two featured pitching and the long ball
Ninth, Yankees down 3-1, now the Twins' fall

Tex singled off closer Joe Nathan, A-Rod next
A timely homer into the Yankee bullpen he did flex
Entering the bottom of the 11th, game tied 3-3
Teixeira hit a walk-off for over 50,000 to see

The series moved on to the Metrodome
And the last baseball game called their home
Game three matched Pettitte versus Pavano
With the Twins striking the first blow

Mauer drove in a run, bottom of the sixth inning
Seventh, the Yanks scored two, just the beginning
Ninth, RBI singles by Posada and Cano, score 4-1
Now on to the ALCS, Yankees hoping for a rerun

Yankees to face the Angels from Anaheim
Like the Yanks, LA in the ALDS had an easy time
Beating Boston 5-0, 4-1, and 7-6, for the sweep
Defeating the Yankees in the best of seven, a leap

LA finished 97-65, yet not an overpowering team
Judging both, the series would go seven it did seem
With tough starters, Joe Saunders and Jered Weaver
And closer Brian Fuentes, 48 saves their ace reliever

CC in the opener (4-1) was in total control
As the ace of the rotation, living up to his role
In eight innings, CC allowed one run and four hits
Walked one and fanned seven, giving the Angels fits

In the second game, after 10 innings, 2-2
In the 11th, LA scored to take the lead anew
In the bottom half, A-Rod hit a home run
On to the 13th tied 3-3, LA came undone

A comedy of errors and poor judgment
That's how the inning from hell went
As Yankee Jerry Hairston Jr. crossed home plate
With the winning run while joyous matesdid wait

A New Joe and Stadium, A Pennant and Championship (2008–2017)

Game three was another extra-inning affair
The Angels won 5-4, but did have a scare
All four Yankee runs were via the long ball
But the Angels won in the 11th, a close call

Game four was an embarrassing rout
Yankee hitting and pitching it was all about
The score was 10-1, a little mayhem
Sabathia, another eight-inning gem

Game five, LA was on the brink of elimination
In desperate need, in any form, of salvation
Angels leading 4-0, through the first six
Entering the seventh, the Yanks need a fix

And the Yankees got what they needed
Base hits galore and six runs, they succeeded
But give credit where credit is due
LA scored three in the seventh to come through

Back in New York, after a coast-to-coast flight
Delayed a day due to rain, played the next night
The Angels scored in the third to take the lead
The Yanks three in the fourth with all due speed

The Angels, not giving up, scored in the eighth
Now trailed 3-2, left with hope and faith
In the Yankees eighth, LA's defense fell apart
Leaving the Angel fans with a broken heart

Allowing the Yankees to tack on two more
Pettitte the winner, 5-2 the final score
With Rivera picking up his second save
The **Yankees 40th AL pennant** they did crave

CC Sabathia was named the series MVP
Pitched almost flawless baseball, won two did he
A-Rod hit three homers, drove in six, batted .429
Damon two homers, five ribbies, he did just fine

Girardi wore number 27 throughout the season
Not by chance, but for a very good reason
It signified the Yankees goal, their 27th World title
With the Yankees overdue and George ill, it was vital

In the World Series the Phillies, the Yankees foe
Philly had hitting and pitching, a tough combo
And gained experience winning the Series in 2008
A distinct advantage, logic would dictate

Game one was all about Phillies pitcher Cliff Lee
Who allowed one run, six hits, no walks, the key
The final score was 6-1, Sabathia took the loss
Although CC pitched well, Lee was the boss

The Yankees came back in game two, winning 3-1
With Tex and Matsui each hitting a home run
The other run came in the seventh, a Posada RBI
Martinez took the loss, former Red Sox bad guy

Burnett was credited with the win, his first
Rivera picked up a two-inning save, so versed
It was Mo's tenth save in World Series play
One more to come to his opponent's dismay

In game three, the Phillies struck first
With three runs off Pettitte in a mild outburst
The Yankees came back with two of their own
When A-Rod went deep off, Cole Hamels to atone

A New Joe and Stadium, A Pennant and Championship (2008–2017)

In the fifth, the Yankees scored three more
Topped by Damon's two-run double, 5-3 the score
Both teams added runs as the game progressed
The Yanks finally won 8-5, ending the mini slugfest

Sabathia pitched well in game number four
Replaced in the seventh ahead in the score
In the eighth, Joba allowed a run, now 4-4
But the Yankees bounced back with three more

Rivera pitched the ninth to only three batters
Throwing eight pitches, that's what matters
In the Series, he earned save number two
Recognized as baseball's closer guru

The final score 7-4, and the Phillies near the end
But in game five Philadelphia did not bend
Burnett pitched two innings and was hit hard
For six runs on four hits as Utley went yard

After the Phillies fast start, New York pecked away
To no avail, the 8-6 Philly win was only a delay
From Philadelphia to New York, a short drive
To play game six, the Phillies hoping to revive

Starters Pettitte and Martinez on the mound
Matsui, as the DH didn't fool around
In the second, he homered with A-Rod on base
In the third, he singled two more RBIs in case

In the fifth, Matsui doubled in two more
Giving him six ribbies as Yankee fans did roar
That tied a World Series record, the six RBIs
By Richardson in the '60 Series, Matsui did reprise

The final score was Yankees 7, Phillies 3
And one of the reasons he was named MVP
It was the **Yankees 27th World Championship**
Over decades of thrills, a glorious trip

Over the winter some changes were made
Hopefully aimed at a roster upgrade
Brett Gardner now in left, Damon moved on
As a free agent to Detroit a move foregone

Melky Cabrera was sent to Atlanta in a trade
For Curtis Granderson, center he played
With Matsui signing as a free agent with LA
Marcus Thames the DH, one season he would stay

But on **July 13, 2010**, player changes seemed trite
The Boss died, no longer the leading light
Much has been said about George, good and bad
For now, let's settle on the good, passing is so sad

Eleven American League pennants he did win
The treasured Fall Classic's next of kin
Seven World Series he won with great pleasure
For Yankee fans, magical memories to treasure

Building the new Yankee Stadium, he led the way
Overcoming multiple roadblocks until all was okay
He sold cable TV rights for Yankee games to MSG
For many, many years at a very lucrative fee

But George was not finished, not by a long shot
Helped create the YES Network, another jackpot
A valuable revenue source to his personal wealth
Leaving his heirs financially in the best of health

A New Joe and Stadium, A Pennant and Championship (2008–2017)

George, love him or not, built a Yankee empire
On reflection, he surely is a man to admire
At his death, the Yankees worth around $3.4 billion
And purchased for only a miniscule $8.8 million

Season over, George would not have been satisfied
Finishing as the wild card, first place denied
There were several players who performed well
CC led the rotation (21-7, 3.18 ERA), he did excel

Young Phil Hughes went 18-8 at age 24
And an aging Pettitte 11-3, hard to ignore
Rivera at age 40, still at the top of his game
With 33 saves, a 1.80 ERA, pitching the same

A-Rod did well despite missing 25 games
He hit home run #600, joining elite names
To name just a few, Ruth, Aaron, and Mays
And more, all deserving accolades and praise

He drove in over 100 runs for the 13th straight year
To be exact, it was 125 in an unforgettable career
The first ever with 14, 100 + RBI seasons to revere
Playing 22 seasons, three teams he did persevere

The Twins (94-68) finished first in their Division
Facing New York once more in a playoff collision
In 2009, the Yankees beat the Twins, three straight
Once again, it would be Minnesota's fate

The ALDS began at Target Field in Minnesota
The series results didn't change one iota
The Twins took the lead, 3-0 in game one
In the sixth, New York scored four to stun

RBI singles by Cano and Posada resulted in two
Granderson's triple plated two more, a fine debut
In the sixth, Minnesota tied the game at 4-4
Then Tex hit a two-run homer, 6-4 the final score

Next day Pettitte won his 19th post season game
Beating the Twins 5-2, his last season of fame
Mo relieved in the ninth as the Twins did cave
It was Rivera's 41st post season save

The series shifted to New York for game three
The Twins down two games to none, a reality
Phil Hughes received the call and pitched very well
For seven innings, four hits, no runs, he did excel

In the eighth, Kerry Wood allowed the Twins a run
The final score was 6-1, the Twins were done
In the ALCS, the Yankees would meet the Rangers
Beating them in prior playoffs, hardly strangers

Opening in Texas, New York trailed 5-0 after six
Scored six runs the next two innings, a quick fix
The Yanks winning 6-5, one inning Mo did appear
Earned a save, his 42nd, last of his illustrious career

Game two, Hughes in four innings was hit hard
Ten hits, seven runs, call for the National Guard
Texas won the game 7-2, series now tied
Ending a losing streak to New York, restoring pride

Game three, at the Stadium, New York shutout
By Cliff Lee on two hits, an embarrassing rout
The score was 8-0 as Pettitte took the loss
Guaranteed, turning in his grave was The Boss

A New Joe and Stadium, A Pennant and Championship (2008-2017)

Game four was another Texas runaway
As the Yankees starting rotation did betray
This time A.J. was the pitcher hit hard
Six innings, six hits, five runs, a sad scorecard

The score 10-3; Yanks need a win to stay alive
Scoring early, the Yankees won 7-2 in game five
Back in Arlington game six, not to be outdone
Entering the bottom of the fifth, score tied 1-1

Hughes still pitching gave up two crucial runs
Replaced by Robertson to stop the Texas guns
Who gave up a two-run homer to Nelson Cruz
Any hope of the Yankees winning he did defuse

Final score: Texas 6, Yankees 1 . . . ALCS ended
The Yankee's 2010 season not as they intended
Texas to the World Series to face San Francisco
The Giants won four games to one, a quick kayo

In **2011**, the Yankees finished the season 97-65
First in the East, World Series hopes to revive
Frankly, they did little to improve the club
As free agent pitcher Cliff Lee gave them the snub

Catcher Russell Martin, the Yankees did sign
Replacing Posada, now the DH, a role redefine
They also signed two pitchers past their prime
Bartolo Colón and Rafael Soriano, passing time

Rookie pitcher Ivan Nova was a surprise
Finishing 16-4, 3.70 ERA, opening a few eyes
CC led the rotation (19-8, 3.00 ERA), as expected
Plus, Mo had 44 saves and a 1.91 ERA, his role perfected

Granderson led the club with 41 homers and 119 RBIs
With Teixeira and Cano, two supportive allies
In 99 games, sore knee A-Rod hit .276/16/62
A long season he struggled to get through

On July 9, Derek Jeter enjoyed his 3,000th hit
As a future Hall of Famer, it did befit
He was also the first Yankee, the honor to claim
Plus . . . the hit was a homer and won the game

In September, Mariano Rivera recorded save 602
The most in MLB history, in '96 with five, so true
Now to the ALDS, to face the Tigers from Detroit
With Cy Young winner Verlander (24-5) so adroit

Plus Scherzer (15-9), Porcello (14-9), both able
And closer Valverde (49 saves), always stable
Along with Miguel Cabrera who hit .344/30/105
With DH Martinez .330/12/103, rallies to revive

Having said all that, the Yankees won game one 9-3
Heavy rain in the second inning, who could foresee?
The game was suspended until the following night
Without Verlander and Sabathia, the fans to ignite

In the bottom of the sixth, the Yanks ahead 2-1
Scored six, led by Cano's grand slam home run
Detroit won game two 5-3, Scherzer the win
To Comerica Park where Yankee troubles begin

Verlander and CC in game three, a second try
Justin gave up two runs in the seventh, a 4-4 tie
But Detroit scored in their half off Rafael Soriano
On Delmon Young's clutch home run blow

A New Joe and Stadium, A Pennant and Championship (2008–2017)

The game ended 5-4 as Valverde shut the door
And the Tigers took the series lead once more
The Yankees won next, 10-1, to play another day
In New York, game five, the Tigers did slay

The Tigers wasted no time taking an early lead
Hitting back-to-back homers in lightning speed
Don Kelly and Delmon Young did set the pace
Not power hitters, as each showed a new face

Top of the fifth, the Tigers tacked on another run
In the bottom half Cano homered, Yanks not done
The Yankees scored again in the seventh, not enough
The Tigers won 3-2 and the series playing tough

Before moving on to **2012**, it must be noted
Posada retired after 17 years, a Yankee so devoted
Six pennants, four Fall Classics he played in
Jorge Posada, at 40, a new life he would soon begin

Pitcher Garcia and outfielder Andrew Jones resigned
As free agents but contributed little, even combined
New York also signed pitcher Hiroki Kuroda, one year
At $10 million, led the staff (16-11) in a short career

The Yanks also signed Raúl Ibañez to a year contract
Adding outfield depth, plus his hitting did attract
Acquiring Ibañez would turn out to be a coup
Particularly in the ALDS, absolutely no one knew

In February, Burnett went to Pittsburgh in a trade
His stay with New York didn't make the grade
Out of baseball for a year, Andy Pettitte was back
At age 40, it took some time to get on track

In **2012**, the Yankees finished 95-67, first place
Led the league with 245 home runs, a hefty pace
Led by Granderson with 43, along with 106 RBIs
Played in 160 games and what that implies

Sabathia turned in a solid season, 15-6, 3.38 ERA
His 13th year of double-digit wins, by the way
In May, when Rivera tore a ligament in his right knee
Rafael Soriano as the closer saved 42 games, did he

New York was pitted against wild card Baltimore
In the ALDS, that looked to be a close tug of war
During the season, 18 games the clubs did split
Both clubs made of toughness and grit

Game one at Baltimore was tied 2-2 after eight
The Yankees scored five in the ninth, never too late
Sabathia pitched 8⅔ innings for the 7-2 win
His outstanding game needs no spin

In game two, Pettitte was against rookie Wei-Yin Chen
The rookie won 3-2 with help from the bullpen
At one game each, the series now tied
Next two games almost every pitcher was tried

Game three, ninth inning, Yankees trailing 2-1
Ibáñez's pinch-hitting belted a clutch home run
Fast forward to inning 12, score is still 2-2
Ibañez hit the first pitch, a blast into the blue

Game four after 12 innings, tied 1-1
Top of the 13th, the Orioles not done
Two doubles quickly scored a run
Series tied once more now begins the fun

A New Joe and Stadium, A Pennant and Championship (2008–2017)

In game five. it was all about the big guy, CC
Threw a complete game in the clutch did he
He gave up one run on four hits, fanning nine
The final score 3-1, and a very, very good sign

Ibañez and Suzuki accounted for two of the RBIs
Granderson's homer added to the Orioles demise
Now on to face the Detroit Tigers in the ALCS
Where the Yankees were swept, a total mess

The Detroit Tigers won the opener 6-4
In 12 innings, a tough loss to ignore
Before moving on, a word about the setback
Not the game, but Jeter's ankle he did crack

Derek twisted his ankle trying to field a ball
Was out the rest of the series, rest the cure-all
Game two came quickly and with no doubt
Aníbal Sánchez, the Tiger pitcher, threw a 3-0 shutout

For seven innings, Sánchez allowed three hits
As the Yankee bats went on the fritz
Phil Coke pitched two innings in relief
Allowed one hit, no runs to the Yankees grief

Game three, by the ninth Verlander had a 2-0 lead
Until Eduardo Núñez homered, the ace did concede
The Tigers still ahead 2-1, with no out
As the anxious Tiger crowd did mill about

Gardner grounded out on "Verlander's 132nd pitch"
At that point, manager Jim Leyland made the switch
Coke retired Suzuki, out two, then gave up two hits
As the Tiger fans, all standing, were having fits

Ibañez up next, the ALDS star with little doubt
Worked the count to 3-2 and then struck out!
Verlander got the win, Coke his second save
It appeared the Yankees were about to cave

Game four was a total embarrassment
The Yankees were physically and mentally spent
Max Scherzer beat CC, the score 8-1
The Yankees were outhit 16-2, totally outdone

The Yankees did little to improve the **2013** team
Saving money or reducing costs the theme
Yes, Kuroda, Pettitte, and Rivera signed for a year
All at the end of their careers or very near

The Yankees also signed Kevin Youkilis for a year
Playing for Boston would get the Bronx cheer
Signing for two years was Ichiro Suzuki, age 39
His best seasons with Seattle where he did shine

The Yankees acquired Vernon Wells in a trade
A 15-year outfielder, his last season played
At the end of April, the Yankees finished first!
By June, their caliber of play would be reversed

In their defense, key players were often on the IL
Jeter, A-Rod, Granderson, and Tex as well
Resulting in the Yankees bringing back Soriano
To play left and DH, plus more offensive ammo

In August, MLB suspended A-Rod for 211 games
For obtaining illegal PEDs were the claims
A-Rod appealed, the rest of the season he played
The suspension upheld for 2014; A-Rod dismayed

A New Joe and Stadium, A Pennant and Championship (2008–2017)

He appealed the suspension, but later dropped it
Ending a charade harmful to the young, let's admit
By 9/25, the Yankees were out of post-season play
Not since 2008 did fans experience such a bad day

The Yankees finished 85-77, third place
Twelve back in the AL East Division race
The season was bad enough, Boston finished first
As the Yankee players for home dispersed

There's more to this painful season, no surprise
Andy (41), Mo (43) retired, can't replace these guys
As a Yankee Andy won 219, lost 127 with a 3.94 ERA
Won 21 games twice and always ready to play

Rivera in 19 seasons finished 952 games, saved 652
Both all-time career records, topping those hard to do
It is doubtful Mo's records will ever be surpassed
This was said about Gehrig, then all were aghast

Apparently, the Yankees front office liked Girardi
And recall 2009 . . . or were just plain foolhardy
For at seasons end they agreed to a new contract
Four years, no World Series, then he was sacked

Well, if you thought 2013 was a surprise
The **2014** season continued the Yankees demise
Among others the Yanks lost Granderson and Cano
To free agency, solid players, it was quite a blow

As free agents, Hughes and Joba departed
For rejuvenated careers to get started
Pitcher Masahiro Tanaka signed, widely extolled
For $155 million brought him into the Yankee fold

211

Yankees signed Jacoby Ellsbury for the outfield
Played four of a seven-year contract, a poor yield
They also signed 37-year-old Carlos Beltran
As part of their new and exciting winning plan

The Yankees signed catcher Brian McCann
To stabilize the backstop situation the plan
Second base and third were shaky at best
With Cano and A-Rod gone, a real test

The Yankees finished 84-78, in second place
Twelve games back of Baltimore, hardly a race
Yankee fans still loyal, as attendance increased
To over 3.1 million fans, a crazy love feast

The 2014 Yankees did get a major scare
Tanaka's ulnar collateral ligament did tear
From July until September, he was on the IL
After his return from rehab, he felt swell

The other event was Jeter's farewell game
At Fenway, heckling for years he overcame
His last day Boston honored Jeter, a classy act
By the Yankees bitter rivals, and that's a fact

The **2015** season would be the first in 20 years
Without Jeter their Captain, to hear the cheers
Didi Gregorius was the shortstop on opening day
It was like someone was missing on that field of play

The Yankees acquired Chase Headley for third base
A-Rod returned as DH after his suspension disgrace
Pitcher Nathan Eovaldi was acquired in a trade
Along with Domingo German in a rotation upgrade

A New Joe and Stadium, A Pennant and Championship (2008–2017)

Andrew Miller was signed to fill the closer role
With 36 saves and a 2.04 ERA he was in control
With no .300 hitters New York played long ball
As nine players hit 11 or more over the wall

A-Rod hit 33 homers, this team's quick fix
Followed by Teixeira 31 and McCann 26
Eovaldi led the club with a 14-3 mark
But Tanaka (12-7) was the ace, the spark

The Yankees finished 87-75, a wild card
And faced Houston in the Yankees' backyard
A one-game playoff to determine who moves on
One mistake could cost the game, the playoffs gone

The pitching matchups were the teams very best
Dallas Keuchel (20-8) vs Tanaka, both blessed
A jam-packed Stadium to give the Yankees support
And any Houston rallies to help the Yankees abort

Sadly, for Yankee fans, Houston pitching dominated
While the Yankee hitters were clearly frustrated
Keuchel struck out seven and allowed three hits
Over six innings, giving Yankee hitters fits

Also, the Astros bullpen was in total command
Allowing no hits in three innings, performing grand
The Astros pitching sealed the Yankees fate
The score 3-0, Yankee fans another season to wait

Tanaka pitched five innings, giving up two mistakes
If your team is not hitting, that's all it takes
Dellin Betances, in relief, gave up the third run
By that time the Yankees were pretty much done

After losing to Houston, the Yanks began to trade
Some of the players involved were an upgrade
In November from the Twins, they got Aaron Hicks
He quickly joined the Yankees outfield starting mix

Later the Yankees made three trades that were key
From the Cubs, Starlin Castro at second immediately
From Detroit, Luis Cessa and Chad Green to help the pen
Both relief and spot starters were the young men

The third trade was with the Cincinnati Reds
For Aroldis Chapman, hard thrower who turns heads
There were other trades, but not as profound
One would think the **2016** playoffs they were bound

Not so, the Yankees finished in fourth place
A once great dynasty now in disgrace
Missed the playoffs, third time in four years
Attendance was down and so were the cheers

For the Yankees (and fans) 2016 was a shame
There were notable events so let's explain
Tex and A-Rod played their last games
For Yankee fans two unforgettable names

Rookie catcher, Gary Sánchez was a sensation
His hot home run bat the causation
In 53 games, 20 home runs the young man hit
Along the way, however, young Gary did not fit

Unlike Gary, Aaron Judge did not burst on the scene
A giant at 6'7" and 282 lbs., in 2017 a home run machine
It's time now to forget the season of 2016
And move on to a more productive Yankee scene

A New Joe and Stadium, A Pennant and Championship (2008–2017)

The Yankees finished the **2017** season 91-71
Second in the AL East, but still a job well done
And good enough for another wild card spot
This beat going home with no playoff shot

With Tex retired, trouble ensued at first base
It was young Greg Bird's position to embrace
But Bird went on the IL, replaced by Chris Carter
A free agent the Yankees signed, a veteran starter

Replacing A-Rod as DH was Matt Holiday
A veteran free agent who knew how to play
But the headline grabbers were three young guys
That in 2017 opened up a lot of baseball eyes

The man who led the club was 25-year-old Judge
Consistent from opening day, he did not budge
Aaron hit 52 home runs never done before!
By a ROOKIE plus great defense, hard to ignore

Judge also hit a respectable .284 with 114 RBIs
A unanimous Rookie of the Year, the prize
Sanchez picked up where he left off in 2016
He hit .278/33/90, his defense routine

Pitcher Luis Severino was the third surprise
Fourth in the rotation, talent to recognize
He won 14 and lost 6 with a 2.98 ERA
His fastball over 97 mph, tough to put in play

At short, Didi had a solid offensive year
He hit .287/25/87 one of the best of his career
Along with Severino, CC won 14, lost five
While Tanaka's numbers (13-12) took a dive

Jordan Montgomery rounded out the rotation
He went 9-7 with a 3.88 ERA, a future sensation?
New York versus the Twins in the Wild Card Game
In four prior postseason games, Yankees did tame

The 2017 Wild Card Game was more of the same
Despite the Twins with three runs in the first frame
As Severino gave up three runs before taken out
A home run with no one on, and a two-run clout

But the Yankees came back with three of their own
Didi's three-run blast off Ervin Santana, to atone
The Twins scored one more run in the third
From then on goose eggs was the watchword

The Yankees added five more during the game
Homers by Gardner and Judge, Twins to inflame
The Yankees finally won 8-4, now to the ALDS
To play the Cleveland Indians, talent they possess

The Indians won their division by 17 games
Filled with a roster of very talented names
Led by Terry Francona they won 102 and lost 60
A battle for Girardi in a short series to win three

During the season, Cleveland won 22 in a row
The most in AL history . . . quite a show
The offense was good, but not really great
The pitching, however, absolutely first rate

Corey Kluber, 18-4 with a 2.25 ERA, the staff ace
Also, won the Cy Young award in a tight race
Next, Carlos Carrasco 18-6 with a 3.29 ERA
The Indians during the season had their way

A New Joe and Stadium, A Pennant and Championship (2008–2017)

Trevor Bauer 17-9 completed the top three
Close games in the series one could easily foresee
And that's where the Cleveland bullpen comes in
Led by Cody Allen, killing rallies before they begin

In game one, the surprise starter was Trevor Bauer
Kluber needed rest, so Trevor the man of the hour
Over six plus innings, he allowed only two hits
And no runs as the bullpen continued the blitz

Cleveland won the game 4-0, a great start
With Kluber in game two ready to play his part
As the saying goes, "Baseball is a funny game"
Corey was hammered, who can explain?

In less than three innings, Corey was gone at last
Allowing six runs, Hicks' three-run homer the big blast
The teams changed leads several times, ending tied
At 8-8, bottom of the 13th, Cleveland not to be denied

Austin Jackson walked, stole second base
Scored on a single by Yan Gomes, a win to embrace
Cleveland used eight pitchers, the Yankees six
New York now in an immediate and terrible fix

At Yankee Stadium for game number three
Home field was an advantage, no guarantee
The Yankees needed a brilliantly pitched game
And that's what they got from Tanaka by name

Masahiro, for seven innings threw a shutout
With help from the pen, the outcome no doubt
The Yankees won 1-0 on a Greg Bird home run
To play another game, New York not quite done

The Yankees won the critical game four 7-3
Behind Severino who threw seven innings did he
Allowing three runs, four hits, and fanning nine
And Cleveland allowed six unearned runs, a bad sign

Game five back at Cleveland, Kluber on the hill
For Gregorius and the Yankees, it was a thrill
In the first inning, Didi whacked a home run
In the third with a runner on, he hit another one

Cleveland scored two in the fifth off of CC
The third game in a row, the bullpen was the key
With Robertson and Chapman pitching shutout ball
For almost five innings, Cleveland's 5-2 downfall

In the other ALDS, Houston beat Boston days ago
Three of four now ready for another exciting show
The ALCS opened in beautiful Minute Maid Park
With the Astros quickly making their indelible mark

Game one, Dallas Keuchel (14-5) pitched a four-hitter
For seven innings while fanning ten, Astro fans aglitter
Houston scored two runs in the fourth inning
New York one in the ninth, score 2-1, Astros winning

Houston won game two, behind a pitching machine
Verlander threw a complete game striking out 13
He scattered five hits and walked only one
Very tough in the clutch, a crucial victory he spun

Bottom of ninth, score 1-1, Chapman in relief
One out Jose Altuve singles, now an inning of grief
Carlos Correa doubles, Altuve scores, game over
Astros led the series 2-0, sitting in clover

A New Joe and Stadium, A Pennant and Championship (2008–2017)

Game three the Yankee bats finally came alive
Yankee crowd providing the impetus to survive
Second inning, a three-run homer by Todd Frazer
In the fourth, Judge hit another three-run laser

The score was 8-0, Yankees at the end of four
As CC allowed three hits in six innings, no more
Houston scored a runoff of, Betances in relief
And that came in the ninth, causing little grief

Game four the Yankees won 6-4, series now tied
Houston ahead 4-0, Yankees not to be denied
With six runs in two innings, they scored
Game five pitching could not be ignored

Tanaka and Keuchel in another showdown
This time Tanaka was the talk of the town
Masahiro, seven shutout innings, three hits
Dallas in four, plus gave up four runs, the pits

The final score was 5-0 as Keuchel took the defeat
Tanaka the win, the Yankees now in the driver's seat
Now back to Houston for the series outcome
And the question: which team will succumb?

Verlander did it again blanking New York, game six
For seven shutout innings, a crucial and timely fix
He allowed five hits while striking out eight
Final score 7-1, now game seven can't wait

Charlie Morton in game three was mistreated
Giving up seven runs and soundly defeated
So, for game seven the Astros, Morton they chose!
The Yankees in this do-or-die game to oppose

Morton pitched very well the second time around
As the 4-0 winner he was eagerly crowned
In five innings, Morton allowed two hits, that's all
His relief, Lance McCullers Jr., continued shutout ball

The ALCS was a painful loss and tough to forget
Needing one win, two chances, a sad regret
And their failure to hit at Minute Maid Park
Three runs in four games, a baffling question mark

Soon after it was revealed Girardi would not return
As manager for 2018 . . . Joe showing little concern
Girardi was disappointed, but not angry or upset
Thanked Hal Steinbrenner for the 10 years, no regret

Told the Yankees were going "in a different direction"
An ambiguous and polite way of voicing rejection
Now the search for a new manager began
Six were considered as part of the search plan

Girardi Gone, Boone New Manager, Championship Drought (2018-2023)

In December 2017, New York hired Aaron Boone
Hero of the '03 ALCS, a walk-off so opportune
With no managerial experience, he was hired
As a player and ESPN analyst greatly admired

Aaron Boone played third in the majors for 12 years
Part of a family who made MLB their careers
Aaron's brother, Bret, for 14 years played second base
Their father Bob, tools of ignorance he did embrace

Add Aaron's grandfather Ray, who started it all
Never dreamed his grandson would get such a call
As a gift to Aaron, New York made an exciting trade
Getting Giancarlo Stanton in an upgrade crusade

With Miami in 2017, Stanton hit .281/59/132
That is a season not many could outdo
Played mostly right field, not known for defense
Yankees to use him as a DH, which makes sense

His last season with Miami voted NL MVP
And a four time All-Star, not too shabby
The Yankees gave up Starlin Castro in the deal
Plus, two prospects, time will tell if it was a steal

The Yankees traded Headley who played third
Leaving second and third vacant, seems absurd
Until two highly touted rookies took their place
Gleyber Torres and Miguel Andújar to showcase

In **2018**, Boone's first season, the team finished 100-62
The new faces on the team played well, no ballyhoo
Winning 100 games, not an easy mission
Especially a first-year manager, a demanding position

The Yankees finished second in the AL East
Good enough to be one of the wild cards at least
Due to surprise performances by several players
During the season quieted the vocal naysayers

Torres hit .271/24/77 at the young age of 21
Played in 123 games and got the job done
Andújar hit .297/27/92, at ease it did appear
And was runner-up to the Rookie of the Year

Stanton hit 38 home runs, the most on the team
Those he hit left the ballpark like a laser beam
He also led the club with 100 RBIs
Used almost exclusively as a DH, no surprise

Severino led the rotation with a record of 19-8
And a 3.39 ERA as injuries would soon be his fate
Tanaka was 12-6 with a 3.75 ERA
His career slowing, soon to be on his way

In July, the Yankees picked up J.A. Happ
A veteran pitcher at 35 as a stopgap
J.A. turned out to be a very pleasant addition
He was 7-0 with a 2.69 ERA, a smooth transition

A one-game playoff is always hard to call
An error or cheap hit could be the downfall
The Oakland A's (97-65), the wild card in the west
In 2018, split six games with the Yanks, who's best?

Girardi Gone, Boone New Manager, Championship Drought (2018-2023)

By the sixth inning there was little to fear
The Yankees led 6-0 as over 49,000 did cheer
Judge started with a two-run blast in the first
The Yankees scored four more, another outburst

Judge, Hicks, Stanton, and Voit all fueled inning six
Two doubles, a walk, and a triple, was the final mix
In the top of the eighth, Oakland scored twice
Then Stanton homered, final score 7-2 to be precise

The ALDS was between two competitive foes
The Yankees and Boston that often come to blows
Boston completed the season in first place, 108-54
Eight games ahead of New York, eager for more

The two teams had not met postseason since 2004
The ALCS Yankee fans want to forget forevermore
Boston down 0-3 . . . but you know the rest
Won the World Series, first since 1918, their quest!

Both teams were contentious during the season
Sometimes words led to fights for little reason
Game one at the historic but dreaded Fenway Park
With the Green Monster in left, a scary landmark

It didn't scare J.D. Martinez who hit a three-run blast
In the first, sending Boston to an early start and fast
They added two more crucial runs in the third
While the Yankees pecked away seemingly undeterred

In the ninth, Judge homered off closer Craig Kimbrel
Who then fanned the next three batters, the death knell
Boston won the first game, 5-4 was the final score
Chris Sale the winner, Craig the save, seeking an encore

Tanaka and David Price were the starters in game two
Judge homered in the first, more runs would ensue
In the second inning, the Yankees scored two more
One of them a Sanchez homer, now 3-0 the score

In the seventh, Sanchez repeated the notable deed
Hitting a three-run homer increasing the Yankee lead
The final score was 6-2, the series now tied
Tanaka and the bullpen were not to be denied

Now to the Bronx, should have stayed at Fenway
New York was clubbed 16-1, it was Boston's heyday
A must win for the Yankees was game four
The importance of the game impossible to ignore

Porcello and Sabathia were matchups for the game
Boston tagged CC for three runs in the third frame
In the fourth, Zack Britton gave up a home run
By Christian Vázquez, the Yankees still had none

In the fifth, the Yankees finally got on the board
Gardner's sac fly as New York finally scored
The score remained 4-1, Boston anxiously in front
Bottom of the ninth, the Yankees still in the hunt

Kimbrel came into pitch, a closer first-rate
Walked Judge, Didi singled, tying run at the plate
Kimbrel struck out Stanton, walked Luke Voit
Bases loaded; the Yankees ready to exploit

Kimbrel hit Neil Walker to force in a run
Sánchez coming to the plate, the Yanks not done
Gary flied out, scoring Didi from third base
Gleyber Torres, Kimbrel now had to face

Girardi Gone, Boone New Manager, Championship Drought (2018-2023)

Torres grounded out to end (4-3) the exciting game
Boston went on to the ALCS and more of the same
Yankee fans still looking for a World Championship
Habitual winners, nine years since their last trip

Prior to the beginning of the **2019** New Year
The pursuit of new players went into high gear
The Yankees traded for lefty James Paxton
To improve their rotation they thought was the one

They also signed Troy Tulowitzki to play short
Didi injured his arm claimed the medical report
From *The Times*, the injury came in the second game
Of the ALDS at Fenway, throwing home the claim

But the most productive signing was DJ LeMahieu
The addition of this versatile player, a real coup
Ability to play all infield positions with skill
Hits for power and average, resilience he does instill

The 2019 season was a virtual home run feast
Helping the Yankees finish first in the AL East
There were 14 players who hit 11 homers or more
Missing games were Judge and Stanton, exactly 204!

The club finished the season with a 103-59 mark
While no one player was the igniting spark
Torres hit .278/38/90, certainly deserves a vote
LeMahieu hit .327/26/102, splendid please note

Stanton incurred multiple injuries in 2019
Forcing the Yankees to change the DH scene
So, they traded for Edwin Encarnación
A veteran slugger, for years well known

Domingo German led the pitching rotation
With an 18-4 record, an instant sensation
But in 2020 would be out of baseball
Violating the MLB domestic violence policy his downfall

Paxton went 15-6 with a respectable 3.82 ERA
The only starter under four to the Yankee's dismay
Tanaka finished 11 and 9, Happ 12 and 8
Not outstanding and for the postseason, not great

Again, the Yankees faced the Twins in the ALDS
In five past postseasons, the Twins had no success!
Again, the Yankees swept the Twins three in a row
By scores of 10-4, 8-2, and 5-1, the final blow

Despite the AL Division Series being so one-sided
There were several exciting moments provided
For example, game one 3-3, fifth inning
Bases loaded Torres doubles; Yanks end up winning

Game two, bottom of the third, Twins in a jam
Yankees score seven, capped by Didi's grand slam
Game three, Yanks used six pitchers, still won
While the Twins could only score one pathetic run

The Twins have been spooked in postseason play
Since '03 they played 18 games, home and away
The Yankees have won 16, and the Twins only two
As Casey would say, "You could look it up," It's true

Next, the Yankees and Houston (107-55) in the ALCS
In the past, a team in which they had no success
And 2019 would be no different than 2015 and 2017
Despite game one 7-0 Yankee win, a smokescreen

Girardi Gone, Boone New Manager, Championship Drought (2018-2023)

Houston won game two on a walk-off home run
By Carlos Correa in the bottom of the 11th to stun
Happ gave up the homer as the Astros won 3-2
To New York where Houston almost pulled off a coup

Gerrit Cole threw seven shutout innings, game three
Please note in December, Cole would be a Yankee
Back to the game, the final score was 4-1
Torres accounting for the tally with a home run

Houston won game four 8-3, the future looked bleak
The Astros needed one more to retain their mystique
Game five, Paxton allowed a run in the first
But the Yankees came back with a four-run outburst

All the runs scored were via the home run ball
DJ, a single shot that started the Astro's downfall
Shortly after, Hicks' homer hit the right-field foul pole
A three-run shot, a 4-1 win, Yankee fans to console

But the victorious uplift didn't last very long
As Houston in game six came back strong
Scoring three in the first inning off Chad Green
A three-run homer, the Yankee hopes to demean

Not so, in the ninth New York tied the game at 4-4
When DJ homered with a runner on, new score
Bottom of the ninth, two out, Chapman on the hill
He walked George Springer, bring on the Advil

The next hitter was Jose Altuve, a bat magician
Who, at the plate, is always on a mission
With one swing the game and series ended
Altuve hit a walk-off homer, timely and splendid

Before moving to **2020**, a word on cheating
It's not fair to players who are honest while competing
So, it came as a shock when *The Atlantic* ran a story
With all the details of cheating by Houston so gory

In 2017, Houston began their sign stealing
Using a center field video camera so revealing
Transmitting the signs to the hitter, the game plan
And this is the hilarious part, by banging on a trashcan

It won a World Series Championship some claim
MLB investigated to find out who was to blame
Commish Rob Manfred revealed the finding 1/13/2020
The guilty team and individuals, there were plenty

MLB suspended Astros GM and manager, one year
Shortly after fined by the owner, fans did cheer
Only two players were mentioned in the MLB report
Beltran and Alex Cora created the scheme, plus consort

At the time Cora served as the Astros bench coach
A job advising the manager with little self-reproach
Season over; Boston hired Cora, who managed for three years
In 2018, Boston won the World Series to Red Sox, cheers!

In 2019, Cora and Boston finished in third place
The MLB report about sign stealing was a disgrace
Cora was suspended for the 2020 season, a laugh
For Boston hired him in 2021, regardless of the gaffe

Beltran, the other culprit in the scandal retired
But in November 2019 by the Mets, he was hired
As their new field manager for the 2020 season
After the MLB report, he was fired for good reason

Girardi Gone, Boone New Manager, Championship Drought (2018-2023)

In 2020, the COVID-19 pandemic hit MLB hard
Like all other sports, they were taken off guard
By the middle of March, spring training scrapped
Now MLB had to quickly find ways to adapt

With the players union, MLB agreed to 60 games
And no fans in the stands were their definite aims
In late July, the season finally and thankfully began
And the postseason still had 10 teams, the plan

Before the Houston mess, the Yanks signed Cole
To a 9-year, $324 million deal to fill the ace role
It was an unusual season, highlighted by Voit and DJ
Both were outstanding during the short season of play

Luke Voit won the AL home run title with 22
DJ the batting title (.364) with scant ballyhoo
The Yankees finished 33-27 in second place
Seven back of Tampa Bay, not much of a race

Due to the shortened season and the COVID-19 outbreak
The Wild Card Game now a series, more to partake
It was now the best of three games, more stress
To decide what teams would play in the ALDS

The Yankees played the Indians, who finished 35-25
In Cleveland for both games the Yanks did arrive
Cole and Shane Bieber faced each other in game one
Bieber, of Triple Crown fame, in less than five was done

The Yankees rocked him for seven runs on nine hits
His relief gave up five more in an offensive blitz
New York won the game 12-3, hard to believe
An easy victory they did achieve

While Cole was at the top of his game, he did amaze
In seven innings, allowing six hits, two runs, and 13 K's
Torres and Gardner accounted for half of the RBIs
As the team picked up 15 hits, the win did crystalize

Game two was a typical see-saw slugfest
With fans at the park and home totally stressed
Yankees leading 6-4 until Cleveland roared back
With two runs in the fifth, where's the Prozac?

The Yankees scored two in the sixth, a Sanchez blast
And led again 8-6, Cleveland fans downcast
Cleveland tied it in the seventh, 8-8, the score
Took the lead in the eighth 9-8, once more

But the Yankees came back in the ninth with two
A sac fly by Sanchez and an RBI single by LeMahieu
Chapman ended the game as the Yankees won 10-9
Striking out three in the ninth as the lefty did shine

In the ALDS, the Yankees met the Tampa Bay Rays
All games played at Petro Park in the coming days
The COVID-19 pandemic the reason for the neutral site
Between two clubs that disliked each other outright

The Yankees won game one in dramatic fashion
In the ninth, as the Tampa Bay fans turned ashen
When Stanton hit a grand slam in a tight game
Winning 9-3, while Cole and the bullpen did tame

But Tampa Bay won game two 7-5
Feasting on Yankee pitching, they did thrive
As Boone chose rookie Deivi Garcia to start
Lasted one inning, a move not very smart

Girardi Gone, Boone New Manager, Championship Drought (2018-2023)

The bullpen added to the Yankees plight
Despite Stanton's four RBIs, having a good night
The rest of the club had trouble hitting the ball
The Yankees fanned 18 times, their pitfall

Tanaka started game three, was gone after four
Kevin Kiermaier's three-run homer the eyesore
In the sixth, the Rays tacked on three more
Despite Stanton's two-run clout the Rays won 8-4

The Yankees pitching in game four was terrific
Montgomery, Green, Britton, Chapman to be specific
The four hurlers held the Rays to three hits, one run
Homers by Voit and Torres upped the final score to 5-1

Now to the exciting and deciding final game five
To continue in the postseason, one must survive
The Yankees scored first; Judge hit a home run
The Rays Austin Meadows hit one too, now tied 1-1

It stayed that way until the bottom of the eighth frame
When Mike Brosseau homered off Chapman, the game
Top of the ninth, Yanks went down easily . . . no doubt
Castillo fanning Stanton and Voit; Gio Urshela lined out

Another season and nothing to show for it
Yankee fans love their team and never quit
But patience is not a virtue to which they adhere
And a very long winter until baseball next year

The **2021** season was back to the good old days
Vaccinations and masks lessened the COVID-19 craze
The full 162 game schedule was back in play
With several key restrictions fans had to weigh

Masks were required and social distancing too
This reduced MLB attendance to a precious few
That was an exaggeration, but it was a concern
And no surprise when attendance took a downturn

In 2019, attendance at the Stadium was 3,304,404
In 2021, it was 1,959,854 if you are keeping score
Not the usual numbers the front office liked to face
Little help on the field, New York ended in second place

Their record was 92-70, good for a wild card spot
Despite Cashman's moves, the staff not that hot
In January, he strengthened the pitching rotation
Acquiring Jameson Taillon and Corey Kluber with elation

Cashman not finished trying to improve the team
In July, he acquired a reliever, a constant theme
Clay Holmes came to the Yankees in a trade
And posted a 5-2 record, a 1.61 ERA, an upgrade

Joey Gallo and Anthony Rizzo acquired for the long ball
New team limited playing time, their value small
But in 2022, Rizzo would find his home run stroke
Aimed at the inviting right field wall, a short poke

In the starting lineup, the Yankees had lots of power
Players who could the opposing pitcher cower
Judge hit .287/39/98 and played solid defense
Stanton hit .273/35/97 as the DH, quite intense

The pitching, thus all the trades, was a concern
After Cole (16-8) the rest would give you heartburn
The only other pitcher with 10 wins was Chad Green
And he was used mostly in relief, not a good scene

Girardi Gone, Boone New Manager, Championship Drought (2018-2023)

The Red Sox (92-70) were the Yankees wild card foe
Both teams throughout the season were so-so
But the fierce rivalry between them did continue
With Rafael Devers a one-man wrecking crew

But he was not the only Boston team star
J.D. Martinez, one of the great clutch hitters by far
Hunter Renfroe also had a good year driving in 96
With 31 homers and 33 doubles, a good mix

Boston pitching . . . that was a different story
With two starters that standout, not laudatory
In a one-game playoff you can get by
But beyond that, a weak rotation will magnify

The wild card pitching match-up was as expected
Two hard-throwing right-handers, highly respected
Nathan Eovaldi (11-9) and 16-game winner Cole
Sadly, the Yankees ace quickly put the club in a hole

When Xander Bogaerts homered, a runner on base
And Kyle Schwarber went yard to keep the pace
The Yankees now trailed 3-0, Cole yanked in the third
Replaced by Holmes as Eovaldi pitched undeterred

When Rizzo homered, the Yankees broke through
Now the score 3-1 and chasing Eovaldi on his miscue
Ryan Brasier relieved as the Yankees failed to score
As Boston's Alex Verdugo's double scored one more

Boston plated two more runs the next inning
The score now 6-1 and on their way to winning
Stanton hit a solo homer, but it was all in vain
Boston won 6-2, no AL pennant, hard to explain

A Brief History of the New York Yankees

In **2022**, the Yankees made an interesting trade
The Minnesota Twins they did invade
Obtaining Josh Donaldson to play third
And Isiah Kiner-Falefa, at short the word

Plus, Ben Rortvedt, a young rookie backstop
As part of an interesting three for two swap
The Yankees sent Gary Sánchez in return
As his play in New York became a concern

Gio Urshela was the final trade piece
His value since 2019 was on the decrease
Also, the Yankees resigned first baseman Rizzo
Traded Luke Voit to the Padres, most apropos

The other trade that turned out exceptionally well
Was catcher Jose Trevino . . . who could foretell?
Said manager Boone, he is one "elite [pitch] framer"
Quickly accepted by fans and peers, a true gamer

In 2022, the Yankees got off to a fast start
With teammates old and new each doing his part
In their first 66 games, they went 49-17
In the stands and the dugout, a joyous scene

And at one point had a 15½ game lead
Then into a tailspin they did proceed
The lead fell to 3½ games, four weeks remaining
As the chasing clubs kept gaining and gaining

Injuries played a part in their backslide
Teams with depth will take losses in stride
Benintendi and LeMahieu were sorely missed
As were Severino, Clay and Holmes, you get the gist

Girardi Gone, Boone New Manager, Championship Drought (2018-2023)

Eventually, the Yankees got back the winning flow
With the help of Trevino, Stanton, and Rizzo
And a late surge from Torres deserves praise
Clinching the AL East in September, the final days

Now, Aaron Judge and his record-breaking season
A fairy tale story in 2022 you can believe in
Aaron finished the season hitting .311/62/131
Incredible stats, his 2022 season far from done

The Yankees drafted Judge in 2013
Doubtful his success to date could be foreseen
$1.8 million bonus he did sign
Judge and the Yankees now on cloud nine

In 2014, sent to the Class A South Atlantic League
Putting up excellent numbers that did intrigue
In 65 games hit .333/9/45, plus other key stats
A .428 OBP and .958 OPS, in limited at bats

During the season he was sent to the Tampa Yanks
Excelling once more; their way of saying thanks
Next Class AA in Trenton in 2015
Then on to Triple A in the IL, a tough scene

In 2016, Aaron Judge remained in Triple A
Made the All-Star team but did not play
Due to a knee sprain, still had a great year
Homers 19 and RBIs 65, from the Yanks he did hear

Judge made his MLB debut August 13, 2016
Homered in first two games with a body clean
And what to expect from this giant of a man
Emerging as a silent leader in a short span

In 2017, Judge was AL Rookie of the Year
Along with the Silver Slugger award to endear
Plus, the home run leader in the AL
And three All-Star game appearances as well

Bringing Aaron's short career up to 2022
When he led in most offensive stats, a quick review
Runs scored (133), home runs (62), RBIs (131)
BB (111) plus key analytics, he could not be outdone

The home run chase grabbed the nation's attention
Building drama, excitement, and above all, tension
In '61, Maris hit 61 homers, the most ever in the AL
Topping Ruth's 60, which stood for a very long spell

On 9/20 when Judge tied Ruth, it was drama time
After a long and often frustrating climb
Now the next target was Maris' number 61
"34 plate appearances" later the job was done

Judge hit number 61 off Tim Mayza of the Blue Jays
As his mom and Roger Jr. in the stands did gaze
And then hugged each other with genuine pride
As Judge headed home pointing to them in stride

Then came the anticipation and wait for number 62
So few games left, the baseball nation waited anew
As Judge stayed outwardly calm, games faded away
Until only two games remained until the historic day

Game two of a twin-bill, Judge made baseball history
Hitting number 62 . . . no longer a mystery
Aaron Judge now the AL single season home run king
At the end the feat was done with one mighty swing

Girardi Gone, Boone New Manager, Championship Drought (2018-2023)

Now that number 99 has had his unforgettable day
Let's not forget the Yankees have the ALDS to play
The Cleveland Guardians (92-70), the opposition
They don't appear to be serious competition

In the six games the two clubs met
New York won five, Cleveland not a threat
José Ramírez and Josh Naylor, the power guns
Who led Cleveland in RBIs and home runs

But singles and doubles can often be an offset
Producing runs and wins it will beget
Cleveland's pitching is somewhat shaky too
Only two with more wins than losses they did accrue

Shane Bieber (13-8) and Cal Quantrill (15-5)
Putting a heavy burden on the bullpen to survive
Led by closer Emmanuel Clase who saved 42 games
With an ERA of 1.36 in less than 73 frames

In game one, the Yankees won handily 4-1 behind Cole
Pitched 6⅓ innings, fanning eight and in control
Helped by Harrison Bader and Rizzo with the long ball
This season's answer to winning games . . . the cure-all

Shane Bieber and Nestor Cortes started game two
The Yankees scored in the first as Stanton came through
With a two-run homer over the right field wall
And the few Cleveland fans at the Stadium it did appall

Cleveland scored in the fourth, Andrés Giménez RBI
An inning later Amed Rosario homered, now a 2-2 tie
Bottom of the eighth, the Yankees threatened to score
Bases full, Higashioka lined out, the Yankees done for

Now to the top of the fatal 10th inning
Cleveland scored two, wound up winning
Ramírez led off with a soft double to left field
A throwing error, an extra base it did yield

Gonzalez singled to right for the first run
Josh Naylor doubled in the second one
This ended the Guardian's scoring
As closer Clase made the Yankees look boring

The final score: Cleveland 4, New York 2
As both teams to Cleveland, they flew
To Progressive Field and game three
And what a game it turned out to be

Cleveland took a very early 2-0 lead
Way too early for the Yankees to concede
In the third, Oswaldo Cabrera whacked a double
Judge homered, Cleveland soon to be in trouble

Fast forward, Yankees lead by a score of 5-3
Bottom of the ninth Yanks ready to claim victory
A double and a single and Peralta was gone
As the Guardians were eager to add on

Three singles later, the winning run crossed the plate
Was it talent and hard work or just fate?
Gonzalez drove in the winning runs, hero of the night
Cleveland 6, New York 5, quite a comeback fight

The Yankees now on the brink of elimination
And a long, long winter of frustration
New York sent Cole to the mound, their ace
To stop Cleveland and continue the ALDS race

Cleveland chose right hander Cal Quantrill
To keep the Yankee bats quiet and still
It didn't work, as the Yankees scored in the first
Added in the second on a Bader two-run outburst

The Guardians scored a run in the third frame
In the fourth, a Naylor homer tightened the game
Until the sixth when Stanton hit a sac fly
The dangerously slim 3-2 lead to amplify

And the final score, New York 4, Cleveland 2
Cole pitched a clutch game, seven innings he threw
Allowing six hits, two runs, ever the kingpin
Forcing game five, and a do or die win

Boone said, "You're looking for an early spark"
And Stanton gave it to him right out of the park
In the first inning, a three-run blast
And just like that, the game was over fast

By inning two, starter Aaron Civale was replaced
With reliever Sam Hentges in quick haste
When Aaron Judge went yard with a solo shot
As Yankee fans were screaming and shouting a lot

After two innings (4-0) the Yankees near done
Then in the fifth, they scored another run
For five innings Cortes pitched very well
Giving up one run, Guardian hitters he did quell

The final score was New York 5, Cleveland 1
Let the celebration begin for a moment of fun
For Houston is waiting at Minute Maid Park
Where noise and winning their trademark

Game one (ALCS) Justin Verlander on the hill
At 39 still pitching with poise and skill
For New York, Jameson Taillon (14-5), a good year
Now one of the tougher assignments in his career

The Yankees scored in the second on a home run
By Harrison Bader, the Astro fans it did stun
Same inning, Maldonado hit a game-tying double
By the sixth the Yankees were in trouble

Yuli Gurriel homered, Astros lead 2-1
One batter later, Chas McCormick a home run
In the seventh, Jeremy Peña went yard, now 4-1
In the eighth, a Rizzo solo, the Yankees last run

Yanks threatened more in the eighth to no avail
Final score: Astros 4, Yankees 2, still a sad tale
But hats off to Verlander giving up one run
In over six innings, fanning 11, still having fun

Game two, the Yankees sent Severino to the mound
But for one mistake pitch he looked fit and sound
In the third with two on, he gave up a home run
Off the bat of Alex Bregman, the Yankees were done

In the fourth, the Yankees scored two
Thanks to Framber Valdez's double miscue
Setting up runners on second and third base
Rizzo's ground out scored a run, a gift to embrace

Torres followed with a single, scoring another run
Cutting the Astros' lead to 3-2, not to be outdone
And that was all the scoring for the rest of the game
Valdez left after seven, and the bullpen did tame

Girardi Gone, Boone New Manager, Championship Drought (2018-2023)

The final score: Houston 3, New York 2
There was a tense moment when fans went PHEW!
It came in the eighth with a runner on first base
Judge hit a towering drive; Astro fans afraid to face

But Judge's mighty and almost timely clout
Caught at the wall by Kyle Tucker for another out
Now to Yankee Stadium, to pitch two of their best
Cole and Cortes with or without adequate rest

Game three pitchers, Christian Javier vs Gerrit Cole
The ace aiming to get his club out of the 0-2 hole
Sadly, in the second inning he lacked support
Bader and Judge in center and right fell short

Fly ball to right center for the third out
Both outfielders to make the catch in doubt
As they crossed, Bader dropped the ball
An error, the clear and obvious call

Up next, strolling to the plate, McCormick
His swing was smooth and quick
Driving a fastball into right field, home run
Two runs when there should have been none

The score remained 2-0 until the sixth inning
When Houston scored three, all but winning
A double, walk, and single, bases full
Boone to the mound, Cole he did pull

Lou Trivino entered the game in relief
But was greeted with nothing but grief
Trey Mancini hit a sacrifice fly
A run scored, then all went awry

Runners tagged and went to second and third
Heads up baseball the descriptive word
Then Vásquez singled, as both runners scored
In center field, 5-0 said the huge scoreboard

Javier pitched 5⅓ innings for the easy win
As manager Dusty Baker used five more to fill in
Cole took the loss with no help from Trivino
Or the Yankee sluggers, the once mighty foe

The goal now to avoid an embarrassing sweep
The Yankees must wake up from their deep sleep
Or heads should roll from the front office on down
Fans are hungry for a new great franchise of renown

Houston is headed to the World Series once more
As they swept the Yankees, 6-5, in game four
It was a close game most of the way
Early on it looked like the Yankees came to play

They scored two in the first, and one in inning two
Hitting starter Lance McCullers Jr. as optimism grew
Until Jeremy Peña hit a three-run homer in the third
Off Cortes, Houston apparently undeterred

In fact, they added another run off the relief
Right-hander Wandy Peralta in disbelief
Houston ahead, now 4-3 the score
Inning four, Rizzo another RBI, now 4-4

In the sixth, Bader homered a go-ahead drive
Giving him in the post-season, a total of five
The Yankees now out front again, 5-4
In the seventh, Alvarez drove in a run, tied score

Girardi Gone, Boone New Manager, Championship Drought (2018-2023)

Holmes now on the mound inheriting the absurd
Facing Bregman with runners on first and third
Bregman singled, scoring Peña, Astros lead 6-5
Further scoring by Houston Holmes did deprive

The last three frames New York went out one, two, three
Against Abreu, Rafael Montero, and Ryan Pressly
The bottles began popping in the Houston locker room
Led by several players each with a sweeping broom

Despite not getting to the 2022 World Series
And all Yankee fans have their theories
It was an exciting season, one must admit
With its ups and downs, the team never quit

Ups and downs are all part of the game
While seasons go unnoticed, this one brought fame
To a young New York Yankee named Aaron Judge
With a humble demeanor he did not budge

He won a Silver Slugger Award, number three
Plus, being named the American League MVP
Humility is what Aaron Judge is all about
As to his peers, "They pushed me day in and day out"

Whether the Yankees went to the Series or not
The season of 2022 will not be forgot
Due to one player, who made all proud
To be part of the talent of which he was endowed

Although Judge brightened the 2022 season
Long-time fans were disappointed for good reason
The team failed again, to make the World Series
Creating a variety of interesting theories

But the past is now baseball history
While the front office tried to stop the losing mystery
In November, they quickly signed Anthony Rizzo
Despite a concussion in 2022, a freaky blow

The most discussed signing, however, was Judge
And for a while neither side would budge
Most fans knew the Yankees had little choice
Aaron was the face of the Yankees . . . and voice

Aaron signed a $360 million, 9-year contract
At the time, the third-largest in MLB, a fact
At age 31, headed for Yankee fame
By staying off the IL and playing every game

Another key signing was Carlos Rodón, a lefty
Signing for $162 million for 6-years, quite hefty
With the Giants in '22, he went 14 and 8
And a 2.88 ERA, undeniably first rate

Now, the Yankees had another pitching ace
Joining Gerrit Cole to set a winning pace
Plus, Cortes, Frankie Montas, and Severino
Forming a formidable rotation, fans now aglow

In addition, the bullpen looked very strong
Led by King and Holmes . . . what could go wrong?
Wait, how about a look at the everyday eight
In '22 there was a weakness at the plate

Frankly, Judge was the Yankee offense
His season was simply immense
Beside the 62 homers, he drove in 131
And batted .311 . . . he was the big gun

Girardi Gone, Boone New Manager, Championship Drought (2018-2023)

No other Yankee came close to 100 RBI's
Or a .300 average, adding to the Yanks demise
Plus, serious injuries, sadly a part of baseball
For the Yankees a big reason for the **2023** fall

And fall they did, to an 82-80 mark
Finished fourth in the AL East, lacking spark
An embarrassing 19 games back of Baltimore
About the ugly season, simply a bore

Injuries were a huge part of the Yanks downfall
Beginning with Rodón, who didn't pitch at all
Until July, then six starts later was on the IL
Ending the season after 14 starts (3-8), pure hell

In 2023, 1⅓ innings did Frankie Montas pitch
After shoulder surgery another huge glitch
Followed by Lou Severino who started the year
On the injured list joining Frankie his peer

Lou finally returned to the mound in late May
But pitched poorly the rest of the way
Finishing with a 4-8 record and a 6.65 ERA
His contribution to the Yankees poor play

Domingo German added to the Yankee demise
Tossing a perfect game on June 28, a rare prize
How so? On the restrictive list in August placed
Beginning treatment for alcohol abuse he faced

With the starting rotation now a mess
It put the bullpen under additional stress
Still, two from the pen stood out
Clay Holmes and Michael King . . . no doubt

In over 104 innings Michael did pitch
With an ERA of 2.75 and made a switch
Starting nine games and pitched very well
And as a continued reliever his death knell

Holmes in 63 innings posted a 2.86 ERA
Then in August his back did betray
Landing on the IL, another injured Yankee
Followed by Peralta, bring on the crying hanky

Throughout this Yankee pitching meltdown
Cole won the coveted Cy Young crown
Gerrit started 33 games (15-4) and an ERA of 2.63
A well-deserved award for a pitcher so gutsy

Cole's 209 innings, third most in baseball
And another step to Cooperstown, and the Hall
Enough of pitching, let's look at the everyday eight
They too played a role in New York's fate

Despite previous remarks the Yanks were united
By June 3, their record was 35-25 most all delighted
And only six games back of Tampa Bay
Then suddenly the future looked dismal and gray

It was on June 3, Judge crashed into a fence
At Dodger Stadium denting the Yankee offence
His injury diagnosed as a torn ligament in the toe
Judge returned 42 games later . . . a tough blow

Upon his return, the Yankees were in last place
Nine games back, the beginning of a chase
Two other players must be singled out
For injuries and what the season was all about

Girardi Gone, Boone New Manager, Championship Drought (2018-2023)

Anthony Rizzo and DJ LeMahieu were missed
Two major Yankee contributors of a short list
Rizzo, his concussion still hampered his play
Missing 63 games to everyone's dismay

LeMahieu was not the same DJ
As old foot injuries did betray
At times looked lost at the plate
Returned after the All-Star break . . . too late

One stat of DJ's really stands out
Fanned 125 times if there was any doubt
The most in his 13-year career, by far
The effect a foot has on hitting, so bizarre

Giancarlo Stanton hit rock bottom in '23
As most fans and Stanton would agree
Plagued by a strained hamstring
Hampering his running and mighty swing

His stats in 101 games told the sad story
Batting .191 . . . far from laudatory
Plus, an OBP (.275) and SLG (.420)
And strikeouts in key moments aplenty

There were two players who did well
Gleyber Torres and Anthony Volpe did excel
Torres played in 158 games, a Yankee rarity
Led the team in runs scored (90) and average (.273)

Shortstop Volpe, a rookie at age 22
Won the coveted Gold Glove, who knew
And the first Yankee rookie to win it
Playing the demanding position with skill and grit

He also whacked 21 home runs with 60 RBI's
Hit .209, whiffing 167 times, and what it implies
Swinging for the long ball is not his game
Hits, walks, and speed will bring him fame

Enough about injuries and a World Series missed
You get the point, if not the gist
The Yankees last World Series title was 2009!
It was number 27 as they did shine

Coupled with their 40 AL pennants to boot
No other Major League club is near to toot
For the 2024 season, the fans want change
From the front office to the field, a rearrange

So where will the Yankees finish in 2024?
World Series number 28 or a continued bore
And mimic the old Brooklyn Dodgers cheer
Year in and year out, "Wait 'til next year"

Soto Arrives, Another Pennant (41), Championship Drought Continues (2024)

The change Yankee fans were looking for in 2024
Appeared from the get-go a closed door
GM Cashman remained, as did manager Aaron Boone
With hope the Yankees would shed their losing cocoon

With the '23 season over, the Yankees acquired Alex Verdugo
An outfielder from Boston, the Yankees hated foe
During the season, Alex patrolled left field
And at times, a key bat he would often yield

Days later came the key Yankee acquisition
Signing a young right fielder on a mission
Who brought power, speed, and unbridled ambition
And at age 25, an immediate welcome addition

From the San Diego Padres came Juan Soto
Paired with Judge made a dangerous combo
Trent Grisham, an outfielder, came with Soto
For five Yankees and a bundle of dough

The Yankees paid Juan $31 million for 2024
To avoid arbitration a number hard to ignore
That raises the question somewhat premature
A contract battle in 2025 will surely endure

But that's getting ahead of the season soon to begin
As the calendar turned over, the Yankees went all in
Signing pitchers Marcus Stroman and Luke Weaver
One a starter and the other a reliever

It appeared the Yankees were all set to go
When in March they announced a shocking blow
Gerrit Cole was headed for the IL
It was quite a depressing bombshell

Due to nerve irritation in the right elbow
It quickly damaged the new season glow
But injuries sadly, are all part of the game
To use it as an excuse, just plain lame

However, the Yankees got off to a terrific start
Opening in Houston they did not fall apart
Sweeping the Astros four games in a row!
About their nemesis they could now crow

After 15 games, the Yankees record was 12-3
Playing steady, solid baseball was the key
Then finishing May with a mark of 40-19
Led by Judge and Soto, a winning machine

But pesky Baltimore was only two games back
As New York kept winning with their offensive attack
By June 14, their record climbed to 50-22
Best in baseball, a pace hard to continue to pursue

With Baltimore now 3½ back in the race
And finding it difficult to keep pace
Then shockingly the Yankees went into a tailspin
And were now finding it difficult to win

A month later, the Yankees were in second place
Trailing Baltimore by a game, now a tight race
Eventually the Yankees straightened out
Although some fans had serious doubt

Soto Arrives, Another Pennant (41), Championship Drought Continues (2024)

But in late July, the Yankees made a trade
With the Marlins the outfield he played
For a player with the unusual first name of Jazz
A young talent with lots of spark and pizzazz

Jazz Chisholm Jr. is his full name
With power and speed, a fan favorite he became
Boone quickly installed Jazz at third base
With determination, a position he did embrace

Then on August 14, Judge hit homer 43
Against the White Sox in a 10-2 victory
It was his 300th and the fastest to reach that mark
He did it in 955 games and that's no lark

Then on September 18, the Yankees beat Seattle 2-1
Clinching a playoff spot and now begins the fun
On September 26, the Yankees secured the AL East title
For home field advantage during the playoffs, so vital

And what a season it was, let's take a peek
First, the offense, which many thought weak
Except for two very, very important exceptions
And the possibility of some key misconceptions

First, Judge had another potential MVP season
And for a very, very, very good reason
He batted .322/58/144 and an OPS of 1.159
Numbers which are absolutely divine

Juan Soto batted .288/41/109, many in the clutch
And in right had a strong arm and a defensive touch
As did Judge in center, regardless of his size
Fast, smooth, and in control and what that implies

DH Stanton wacked 27 homers and drove in 72
And at key times a clutch homer he would tattoo
Jazz played in only 46 games but was a quick fit in
He batted .273/11/23 and stole 18, that's no spin

The Yankee pitching, both starters and relievers
Were too often during the season deceivers
For example, a starter would look great
For a few innings, then hit hard and look third rate

Resulting in a bullpen being overused
Plus blown saves and lost games, a situation unexcused
Clay Holmes was the closer for most of the season
He saved 30 games, a pretty good reason

But late in the season, he lost his closer position
After blowing late inning games to the opposition
Luke Weaver took over the closer role
And after several appearances was in total control

Now to the starters and how well they threw
As expected, mixed results did accrue
Cole, the ace of the staff returned in June
And by seasons' end was in fine tune

He finished with an 8-5 record and a 3.41 ERA
Eager to be back and ready for postseason play
Carlos Rodón led the staff with a record of 16-9
And a 3.96 ERA in 175 innings an encouraging sign

At 26, Louis Gil was 15-7 with a 3.50 ERA
A right hander if he stays healthy will have his day
But after Gil the staff becomes suspect
And honestly one never knew what to expect

That leaves Marcus Stroman, who won 10 and lost 9
With an ERA of 4.31 . . . and that's not a good sign
Nestor Cortes did not have a winning record at 9-10
With an ERA of 3.77, but elbow problems nagged him again

Finally, Clarke Schmidt returned from a lat strain
And threw only 85.1 innings free of pain
With a 5-5 record, but an ERA of 2.85
A hopeful sign his career will continue to thrive

That's a quick review of the Yankee team
The long ball mostly their winning theme
The starters are competitive, the relief strong
Enough said, now to the playoffs let's move along

Winner of the Wild Card Series the Yankees to meet
Between Baltimore and KC, NY ready to compete
KC swept the Orioles, by scores of 1-0 and 2-1
And at Camden Yards no less, their season done

KC finished second in the AL Central 86-76
Led by Bobby Witt Jr. batting champ with power, a deadly mix
He led KC in three key stats: batting .332/32/109
Salvador Pérez was the other threat to shine

Pérez hit .271/27/104 with an OBP of .330
The rest of the offense, not very scary
Seth Lugo 16-9, Michael Wacha 13-8
Along with Cole Ragans 11-9, good, but not great

The Yankees won game one of ALDS 6-5
A thrilling win that kept Yankee fans' hope alive
The unlikely hero was the slumping Verdugo
Soon to administer the crushing blow

The seventh-inning game tied 5-5
Chisholm Jr. singled, the inning alive
Volpe struck out as Jazz stole second
Cabrera now up a hit does beckon

But Oswaldo fans for out number two
Verdugo up next and he comes through
Smacking a single scoring Jazz with run six
Eventually the game winner and a quick fix

The inning ended when Torres grounded out
The irony of it all was Verdugo's bailout
Alex was in a skid prior to the game
Going three for 25, somewhat lame

But the crazy game of baseball
At times it will surprise and appall
Another example specific to the win
Holmes no longer the closer kingpin

Holmes redeemed himself as a fill-in
Getting five key outs to help win
The save went to Luke Weaver
In the closer role as the chief reliever

Luke faced four batters, fanned 3 of
As his credibility in the new role did soar
One disappointment of the game was Cole
The Yankee ace not living up to his role

Judge another disappointment in the game
Fanning 3 of times, a performance lame
One is a Cy Young winner, the other an MVP
Talent that must show up, no hyperbole

Soto Arrives, Another Pennant (41), Championship Drought Continues (2024)

Rodón started game two and looked great
In the first, striking out the side to illustrate
In the meantime, the Yankees scored a run
On Stanton's two-out single, well done

In the fourth-inning, Rodón came unglued
As Pérez homered a ball he tattooed
Then four singles, as three more crossed the plate
The score now 4-1, the Yankees quiet and sedate

KC's Cole Ragans after four innings was gone
After 87 pitches, time for the pen (5) to come on
The final score Kansas City 4, Yankees 2
Allowing only Jazz's blast, did the crew

Now on to Kansas City for game three
A very crucial game all do agree
Starting for KC was right hander Seth Lugo
Who faced the Yanks September 10, a tough foe

Lugo beat the Yankees 5-0 for win number 16
He allowed only three hits, downright mean
Across seven innings, he struck out 10 hitters
Yankee fans recalling the game had the jitters

For the Yankees, Schmidt got the call
Prior to his lat strain he pitched decent ball
In 11 starts he was 5-3 with a 2.52 ERA
The injury cost him three months of no play

Stanton was the hero of the Yankees 3-2 win
He doubled in the fourth, scoring Soto to begin
In the fifth, Soto drove in a run with a sac fly
Then came the Royals two-run reply

After five innings the game was tied at 2-2
Until the top of eighth as the tension grew
Stanton launched the critical go-ahead home run
As the Kaufman hometown crowd came undone

But the game was far from over with six outs to go
After one out in the eighth, Boone wanted more ammo
He quickly summoned Weaver for the five-out save
The right-hander was the new Yankee closer rave

Witt greeted Weaver with a base hit
Not the way to show dominance, one must admit
Volpe made a "beautiful catch" on a line drive
But the inning was still well and alive

Then Pérez singled on to third went Witt
But Yuli Gurriel flied out lickety split
In the ninth, Weaver got three quick outs, game over
Yankees now positioned in proverbial clover

Michael Wacha started game four for KC
Greeted by Gleyber Torres immediately
With a solid double to center field
Followed by a Soto single, a run it did yield

In the fifth inning, the Yankees added another run
With runners on first and third, Torres got it done
This time he singled to right scoring Verdugo
Chasing Wacha did the timely blow

In the sixth, Stanton came through once more
With an RBI single for a run, 3-0 now the score
But in the bottom of the inning, KC scored a run
Unknown to all, the scoring (3-1) was done

Soto Arrives, Another Pennant (41), Championship Drought Continues (2024)

Cole continued to pitch like a Cy Young ace
In seven innings, six hits, and one run, a dominant pace
He threw 87 pitches, striking out four
Walking none, one heck of a pitching chore

Game over Boone said, "We get to play for a pennant now."
The third time under Boone, who must win somehow
Since there has been no trip to the World Series since 2009
And for die-hard Yankee fans that's the bottom line

After five games, Cleveland moved on to the ALCS
Beating Detroit in game five (7-3), after much stress
The Guardians to the ALCS for the first time since 2016
To meet the Yankees, a series anything but serene

Cleveland finished the regular season 92-69
First place in the Central Division they did shine
Led by Stephen Vogt managing the team
His first season at the helm and a job supreme

José Ramírez is Cleveland's player with power
Batting .279/39/118, often the man of the hour
Not far behind is Josh Naylor, a long ball threat
With 31 homers and 108 RBI's, a dangerous duet

Not much long ball after those two power guys
Often though an unlikely hero will surprise
Cleveland's pitching is also an interesting situation
That, of course, involves the starting rotation

Tanner Bibee won 12, lost 8 with a 3.47 ERA
One of two starters whose results were okay
The other is Ben Lively, who won 13 and lost 10
With a 3.81 ERA, he can be tough now and then

The Guardian's pitching strength is in the bullpen
Says Greg Joyce of the Post, saving games time and again
Doing so, the pen posted a demanding 2.57 ERA
Coming in late in games they were the mainstay

Emmanuel Clase is clearly the bullpen ace
The right hander is the closer that sets the pace
During the 2024 season, he had an ERA of 0.61!
Including a 4-2 record and 47 saves, he got the job done

Now let's move on to game one of the ALCS
At the Stadium before 47,000 plus wanting success
For New York, Carlos Rodón on the mound
Badly wanting a pitching performance profound

The Yankees won game one of the ALCS 5-2
And the defeat of the Guardians a lulu
It began with Cleveland starter Alex Cobb
For whatever reason did a terrific job

Despite having trouble with his location
And the Yankee fans continued ovation
Like in the third, when Soto homered to right
For the Yankees first run of the night

Judge walked, Wells fanned, Stanton walked too
Jazz flied out, Volpe walked, what's to ensue?
Joey Cantillo now pitching, Rizzo at the plate
Cantillo uncorks a wild pitch, Guardian fans irate

Judge scores run two, the Yanks looking for more
Rizzo walks, for Cleveland fans the inning a bore
Cantillo another wild pitch, Stanton scores third run
Verdugo fans, score 3-0, ending all the fun

Soto Arrives, Another Pennant (41), Championship Drought Continues (2024)

Hold on more fun to come in inning number four
Cantillo still pitching walks, Torres to open the door
Cantillo throws two wild pitches, Torres to third
Soto walks, ending Joey's evening of the absurd

Pedro Avila pitching as Judge flies to centerfield
Scoring Torres and run four, (4-0) it did yield
All the while, Rodón was pitching a beautiful game
He had the Guardians under control, frame after frame

Until the sixth, when Brayan Rocchio went deep
The score now 4-1, from Yankee fans not a peep
The next three Guardians made out, one, two, three
Ending Rodón's solid pitching evening, all would agree

In the seventh, Stanton rocked a 439-foot blast
That left the field of play quite fast
In the eighth, Cleveland tacked on another run
Off Tim Hill, but for the evening Cleveland was done

Weaver replaced Hill, finishing the frame
Then in the ninth, Luke increased his closer fame
By striking out the side to end the 5-2 win
A positive start for the Yankees, the ALCS to begin

In game two, the Yankees started their ace Cole
His pre-season injury apparently took its toll
In 4.1 innings, Gerrit gave up two runs and six hits
But Cleveland starter Tanner Bibee was the pits

By the second inning, Bibee was out of the game
As the Cleveland pen was unleashed, name after name
Seven pitchers entered, hard to understand
Slightly better, the Yanks used four to give a hand

After six innings, the Yankees led 4-2
Then came the Yankees seventh, let's review
With Torres on base, Judge came to the plate
Hunter Gaddis on the hill as the big guy did wait

He homered a 414-foot drive, a monster indeed
A timely blast that gave the Yanks a 6-2 lead
Torres and Volpe helped the offense to ignite
Gleyber scored twice with a 3 for 5 night

Volpe went 2 for 3, scoring twice to help win
While Verdugo drove in a run as he weighed in
But Aaron Judge was the man this night
Driving in half the Yankee runs, back to unite

In the ninth, Cleveland added a meaningless run
When José Ramírez went deep, adding a little fun
But it was too little to late
Two outs later, game three did await

And what a game it was . . . unforgettable
And for the Yankees . . . regrettable
Still the Yankees held a 2-1 Series edge to date
So on to game four and who will celebrate?

First, let's recap game three, painful for Yankee fans
Nothing went according to either team's plans
The Yankees trailed 3-1, entering inning eight
With two out (Wells and Torres), it was getting late

Soto worked a walk off pitcher Gaddis
For Cleveland fans not easy to dismiss
For up stepped Judge in postseason overdue
To replace Gaddis, no secret, everyone knew

Soto Arrives, Another Pennant (41), Championship Drought Continues (2024)

It was Clase to greet the home run king
Judge ran the count to 2-1, then The Swing
A line drive bullet to right field 356-feet
For Yankee fans, an unbelievable treat

Game tied 3-3 as Stanton stepped to the plate
With a 1-2 count, Stanton did not wait
Homering to right 350 feet, Yanks ahead 4-3
Back-to-back off a premier closer, who could foresee

In the ninth, the Yankees added another run
And led Cleveland 5-3, but soon to be outdone
Bottom of the ninth, Weaver still on the hill
Induced Bo Naylor to hit into a double play, but still

One more out to go, but it was not to be
Always the allusive final out was the key
As Lane Thomas doubled, the inning still alive
Jhonkensy Noel homered to left, score 5-5

Top of the tenth, the Yankees failed to score
Bottom of the inning, Cleveland fans did roar
Holmes now pitching, Naylor singled to right
Rocchio sacrificed Naylor to second, sit tight

Now the winning run in scoring position, one out
Steven Kwan grounded out Naylor to third, any doubt?
No! David Fry ended it all with a home run
A blast 399 feet and a never die comeback well done

Gavin Williams started for Cleveland in game four
With a 3-10 record and a 4.86 ERA, hard to ignore
Not much of a surprise when Torres singled to right
And Soto homered 414 feet to start the night

For the Yanks, Luis Gil with a 15-7 record started
And an ERA of 3.50, but in waters uncharted
As Cleveland came right back to score a run
On a Ramírez sac fly as early scoring had begun

But in the second the Yankees scored once more
When Wells homered 407 feet, now it's a war
Cleveland not giving up, scored again in the third
When Kwan singled and stole second undeterred

Now with two out, Naylor singled, Kwan scored
Putting the Guardians back on the scoreboard
Until the top of the sixth, the score remained 3-2
When Stanton once again in the clutch came through

The inning began with Cade Smith pitching
From the Yankees standpoint hardly bewitching
Soto walked; Judge singled to begin the inning
And Jazz sacrificed both, just the beginning

Stanton stepped to the plate and homered 404 feet
Score now 6-2, as the Yankees increased the heat
Relax! This game is far, far from over
An inning later the Guardians were back in clover

Bottom of the seventh, Cousins pitching for the Yanks
Rocchio walked, Kwan singled, no thanks
Holmes now on the mound, Ramírez and Naylor doubled
Guardians back in the game and untroubled

Leiter Jr. now pitching and got the last two outs
Yankees still leading 6-5, if there were any doubts
Top of the eighth, Gaddis retired the Yankees quickly
Bottom of the eighth, a one run lead no guarantee

Soto Arrives, Another Pennant (41), Championship Drought Continues (2024)

Sure enough, Cleveland scored the tying run
On a Leiter throwing error and now begins the fun
Clase the ace now pitching, three hits and an error later
The Yankees now lead 8-6, what a deflator

Kahnle now pitching, three outs to go
Perhaps the toughest outs to get you know
With one out, Kahnle allowed a walk and a hit
But Kahnle found that little extra and didn't quit

He retired Naylor and Rocchio to end the game
And the exciting ALCS momentum to reclaim
Now on to game five, and another unbelievable ending
Once again, the result is simply mind-bending

The starters for game five were Bibee and Rodón
Not long, however, before they were gone
The Guardians scored first in the second inning
And another in the fifth, a good beginning

Bibee had the Yankees shutout after five
But in the sixth he simply couldn't survive
Stanton homered again with a runner on base
Game tied 2-2, creating another tight race

Each team failed to score through nine
As tough pitching kept the hitters in line
Finally, the top of the tenth arrived
And the Yankees with help would not be denied

With Gaddis pitching, he ran into some bad luck
A walk, an error, and the inning went amuck
But with two Yankees on base, Torres struck out
Soto homered 402 feet, a crushing clutch clout

Weaver now pitching, retired the side with ease
Allowing a single, otherwise it was a breeze
Yankees won 5-2 for the AL pennant, their **forty first**
Celebrating on the field and clubhouse in a wild outburst

Shortly after Stanton was named the ALCS MVP
And accepted the trophy in calm glee
His series stats tell the story and why no surprise
Four home runs scored, five with seven RBIs

The Yankees back in the World Series since 2009
A long time for Yankees fans to fret and pine
And the LA Dodgers to be their talented foe
Facing the long absent Yankees, expect quite a show

But first a quick review of the LA team
It might give hope or not it would seem
The Dodgers finished the season 98-64
Winning both playoff series, never a bore

Clearly the Dodger's strength is in their offense
Nine players hit 10 or more homers, common sense
Led by Shohei Ohtani batting .310/54/130
Along with several others, their stats not too shabby

Teoscar Hernández hit .272 with 33 home runs
And 99 RBIs, another of the big guns
Plus, Freddie Freeman who hit .282/22/89
And Mookie Betts who batted .289/19/75, just fine

And it doesn't end with these names or stats
It's clear Yankee pitching will be facing serious bats
Conversely, Dodger pitching is their Achilles heal
A situation for manager Dave Roberts that's not ideal

Soto Arrives, Another Pennant (41), Championship Drought Continues (2024)

Out of the Series is LA's top pitcher Gavin Stone
Along with Tyler Glasnow, he is not alone
Leaving Yoshinobu Yamamoto with a record of 7-2
And a 3.00 ERA, a rookie in his World Series debut

So, to sum up the Dodgers and what to expect
Starting pitching leads one to be slightly suspect
While the hitting and power of LA is scary
The Yankees are a determined and solid adversary

So on to Dodger Stadium for game one
For the Yankees, Cole on the mound, the big gun
And Jack Flaherty (6-2, 3.58) for LA
Both hurlers came to play, pardon the cliché

LA took an early lead, 1-0 in the fifth inning
When E. Hernández tripled, just the beginning
Next, batter Will Smith flied out
Scoring Hernández as the LA fans did shout

But in the sixth the Yankees answered right back
A single by Soto began the attack
Judge next and his postseason demise
Continued when he struck out, as fans did agonize

Next up Stanton, the Yankee hero to date
Who promptly homered to left, time to celebrate
The Yankees now led by a thin margin, 2-1
But not for long, LA was far from done

Bottom of the eighth, Kahnle back on the mound
Had been since the seventh continued to confound
Getting Tommy Edman to ground out to Volpe at short
Until Ohtani doubled to right and would not abort

A Brief History of the New York Yankees

As he went on to third, on a throwing error by Soto
Weaver now pitching to face his first foe
Betts who flied out to Judge in center field
Scoring Ohtani, the tying run it did yield

Until the top of the tenth, the game remained 2-2
Treinen now pitching for LA as the tension grew
Stanton struck out, Jazz singled and stole second base
Rizzo intentionally walked; Jazz swiped third with grace

Volpe hit into a fielder's choice, out two
But Jazz scored, showing what speed can do
Yankees now led 3-2 as Volpe steals second base
Wells fans, Jake Cousins in the tenth LA to face

Will Smith flies to right field for the first out
Gavin Lux walks, Edman a single raises Yankee doubt
Cousins out, Nestor Cortez now pitching a total surprise
After the game the move challenged, was it wise?

Back to the game, to left field Ohtani fouled out
Runners advanced to second and third, game in doubt
Betts is intentionally walked, bases now loaded
Freeman homers to right as the stadium virtually exploded

Final score: Dodgers 6, Yankees 3
As post-game critics berated Boone with glee
Because Cortez hadn't pitched in a month or so
Why select Nestor Cortez to throw?

Game one is over and will be part of baseball history
And Boone's choice will always be a mystery
For now, let's focus on game two and who will throw
Starting for the Dodgers will be Yoshinobu Yamamoto

Soto Arrives, Another Pennant (41), Championship Drought Continues (2024)

Right hander Rodón will start for the Yankees
And he must win, if not bring out the hankies
In a World Series, a team losing the first two games
About 20% of the time will go down in flames

The Dodgers scored first in inning two
When Edman homered for the Blue
In the top of the third, the Yankees came back
Soto went deep, 386 feet, with a solid whack

LA countered in their half of the third
With three huge runs, long ball the key word
With two out no less, Betts singled to left field
T. Hernández homered 392 feet, two runs it did yield

But the Dodgers were not finished just yet
That man Freeman won't let the Yankees forget
He launched another key homer 401 feet
For the Dodger fans an unbelievable treat

LA now had a somewhat comfortable 4-1 lead
With Yamamoto pitching brilliantly all agreed
The rookie blanked the Yankees until the seventh inning
When removed with one out on the way to winning

Until the last inning the score remained 4-1
But the Yankees were not quite done
Blake Treinen now pitching for LA
Soto singles, not yet doomsday

On a wild pitch, Soto to second
Judge next as fans for a home run do beckon
But the home run king struck out
Stanton up next fans looking for a clout

Stanton singles, Soto scores run two
Jazz singles, a rally starting to brew?
Rizzo hit by a pitch; all bases now occupied
Treinen still pitching, will the Yankees be denied?

Volpe up next, strikes out on a 2-2 pitch
Trevino hits for Wells, LA a mound switch
Treinen removed, Alex Vesia now on the hill
Trevino flies out, game over and the thrill

Back to New York and the critical game three
A must win for the Yankees all agree
Yankees' Schmidt and LA's Walter Buehler meet
Of the two, Schmidt the most pressure to compete

The Dodgers struck early and fast
A walk to Ohtani, Freeman another blast
The score 2-0 before New York came to bat
As the Yankees offence started off flat

Then in the top of the third inning
Every LA player confident and grinning
The Dodgers tacked on another run
The score now 3-0, LA having all the fun

In five scoreless innings, Buehler breezed
And the Yankee faithful not very pleased
LA added another run during inning six
Hit batter, a single, and a steal, no tricks

Now the score 4-0, the crowd poised to roar
Patiently waiting for the Yankees to score
In the meantime, since Buehler left
LA used six pitchers, Yankee fans bereft

Soto Arrives, Another Pennant (41), Championship Drought Continues (2024)

Finally, the bottom of the ninth arrived
Last chance, will the Yankees be revived?
Volpe fans, Michael Kopech walks Rizzo
Moves to second on a Kopech wild throw

Wells fouls out to first, now two out
Verdugo homers, an encouraging clout
Yankees still alive, the score now 4-2
But Torres grounds out, Yanks through

LA now with a 3-0 lead in the Series
What next? Fans all over have their theories
Now to game four, truly a must win
To experience a sweep, a baseball sin

LA's first inning, Freeman homers once more
With Betts on base, 2-0 quickly the score
Gil on the mound treated with little respect
But for the next three innings he was perfect

In the meantime, the Yankees scored a run
In inning two and now trailed 2-1
In the third, LA made a pitching switch
Dan Hudson replaced Ben Casparius to enrich

A hit batter, single, stolen base, and a free pass
Loaded the bases, fans shouting yelling in mass
Volpe at bat lined a bullet left center (390 feet)
Grand slam as the Stadium rocked, how sweet

Yankees now ahead 5-2 as Volpe touched home plate
Even though LA added two runs it was too late
The Yankees added another run in the sixth inning
When Wells went deep, determined on winning

As four Yankee relievers blanked LA from the sixth on
Perhaps Volpe's slam woke the team to carry the baton
For the Yankees scored five more runs in the eighth
Final score Yankees 11, LA 4, a club with restored faith

There was another sold out crowd for game five
And like the others they were anxious and alive
Cole, the Yankees Cy Young ace, took the ball
Pitched like a winner, the Series to forestall

Jack Flaherty started game five for LA
Looking to end the Series, no delay
And that's exactly what they got
As New York wanted no part of their plot

The Yankees took a quick lead in game five
Soto singled to right, a line drive
Judge homered to right center, 403 feet
Fans screaming and now upbeat

Jazz followed with another homer, 392 feet
Giving Flaherty some very early heat
In inning two, the Yankees added another run
Volpe doubled, Verdugo singled, still not done

In the third, Stanton homered 385 feet to right
Score 5-0, it looked like a Yankee night
Then came the fifth inning from HELL
It was a total and still unbelievable bomb shell

Up to and including that inning Cole was in control
He threw four no-hit innings like taking a stroll
Then what happened in the fifth will boggle the mind
Even before your eyes it cannot be defined

Soto Arrives, Another Pennant (41), Championship Drought Continues (2024)

K. Hernández singled to right was the harmless start
Judge dropped an easy fly, the sad beginning part
Edman safe at first, Hernández at second base
Smith grounds to Volpe, a fielder's choice in place

Volpe an errant throw to Jazz, bases full, no out
Gavin Lux strikes out swinging as thousands shout
Ohtani whiffs too, Cole is one out away
Fans all standing, some quietly will pray

Betts hits a ground ball to Rizzo
Cole fails to cover, thus no throw
K. Hernández scores run number one
But the inning from hell is not done

Smith and Edman to second and third
The inning is quickly becoming absurd
The bases are loaded once more
LA to take advantage for sure

Freeman singles to center two more score
Betts on to third, LA looking for more
T. Hernández doubles two more cross home plate
Inning finally ends 5-5 and impossible to relate

But the nightmare not over just yet
Despite the thousands of fans upset
In the sixth, the Yankees regained the lead
Stanton sac fly scored Soto; not ready to concede

Now to the eighth, only six more outs to go
Between Kahnle and Weaver, painfully slow
Hits, walks, and two sacrifice flies scored two
LA leads 7-6, Yankees in deep doo-doo

With one out in the eighth Judge ripped a double
For the Dodgers this could spell trouble
Jazz walked and Stanton flied to right
But Rizzo struck out, the end in sight

Bottom of the ninth, Buehler pitching for LA
Volpe grounds out, soon to be doomsday
As Wells and Verdugo strikeout to end the game
And one feeling will always remain: what a shame

There were many reactions to the ugly defeat
From the average fan to baseball's elite
Boone never accused of being outspoken
Said it all very succinctly, "I'm heartbroken"

Despite how the 2024 World Series ended
Winning the American League pennant was splendid
It was **number 41** in their history of success
Along with 27 World Series wins must impress

Yankee fans finally got something to cheer about
When Judge was voted AL MVP without a doubt
By the BBWAA, it was a reassuring unanimous vote
Hitting .322/58/144 with an OPS 1.159, please note

The 2025 season should be an interesting one
To follow the off season moves will be fun
Rookies, trades, and key veteran hires
Through the winter and spring to see what transpires

But signing Juan Soto will be the main concern
Competition will be a factor, whether he will return
Signing Soto will be a very challenging one
If money is his sole interest the Yankees are done

Soto Arrives, Another Pennant (41), Championship Drought Continues (2024)

But if Juan is motivated by more than dough
Like Yankee history, dollars he might forego
Regardless, the decision will be lucrative, but tough
And he faces the age-old question, how much is enough?

It didn't take long for the courting to begin
Five clubs were serious contenders to win
The Yankees, Mets, Boston, Blue Jays, and LA
All romancing Juan to join their club to play

Sure enough by mid-December, the Mets had won
Signing Soto to a contract, the baseball world it did stun!
To an historic $765 million, 15-year deal
That could reach $805 million *The Post* did reveal

But we won't delve into Juan's contract that deep
About this decision from here, not another peep
The Yankees quickly activated Plan B
Strengthening the pitching they believe the key

Quickly, Max Fried signed an 8-year contract
For $218 million at age 31, that's a fact
Behind Cole the lefty will be a perfect fit
Strengthening the rotation, you must admit

Next the Yankees acquired Devin Williams in a trade
From Milwaukee, a star closer the pen to upgrade
Despite back problems, Devin finished 2024
With 14 saves, 1.25 era, stats hard to ignore

Shortly after the Yanks traded with Chicago
From the Cubs acquiring lefty power ammo
Cody Bellinger can play center or first base
The former position Aaron Judge to replace

If the Yankees move Judge to right
A possibility that does excite
Cody is a formers NL MVP and young at 28
With a positive spin this move could be great

Will Cashman continue dealing into 2025
To improve the club and keep fan excitement alive?
The goal from Hal Steinbrenner on down must be
That allusive number 28, nothing less all agree

Appendix A

Year	Pennant #	World Series #	Winner	Manager
1921	1	–	New York Giants	Huggins
1922	2	–	New York Giants	Huggins
1923	3	1	New York Yankees	Huggins
1926	4	–	St. Louis Cardinals	Huggins
1927	5	2	New York Yankees	Huggins
1928	6	3	New York Yankees	Huggins
1932	7	4	New York Yankees	McCarthy
1936	8	5	New York Yankees	McCarthy
1937	9	6	New York Yankees	McCarthy
1938	10	7	New York Yankees	McCarthy
1939	11	8	New York Yankees	McCarthy
1941	12	9	New York Yankees	McCarthy
1942	13	–	St. Louis Cardinals	McCarthy
1943	14	10	New York Yankees	McCarthy
1947	15	11	New York Yankees	Harris
1949	16	12	New York Yankees	Stengel
1950	17	13	New York Yankees	Stengel
1951	18	14	New York Yankees	Stengel
1952	19	15	New York Yankees	Stengel
1953	20	16	New York Yankees	Stengel
1955	21	–	Brooklyn Dodgers	Stengel
1956	22	17	New York Yankees	Stengel
1957	23	–	Milwaukee Braves	Stengel
1958	24	18	New York Yankees	Stengel
1960	25	–	Pittsburgh Pirates	Stengel
1961	26	19	New York Yankees	Houk
1962	27	20	New York Yankees	Houk

A Brief History of the New York Yankees

Year	Pennant #	World Series #	Winner	Manager
1963	28	–	LA Dodgers	Houk
1964	29	–	St. Louis Cardinals	Berra
1976	30	–	Cincinnati Reds	Martin
1977	31	21	New York Yankees	Martin
1978	32	22	New York Yankees	Lemon
1981	33	–	LA Dodgers	Lemon
1996	34	23	New York Yankees	Torre
1998	35	24	New York Yankees	Torre
1999	36	25	New York Yankees	Torre
2000	37	26	New York Yankees	Torre
2001	38	–	Arizona Diamondbacks	Torre
2003	39	–	Florida Marlins	Torre
2009	40	27	New York Yankees	Girardi
2024	41	–	LA Dodgers	Boone

Bibliography

BOOKS

Anderson, Dave, editor. *Story of the Yankees: 382 Articles, Profiles, & Essays from 1903 to the Present.* New York: Black Dog & Leventhal Publishers, Inc., 2012.

Anderson, Dave, et al. *The Yankees.* New York: Random, 1979.

Appel, Marty. *Pinstripe Empire.* New York: Bloomsbury, 2012.

———. *Casey Stengel Baseball's Greatest Character.* New York: Doubleday, 2017.

Berra, Yogi with Tom Horton. *Yogi: It Ain't Over.* New York: McGraw-Hill, 1989.

Coleman, Jerry with Richard Goldstein. *An American Journey.* Illinois: Triumph Books, 2008.

Connor, Anthony J. *Baseball for the Love of It.* New York: Macmillan Publishing Co., Inc. 1982.

Creamer, Robert W. *Stengel His Life and Times.* New York: Simon and Schuster, 1984.

Devito, Carlo. *Yogi The Life and Times of an American Original.* Chicago: Triumph Books, 2008.

Eig, Jonathan. *Luckiest Man.* New York: Simon and Schuster, 2005.

Engleberg, Morris and Marv Schneider. *DiMaggio Setting the Record Straight.* Minnesota: MBI Publishing Company, 2003.

Feinsand, Mark and Bryan Hoch. *Mission 27.* Illinois: Triumph Books, 2019.

Fischer, David. *Aaron Judge.* New York: Sports Publishing, 2017.

Fleming, G.H. *Murders Row The 1927 New York Yankees.* New York: William Morrow Co., 1985.

Frommer, Harvey. *A Yankee Century.* New York: Berkley Books, 2002.

Gaff, Alan D. *Lou Gehrig The Lost Memories.* New York: Simon and Schuster, 2020.

Gallagher, Mark. *The Yankee Encyclopedia 6th Edition.* Canada: Sports Publishing, 2003.

Golenbock, Peter. *Dynasty: The New York Yankees 1949-1964.* New Jersey: Prentice Hall, Inc., 1975.

Golenbock, Peter. *George*. New Jersey: John Wiley & Sons, Inc., 2009.

Gomez, Verona & Lawrence Goldstone. *Lefty An American Odyssey*. New York: Ballantine Books, 2012.

Graham, Frank. *The New York Yankees an Informal History*. Illinois: Southern Illinois University Press, 2002.

Henrich, Tommy and Bill Gilbert. *Five O'Clock Lighting*. New York: Carol Publishing Group, 1992.

Hoch, Bryan. *The Baby Bombers*. New York: Diversion Books, 2018.

Honig, Donald. *The New York Yankees An Illustrated History*. New York: Crown Publishers, Inc., 1987.

Koppett, Leonard. *Koppett's Concise History of Major League Baseball*. Philadelphia: Temple University Press, 1998.

Leavy, Jane. *The Last Boy Mickey Mantle*. New York: Harper Collins Publishers, 2010.

Levitt, Daniel R. *Ed Barrow*. Nebraska: University of Nebraska Press, 2008.

Levy, Alan H. *Joe McCarthy: Architect of the Yankee Dynasty*. North Carolina: McFarland & Company, Publisher, 2005.

Mayer, Ronald A. *Baseball Memories A Collection of 101 Poems Celebrating Immortal Players, Classic Games, and Wacky Events of the National Pastime*. Pennsylvania: Sunbury Press, Inc., 2020.

_____. *The 1923 New York Yankees*. North Carolina: McFarland & Company, Publishers, 2010.

_____. *The 1932 New York Yankees*. Pennsylvania: Sunbury Press, Inc., 2018.

Morrissey, Michael. *The Pride and the Pressure*. New York: Doubleday, 2007.

Negron, Ray and Sally Cook. *Yankee Miracles Life with the Boss and the Bronx Bombers*. New York: Liveright Publishing Corportation, 2012.

Nemec, David and Saul Wisnia. *100 Years of Baseball*. Illinois: Publications International, Ltd., 2002.

Pepe, Phil. *The Yankees: An Authorized History of the New York Yankees*. Texas: Taylor Publishing Company, 1995.

_____. *The Ballad of Billy & George*. Connecticut: The Lyons Press, 2008.

Pessah, Jon. *Yogi A Life Behind the Mask*. New York: Little, Brown and Company, 2020.

Poekel, Charlie. *Babe & The Kid*. South Carolina: The History Press, 2007.

Robinson, Ray and Christopher Jennison. *Pennants & Pinstripes The New York Yankees 1903-2002*. New York: Viking Studio, 2002.

Shalin, Mike. *Donnie Baseball The Definitive Biography of Don Mattingly*. Chicago: Triumph Books, 2011.

Silverman, Al. *Yankee Colors*. New York: Abrams, 2009.

Smith, Ron. *Yankees: A Century of Greatness*. Missouri: The Sporting News, 2003.

Spatz, Lyle and Steve Steinberg. *The Yankees, The Giants, & The Battle for Supremacy in New York*. Lincoln: University of Nebraska Press, 2010.

Steinberg, Steve & Lyle Spatz. *The Colonel and Hug*. Nebraska: University of Nebraska Press, 2015.

Stout, Glenn. *New York Yankees Yesterday & Today*. Illinois: West Side Publishing, 2007.

Torre, Joe and Tom Verducci. *Chasing the Dream*. New York: Bantam Books, 1997.

———. *The Yankees Years*. New York: Doubleday, 2009.

Wallace, Joseph. *World Series: An Opinionated Chronicle of the Fall Classic 100 Years*. New York: Harry N. Abrams, Inc., 2003.

Winfield, Dave with Tom Parker. *Winfield A Player's Life*. New York: W.W. Norton & Company, 1988.

NEWSPAPERS

Chass, Murray, "Jackson Signs Yanks Contract," The New York Times, November 3, 1976.

Chass, Murray, "Clemens at His Best, and Most Bizzare," The New York Times, October 34, 2000.

Curry, Jack, "For Yanks Game Isn't Over Till They Win in the 10th," The New York Times, October 24, 1996.

———, "Yankees in Series After 15 Years in Wilderness," The New York Times, October 14, 1996.

———, "Mussina and the Yankees Reach Agreement in Pact," The New York Times, November 30, 2000.

Durso, Joseph, "Steinbrenner Suspended for 2 Years," The New York Times, November 28, 1974.

Kepner, Tyler, "An October Surprise, Angel's 8-Run Fifth Inning Ends Yanks Season," The New York Times, October 6, 2002.

———, "For Fifth Year In Row, Yanks Have Hit Wall," The New York Times, October 11, 2005.

Olney, Buster, "Yanks Sweep Series and Assure Legacy," The New York Times, October 22, 1998.

———, "Steinbrenner Aide, Watson Says He's Worn Out," The New York Times, February, 4, 1998.

Strauss, Michael, "Yanks Win Again; New York Gains a Game in East on 8-5 Victory," The New York Times, August 31, 1974.

Wallace, William, "C.B.S. Buys 80% of Stock in Yankees Baseball Team," The New York Times, Ausust 14, 1964.

Wagner, James, "Yanks Blow 2 Run Lead in the 9th, The New York Times, October 16, 2022.

ONLINE SOURCES

Amour, Mark. "Lee McPhail." https://sabr.org > bioproj > person > lee-macphail

Ban Johnson. Baseball Hall of Fame. https://baseballhall.org – hall-of-famers – johson-ban

Baseball Almanac. https//www.baseball-almanac.com>yr 1921ws

Baseball-Reference.com, https//www.baseball-reference.com

Glueckstein, Fred. "Tony Lazzeri." https://sabr.org > bioproj > person > tony-lazzeri

History of Baseball in the United States. https//en Wikipedia.orr > wiki > History_of_baseball

History of the American League. https://en.wikipedia.org > wiki > History of the American League

History of the MLB: From early beginning to current. https://www.foxnews.com > sports > mlb-baseball-history

Jacob Ruppert. https://baseballhall.org > hall-of-famers> Jacob Ruppert- Baseball Hall of Fame

Levitt, Daniel R. "George Weiss." https://sabr.org > bioproj > person > george-weiss

National Baseball Hall of Fame and Museum. https://en.wikipedia.org > wiki > National Baseball Hall of Fame and Museum

1936 World Series by Baseball Almanac. https://www.baseball-almanac.com > yr 1936 ws

Pinestripe Alley. https://www.pinestripealley.com

StatMuse. https://www.statmuse.com

Thornley, Stew. "Billy Martin." https://sabr.org > bioproj > person > billy-martin

Thornley, Stew. "Polo Grounds." https://sabr.org > bioproj > park > polo-grounds

The Atlantic. https://www.theatlantic.com

Wancho, Joseph. "Clete Boyer." https://sabr.org > bioproj > person > clete-boyer

Yankees and the Cursed 1921 World Series. https://www.,pinestripealley.com > Yankees-1921-world series

About the Author

Ronald A. Mayer is an author of baseball history books. He's written about immortal players, single-season sagas, and even a collection of poems called *Baseball Memories* that celebrates America's favorite pastime in its biggest and smallest moments. He is a diehard New York Yankees fan through the good and not-so-good years, and an avid appreciator of the two greatest screwball pitchers of all time, Christy Mathewson and Carl Hubbell.

His love of the sport comes from his father, who in his later years, would intrigue him with stories of Babe Ruth, Lou Gehrig, Earle Combs, and Bill Dickey. As many boys did, he played the game as a youth and through his college days at Montclair State University. He gave up his dream of playing major league baseball, like so many others, when pitchers began throwing that dastardly curve ball. The same curve scientists once claimed was an optical illusion. He is a former member of the Society for American Baseball Research (SABR) and a life-long resident of New Jersey. Ron currently resides in East Hanover, PA with his wife Arlene.

www.ingramcontent.com/pod-product-compliance
Lightning Source LLC
Chambersburg PA
CBHW032036150426
43194CB00006B/306